Beyond the Ivory Tower

Beyond the Ivory Tower

THE CASE FOR CIVICALLY
ENGAGED POLITICAL SCIENTISTS

Richard Davis

University Press of Kansas

To my wife, Molina, and our children—
Audrey, Jonathan, Romney, Bethany, and Devin

Published by the University Press of Kansas (Lawrence, Kansas 66045), which was
organized by the Kansas Board of Regents and is operated and funded by Emporia State
University, Fort Hays State University, Kansas State University, Pittsburg State University,
 the University of Kansas, and Wichita State University.

Library of Congress Cataloging-in-Publication Data
Names: Davis, Richard, 1955– author.
Title: Beyond the ivory tower : the case for civically engaged political
    scientists / Richard Davis.
Description: Lawrence : University Press of Kansas, 2023.
Identifiers: LCCN 2022043575 (print) | LCCN 2022043576 (ebook)
    ISBN 9780700634835 (paperback) | ISBN 9780700634996 (ebook)
Subjects: LCSH: Political science—Study and teaching (Higher)—United
    States. | Political scientists—Political activity—United States. |
    College teachers—Political activity—United States. | Utah—Politics
    and government.
Classification: LCC JA88.U6 D38 2023 (print) | LCC JA88.U6 (ebook) | DDC
    320.973071/1—dc23/eng/20221115
LC record available at https://lccn.loc.gov/2022043575.
LC ebook record available at https://lccn.loc.gov/2022043576.

British Library Cataloguing-in-Publication Data is available.

Printed in the United States of America

10 9 8 7 6 5 4 3 2 1

The paper used in this publication is acid free and meets the minimum requirements of
the American National Standard for Permanence of Paper for Printed Library Materials
Z39.48-1992.

Contents

Preface

The impetus for this book is my own experience as a political scientist and a civic activist. In my life, that order was reversed early on. Initially, my goal was to pursue a political career. I worked for candidates while I was an undergraduate in the 1970s. However, while an undergraduate, I also discovered that I enjoyed academic life and, after a brief foray into public relations, decided I would best serve as a teacher and scholar.

But the political activism bug never really went away. And I began to see that as a positive trait. It made me relate more to the many students I encountered who sought a political career, not an academic one. It also made me more comfortable around politicians, since I could understand what drove them toward public office.

That bug was coupled with the sense that I could contribute to the larger society both in and out of the classroom. Service was critical to me. Educating young people was just such a service. But it was not the only path for service. Joining initiative campaigns, serving in political party organizations, advising candidates, and even running for office became additional, perhaps more immediate, vehicles in attempting to bring about improvements in my community. And although I would pursue teaching and scholarship vigorously, I concluded that both could well be informed by civic activism, since, through it, I might better comprehend how politics really operated.

Fortunately, that bug was not dampened in graduate school at Syracuse University. I remember conversations with my dissertation advisor, Thomas E. Patterson, about the dearth of political scientists contributing to public policy debate. Tom set an example himself with his research on the role of the media in campaigns. Another influential professor was Robert McClure, who had been a legislative aide prior to his academic career. While I was a teaching assistant for him, he often shared insights with students on the "real world" of Congress.

When I took my first job, at SUNY Geneseo, I concentrated on finishing a dissertation and creating course preps. But, that bug emerged as I interacted with my children's school. After only my first year of teaching, I decided to become civically engaged by running for the school board. I lost that race—the first of several I would lose! But as a political scientist the experience was stimulating. It also was highly educational for me.

When I changed jobs after finishing my dissertation, the bug was temporarily suppressed because I was a federal employee working at the US Coast Guard Academy. But when I moved again after five years, this time to Brigham Young University (BYU), I could renew my political activity. My subsequent involvement, which is discussed in later chapters, offered me the opportunity to fulfill what I long had sought to do—attempt to make a difference in my community through my vocation and my avocation.

However, this book is not simply about me. It is about a cause—to bring political scientists back into the sphere of civics. I do so by relating my own experiences as both a political scientist and a civic activist but also by presenting at first the stories of others who have done the same. These models offer a glimpse into the lives of those who seek to straddle two worlds—academe and practical civics/politics.

Why should we care about these models? I believe they may help those who want to become civically engaged but are not sure how to do so or what to do to accomplish that end. And they remind us that our role as political science professors is to do more than teach models, theories, concepts, and facts. We are educating citizens. And the models we provide are helping our students see citizenship in action. To put it bluntly, we walk the walk and do not just talk the talk.

Through the models provided in this book, including my own, I hope to stimulate current and future political scientists to view service in broader terms than is generally taught in the discipline—and, by so doing, serve in various ways in helping make their communities (group, local, state, national, and global) better places for all to live. May they become models themselves for future generations of young people for whom politics should not be a dirty word.

Acknowledgments

A book, like a career, is hardly the work of one individual. So many people—from my parents, schoolteachers, and university professors to department colleagues and the many students I taught (and who taught me)—have contributed to my career and my drive and approach to this topic of political science and civic engagement. They had no idea they were doing so when they made comments or shared experiences that influenced my thinking concerning the value of being civically engaged.

Additionally, many individuals outside academe have been influential in my civic engagement endeavors. Those I worked with in political parties generally were models of citizenship who receive no salary and were dedicated to a cause. That designation was especially appropriate for those who were involved in the United Utah Party. They were not there for personal ambition. They knew the formation of a new political party was an uphill climb. And yet they pursued it anyway.

I incurred an enormous debt with the many people in both the Democratic and United Utah parties who accepted my invitation to run for office. Nearly all of them knew the odds of winning were small. But they were willing to donate time and money and energy to a larger cause. I was overwhelmed by their commitment to civic responsibility.

The cofounders of the Utah Debate Commission have earned my longstanding appreciation for their willingness to do something new and different to improve campaigns in Utah. Former Utah governor Olene Walker, former US senator Bob Bennett, former state Senate minority Scott Howell, and then *Deseret News* editor Paul Edwards all were particularly important in playing significant roles in the new organization. I am delighted that the organization still exists a decade after its founding and that the current leaders are as dedicated to its continuance as an independent organization as were the founders.

Similar to the party activists, I found those who work in or seek to influence local government are dedicated civic activists. We may disagree about how the city or school district should be run. But we can see in each other the dedication to something larger than self or even family. In particular, I appreciated Jerry Ortiz's invitation to join his Orem Recreation Advisory Commission. That act started my long-term involvement with my city's politics and government.

Civic engagement centers are cropping up at universities and colleges around the nation. I am grateful that Dean Ben Ogles was willing to advocate for the creation of one at BYU and allowed me to lead it. And I was appreciative of colleagues, both in my department (particularly David Magleby) and throughout the university, who devoted time and resources to instilling civic engagement values in current and future students at BYU.

I am also grateful to the political science professors who answered my questions about their political and civic involvement and were willing to be featured in this book. I hope that their stories activate others to take similar risks beyond academe in the pursuit of service to their communities—local, national, and even global.

I wish to thank David Congdon, who suggested this volume. He casually mentioned the idea when we were conferring about another book at the press's exhibit booth at an American Political Science Association meeting. And I quickly rejected the idea. It seemed too personal: I did not want to talk about myself. It took me some time to warm to the idea. And even then, I suggested the version you see here—one where others are highlighted as well.

Finally, I am particularly grateful to my wife, Molina, who has contributed so much to my civic engagement through her encouragement, even when I lost elections or failed in achieving my goals in community service.

Introduction: Academic Disengagement

Quite frequently, when I have told a new acquaintance that I teach political science, he or she begins a political discussion, or at least a monologue, where they precede to express their views on current political events to me, expecting I will be interested in hearing their personal political views. I doubt I am the only political science professor who has had that experience. I believe it stems from widespread confusion about what political science is. Many people believe that all we discuss in political science classes are current events and that the professor seeks to "educate" his or her students about the superiority of his or her particular political ideology. In other words, political science is nothing really but a normative discussion of politics.

Of course, political scientists know that the classroom, for most of us, looks very different from that. Yet, there is still the lingering feeling that political science isn't really either political or a science. Edward S. Corwin once joked that "a political scientist has been described as one who among politicians is reckoned a scientist, and among scientists is reckoned a politician."[1]

Political scientists have reacted to that charge by seeking to become recognized as scientists. However, the purpose of this book is to suggest that perhaps political science has gone too far in that direction. By insisting that political science is another science, political scientists have discarded aspects of civic involvement that would enhance, rather than damage, the profession. This is not an argument for transforming political science into a normative debating society. Rather, it is a suggestion that political scientists can remain scientists while simultaneously participating in the larger society. It is a recommendation that political scientists become more than spectators of the political sphere in their personal lives while maintaining rigorous standards of scientific inquiry in their professional lives. It is time to assess what political scientists can and should do that does not undermine the scientific approach but also allows them to be contributors beyond the classroom or the database.

When John Burgess became the first political science professor in the United States in 1880, the purpose of the new discipline was to understand government. Burgess was an advocate of incorporating science into the study of politics, including use of the scientific method and theory building. This was a departure from the prior study of politics that concentrated on morals and good citizenship.[2]

However, Burgess and others also considered this new discipline to be an important tool for improving the state of government. His secondary goal, beyond injecting the scientific method into the discipline, was "to do something for democracy, even in letters and science." Newly formed political science departments were designed not only to produce academicians but also to improve the quality of state and federal government officials.[3]

The dual purpose of political science—education and reform—helped explain the intersection of teaching, research, and practice among early political scientists. In 1909, members of the American Political Science Association (APSA) elected Woodrow Wilson, a political science professor at Princeton University then serving as university president, to be the association's president. One year later, Wilson was a candidate for governor of New Jersey, a race he won. Two years after becoming governor, he was inaugurated president.[4]

Wilson was not alone in being recognized by other political scientists for his academic leadership and for playing a role in practical politics. Wilson's successor as APSA president, Simeon Baldwin, was highly recognized as a scholar of government and law and at different times served as well as president of the American Historical Association, the American Social Science Association, and the Association of American Law Schools. But Baldwin also was a member of the Connecticut Supreme Court, including four years as the chief justice. Following his APSA term, he was elected governor of Connecticut.[5]

Actually, the tradition of mixing practical politics and political science began early in the APSA. The first president of the APSA was Frank Goodnow. In addition to his long career teaching at Columbia University, his presidency of Johns Hopkins University, and his scholarship in public administration, Goodnow served as an adviser to the Chinese government. And the fourth APSA president, James Bryce, taught at Oxford University for twenty-three years and was a prolific scholar across a wide variety of topics. But he also served as a member of the British Parliament for a quarter of a century before his election as APSA president. During and following his APSA presidency, he held the position of British ambassador to the United States. According to one estimate, approximately two-thirds of the early leaders of APSA, including officers and members of standing committees, were then or soon would be involved as well in practical politics.[6]

This practice of public service continued into the 1920s and 1930s. Harry Garfield, president in 1923, directed the US Fuel Administration during World War I. Charles Merriam, APSA president in 1924, was alderman in Chicago, ran for mayor unsuccessfully, and helped build the Progressive Party in Illinois. In the 1930s, political scientists were involved in the study and reorganization of municipal and state governments throughout the nation. And an APSA committee urged political science departments to give consideration to job candidates who, in addition to teaching and scholarship, had or could acquire contacts with government officials.[7]

However, by the 1950s, fewer APSA presidents were drawn from applied politics, nor did they serve in elective or appointive office at some point in their careers. They came well known for their scholarship, which earned them multiple honors within academe. However, actual participation in practical politics and government became a rarity. The exceptions were Emmette Redford, who served in the Office of Price Administration during World War II, and Carl Friedrich, who was an official in the military occupation of Germany after World War II, as well as Lucian W. Pye and James Q. Wilson, who became advisors to some politicians but never served in an appointed office or ran for elective office.[8]

The absence of involvement in practical politics among APSA presidents was indicative of what was changing within the discipline as a whole. Political scientists were rejecting participation in policy making and political organizations in favor of teaching and scholarship. Running for office, serving in government positions, or even nonprofit leadership became increasingly uncommon.

This transition affected not only the individual political scientists' public participation but also scholarly interest in current events. Concern for contemporary affairs dominated the early work of political scientists. The pages of the discipline's scholarly journals at the time were filled with articles addressing current events in government. According to Albert Somit and Joseph Tanenhaus, later political scientists might "find it hard to realize, in going through these early volumes, that they are reading a scholarly journal rather than a somewhat badly written version of *Harpers* or the *Atlantic Monthly*."[9]

Simultaneously, political scientists were distancing themselves from politicians. Increasingly, the venue for research was exclusively the library or the database. What was rare as well was the use of participant observation or as Richard Fenno termed it "soaking and poking." Fenno not only interviewed practical politicians, such as members of Congress and candidates, but he observed their routines and rituals. He even volunteered to help with mundane tasks to ingratiate himself with them.[10]

Fenno's research method placed him in the room when campaign workers stuffed envelopes, campaign managers plotted strategy, and members of Congress deliberated on legislation. Through participant observation, he experienced campaigns and constituent relations firsthand and offered real-world perspectives on how candidates and members of Congress actually operated. But it was a method eschewed by political scientists in favor of more aloof methods such as data-set analysis or quasi-experimentation.

REFORMIST VS. SCIENTIST

The Progressive movement's impact on early political scientists was highly significant. Early political scientists such as Wilson, Merriam, and Goodnow considered the discipline as a mechanism for reforming the political system. Science was a new means for achieving more effective public administration but also for contributing to a more democratic system of government. Political science research would enable policymakers to understand what drives mass political involvement and how institutions can function more effectively. Then, that information could be utilized by policymakers to change procedures, practices, and even attitudes about government to facilitate reform.

What was lacking in that approach, but would come later, was a sense that science was useful for its own sake. Rather, science was a new tool for society to improve itself. And, with the ability to glean knowledge, political science possessed the power, and therefore the responsibility, to reform democratic societies to make democracy more effective.[11]

This optimism about science's ability to ameliorate societal ills was undermined by reality. A world war that culminated with the use of a weapon that could destroy the human race began an extensive debate about whether science had improved the human condition. The Progressive movement faded in American politics in the face of war as well as economic downturns. Progressives also failed to become an electoral force over time.

Within political science, the reliance on institutions to effect change was challenged. Liberal reforms did not always turn out as expected. During the period between the 1930s and the 1960s, political scientists had urged the expansion of presidential power to achieve rapid results in policy change and override a parochial Congress. But the rise of presidents like Lyndon Johnson and particularly Richard Nixon using such broadened political power frightened the very advocates of presidential power.

Similarly, the Warren Court years were accompanied by political science defenses of a strong judiciary capable of effecting much-needed policy change without having to endure the slow legislative processes or achieving policy goals on a state-by-state basis. But, again, such reform ultimately backfired when the Supreme Court became a haven for conservatives under Warren Burger, William Rehnquist, and John Roberts.

BEHAVIORALISM AND ENGAGEMENT

Political science established itself as a discipline with the creation of the American Political Science Association in 1903. The association quickly became a vehicle for scholarly presentations, publications, and networking. But it struggled to define itself, particularly in contrast to other disciplines such as sociology and history.

Early on, calls emerged for abandoning the historical, institutional approach that characterized the study of politics and replacing it with a concentration on behavior. A. Lawrence Lowell, Charles Merriam, and Arthur Bentley were voices emphasizing empirical rather than normative approaches as well as function over structure in understanding government. However, even Merriam's motives were not entirely academic. He felt attention to the "science of politics" would result in a "more intelligent control of the process of government."[12]

Yet, successors of Merriam did not have dual aims: They argued the profession needed to abandon its political biases reflecting a middle-class, American mindset and strive for scientific neutrality. William F. Whyte challenged political scientists to engage in systematic theory that does not include moral judgments. He suggested that political scientists "should take an interest in politics" and "leave ethics to philosophers." Political scientists should study behavior rather than seek to impose morals.[13]

Early advocates of science were met with early opponents who argued that the objectivity claimed by the scientism advocates was a sham. Charles A. Beard contended that political science needed ethics and therefore a morally neutral political science was impossible to achieve. And Edward S. Corwin concluded that the "primary task of political science is today one of popular education" and urged political scientists to continue their interest in "the true ends of the state and how they can be achieved."[14]

The emphasis on behavioralism that emerged in the early twentieth century dominated political science by century's end. Yet, behavioralism was an amorphous concept. As Robert Dahl noted, it was like the Loch Ness Monster: "One can say with considerable confidence what it is not, but it is difficult to say what it is."[15] As Evron Kirkpatrick, longtime executive director of the APSA, put it: "The term served as a sort of umbrella, capacious enough to provide a temporary shelter for a heterogeneous group united only by dissatisfaction with traditional political science." However, the concept gelled over time to include the assertions that political science is a predictive and explanatory science, theory should anchor research, observation (and particularly that which is quantifiable) is the task of a political scientist, applied research is useless and therefore should be avoided, and the "great issues" (democracy, equality, liberty, and so on) are not the concern of political scientists because they cannot be scientifically observed and measured.[16]

Behavioralism turned attention away from reform toward observation and analysis. No longer was it the political scientist's job to attempt to reform. The reform impetus of an early age was viewed as value-laden, since it rested on largely unstated assumptions about good government. According to its advocates, behavioralism was apolitical. However, even behavioralism was criticized as value-driven.[17]

There remained a strain in political science that sought to return the discipline to its roots. Political science, the argument went, should address questions regarding civics that were lost in the rush toward behavioralism. Ralph Ketcham termed the discipline's handling of civic engagement questions regarding leadership and civil society as "odd, paradoxical, and perhaps even tragic."[18]

Yet, behavioralism itself is not the opponent of academic "real-world" engagement. Rather, it is its use as a justification for nonparticipation. Behavioralism can lead political scientists to believe that they cannot be neutral observers of phenomena as professionals while simultaneously becoming involved in that same phenomena as individual citizens.

But the two—behavioralism and civic engagement—are not contradictory. As individuals, behavioralists can be as engaged in practical politics as much as those who may not share that approach. A political scientist's methodological proclivities do not necessarily predict involvement. What is more common may be the field of study. Public policy, American government, particularly state and local politics or urban politics, may be better predictors of involvement, at least in government positions. Political scientists who seek to remain in their posts but desire to use their expertise to serve the community would seem more likely to gravitate to local government posts such as a planning commission, a city council, or a school board. And the attraction to such positions may be greater for those who feel they can utilize the knowledge related to their subfield for the good of the community.

That is not to say that those studying political theory, comparative politics, or international relations may not be involved as well. They may do so for reasons unrelated to their specific field of study. Instead, they may perceive they possess the capability, and even the responsibility, to contribute civically.

But beyond behavioralism there are other potential disincentives to academic participation in civic endeavors. One is the perception of a lack of time. The tenure clock ticks loudly for an untenured professor. Developing courses, establishing a pipeline of publications, and becoming integrated into service opportunities within the university are time-consuming enterprises. Add to that the demands of family and an untenured professor may feel overwhelmed with the current load. Piling on a race for office or even service in a nonelective position such as a city or county board or committee may seem too much.

Once that pattern has been established, it may be easy to continue it throughout one's career. That is particularly true when the rewards of civic involvement may be elusive while the rewards of other activities (teaching, scholarship, and service specifically to the university) are immediate and visible. A campaign may be waged and lost. An effort to shape a particularly public policy may fail. On the other hand, the incentives of service within the institution are apparent and promised. Service on a college committee "counts" toward promotion or a salary increase, but service to the broader community beyond the university may or may not matter to the institution. In fact, in some cases it may be rhetorically supported but practically frowned upon as a distraction.

Hence, a major contributor to avoidance of civic engagement is the set of disincentives of the profession generally and institutions specifically. The lack of encouragement by the profession comes in the form of the dearth of recognition of political scientists who engage civically. There are many forms of tribute for scholarship and teaching. But the recognition of achievements in civic engagement is less common.

Recently, there has been some movement in the direction of increased awareness of the importance of such acknowledgment. In the 1980s, the American Political Science Association initiated an award for a political scientist who contributed to public service. But those awards nearly always were given to individuals who held a PhD in political science but were not faculty members. They included prominent members of Congress, such as David Obey, Mark Hatfield, and Daniel Patrick Moynihan, or federal cabinet members or presidential advisers, such as Dick Cheney, Donna Shalala, and Brent Scowcroft.

Only in 2020 did the APSA create an award for civic engagement designed specifically for a faculty member. The award is recognition "for significant civic or community engagement activity by a political scientist which merges knowledge and practice and has an impact outside of the profession or the academy."[19] Additionally, the Civic Engagement Section of the APSA similarly initiated an award for faculty civic involvement.

Although these discipline-wide acknowledgments of civic engagement are occurring now, they are only recent and are only beginning to filter to colleges and universities. In conjunction with signals from the discipline, as well as other disciplines, institutions reward faculty for teaching, scholarship, and service within the institution (such as administrative or committee work), but rarely do they do so for the individuals who serve beyond the institution itself. A political scientist who serves in local government, a local nonprofit, or an NGO does so largely on his or her time. Such activity may not count against them explicitly, but it may do so implicitly as others in the university community fear they are not doing enough within the institution. However, the fact that it did not count "for" them in official terms either serves as an implicit form of discouragement.

This is particularly true for junior faculty who are warned that they must "publish or perish." That admonition is less applicable to faculty at primarily teaching institutions. Even there, however, any encouragement to participate beyond the university is atypical. Instead, faculty are admonished they would be best served by concentrating on improving teaching, particularly since they carry heavier teaching loads, as well as some scholarship and potentially extensive service within the department or college/university generally.

Even when a tenure review is finished, the faculty member who wishes to engage more broadly still faces the prospect of a full professor review that may come up short if the faculty member is viewed as spending too much time elsewhere. Even beyond tenure and promotion reviews, annual reviews for merit increases are not likely to value civic engagement.

Once the rank of full professor is achieved, then, the faculty member might be free to pursue civic involvement. Yet, even that is unlikely, because many institutions have incorporated post-tenure reviews that are centered on the same standards as tenure/promotion. In some cases, university trustees are seeking to inject politics into that post-tenure review process that might inhibit faculty involvement beyond the bounds of university service.[20] Even where post-tenure reviews are not employed but annual reviews that determine merit increases are, service beyond the institution may not be credited.

In many cases, the barrier may be the inculcation of the philosophy that political scientists are not expected by peers to engage in practical politics or even broader civic engagement. Rather, such engagement is left to politicians. Political scientists study politics; they do not engage in it. Indeed, in many cases, there will be no encouragement from other faculty. In fact, the reaction may be wonderment as to why a faculty member would take time to run for office, serve on a city committee, or head a nonprofit. The peer pressure may be too strong to take action that strays from the conventional wisdom.

In line with the discipline's disinterest in teaching civic engagement, political science departments, along with universities in general, have not valued engagement by individual faculty. If that engagement is personal, conducted beyond time devoted to teaching and scholarship, and does not impact expected duties, then institutions tend to be indifferent. This typically entails minimal civic involvement such as serving on a city volunteer-based committee or being a member of a board of a nonprofit organization. However, this approach devalues personal engagement as a tool for enhancing the faculty member's teaching and scholarship.

In contrast, business schools tend to offer time for faculty to consult. Not only does such consulting offer additional remuneration for faculty, but it also means they are integrating themselves into practical business methods at real-world organizations. Such activity cannot help but inform their teaching and perhaps their scholarship.

Political science purposely has moved away from the identity as a profession toward one solely as a scientific discipline. Granted, political science does not look like a profession such as law or medicine. There are no professional standards for practice. There is no required examination or certification to become a political scientist versus a lawyer or a doctor.

However, there are aspects of political science that tie the discipline into professionalism. One is that students do go on to work in a particular field, much like business. Not only is political science a scientific discipline, but it also is a liberal arts major. And it leads to professions. These are not just in law or business but also in occupations related to government. These include government service at various levels, as well as those that touch on government, such as employment in lobbying groups and associations, campaign management, and applied research.

But for faculty such roles do not "count" toward tenure, promotion, or merit increases. That is true even for political scientists, for whom political engagement might serve as a useful supplement to teaching and scholarship. Nor do more extensive forms of involvement, such as a part-time job as an elected official, such as a member of a town council or a local school board.

Yet, even if a political science professor possesses the time, is seized by the idea that he or she should be a model, and is inclined to serve, there is still another barrier to involvement. It is the notion of professional neutrality. And the issue touches on both teaching and research.

In terms of teaching, the faculty member may worry about whether the classroom becomes not a forum for the presentation of political science theories and studies but a platform for advocacy. Doesn't civic engagement become advocacy? If it is, then how will the faculty member be perceived by students? Will teaching be impaired by an identification with particular causes, particularly if those causes may be unpopular with students?

What about the effect on the scholar's work? Will other scholars conclude that research projects are tinged by partisanship? Will they become less willing to accept findings from a scholar who is considered an advocate? These are real concerns that may give political scientists pause when contemplating personal political engagement that then becomes known to others. The purpose of this book is to demonstrate that the benefits of engagement for political scientists outweigh these concerns. However, we will see how others, including myself, have become engaged civically and addressed these potential drawbacks in their own professional lives. The first chapter will examine political scientists who became full-time practitioners and actually or effectively surrendered their academic positions. The second chapter features those who have engaged civically on a part-time or temporary basis. Chapters 3 through 7 describe my own political and civic engagement and the lessons I learned from those experiences. The concluding chapter offers suggestions on how the discipline and academic institutions can facilitate civic engagement by their political science faculty.

1. Engagement as a Practitioner

The discipline of political science has not encouraged political engagement by political scientists for the reasons discussed in the introduction. Yet, that engagement has been undertaken by some political scientists, as the next two chapters will demonstrate. In some cases, political involvement has been a full-time endeavor. And in those cases, with few exceptions, academic institutions have required political scientists to leave academe.

This chapter presents the cases of political scientists who have served as full-time practitioners for more than a typical leave period of two to three years during the past half century or so. They may have started these careers with professional leaves from their institutions, but (for the most part) eventually they became unaffiliated with those institutions. Some returned to academe after practitioner service.

We discuss first those who served in the legislative branch and then those in executive positions, although some (as will be discussed) served in both. Some of the individuals discussed will be well known to political scientists because they have held prominent positions in American government. Although less well known to the general public is the fact that they were political science faculty prior to their government service. Others, however, will be less well known because they were in lesser positions, they were not Americans, or their academic background was downplayed. But all these individuals share a common feature—they received doctoral degrees in political science and, prior to government service, they were full-time faculty in a political science department.

The following list is not intended to be exhaustive. Rather, it is a sample of political scientists who became full-time practitioners, at least for some period of their careers. These vignettes are designed to demonstrate that civic involvement has been engaged in successfully by political scientists.

Additionally, these vignettes will not seem very diverse. In that sense, it reflects academe generally and political science specifically. Women and racial and ethnic minorities have not been well represented in academe. According to the National Center for Education Statistics, in 2017, 76 percent of faculty members in the United States were white. Only 5 percent were Hispanic, while only 6 percent were African American. The disparity is even more acute at higher ranks, when professors are more likely to feel comfortable being civically engaged. The survey found that 81 percent of full professors were white. Similarly, higher education is male-dominated. In 2019, only 31 percent of full-time faculty were female. The percentage of tenured faculty is even lower—27 percent. There has been an increase in the percentage of full-time faculty over the past two decades, when the percentage stood at 26 percent, but those figures suggest gender parity is still a long way off.[1]

The problem is true as well in political science specifically. One study in 2013 found that 71 percent of political science department faculty in the United States were male. Another, in 2016, found a little improvement—68 percent were male. And, in the 2016 study, only 14 percent of political scientists self-identified as part of a racial or ethnic minority. The disadvantages for women and racial and ethnic minorities extend beyond hiring. Gender bias exists in methodological emphases of political science journals, coauthoring opportunities, and the ability to get published in the discipline's top journals. Not surprisingly, women are cited less often in political science and international relations journals.[2]

The models discussed below reflect that lack of diversity, which may be more problematic when examining faculty who are engaged civically because of timing (tenured faculty, particularly full professors, may feel freer to become civically involved due to the absence of review pressures) as well as concerns about succeeding in the field with the presence of long-term obstacles to career advancement. Nearly two-thirds of the academics discussed below who became full-time practitioners are male. That is not surprising given the fact that some of them come from time periods when women were rare among political science faculty. However, among those discussed below who engaged in civic service temporarily or on a part-time basis, more than one-third are female.

LEGISLATORS

Daniel Patrick Moynihan

One of the most extensive government careers by a political scientist was that of Daniel Patrick Moynihan. Over his career, he served as ambassador to India, ambassador to the United Nations, assistant secretary of labor, and a presidential advisor. Then, for twenty-four years, he represented New York state in the US Senate.

However, Moynihan also was an academic. At various times, he was on the faculty of Harvard University, Wesleyan University, Syracuse University, and Princeton University. Indeed, his academic career both preceded and succeeded his governmental one. Early in his professional career, he taught at Wesleyan and Harvard and then returned to academe after his retirement when he became a faculty member at the Maxwell School of Citizenship and

Public Affairs at Syracuse and a senior policy scholar at the School of Public and International Affairs at Princeton University.[3] Unfortunately, he was not able to return for long to academe. He passed away on March 27, 2003, at the age of seventy-six, only a little more than two years following his retirement from the US Senate.

As is characteristic of most political scientists who have jumped to full-time political careers, Moynihan was not known for publishing in academic journals. He coauthored one article in the *American Political Science Review*. He also coauthored *Beyond the Melting Pot*, which became a classic treatise on race and urban politics.[4] His interests gravitated toward applied research. And even while serving on university faculties, he was prolific at persuasive writing and speechmaking rather than scholarly article writing.

Not surprisingly, he was viewed with some suspicion by other academics. The fact that he left academe twice to pursue government work and that he had produced little traditional scholarship made that suspicion understandable.[5] Yet, Moynihan kept returning to academe, and particularly political science and public policy, including at the end of his life, which suggested his high degree of comfort in academic settings and, perhaps, his desire to be viewed, at least partly, as an academic.

In 1983, the APSA recognized Moynihan's contribution as a political scientist when he became the first recipient of the Hubert H. Humphrey Award in acknowledgment of his role in the discipline and in public service. The award recognizes a political scientist who has made notable contributions to public service.[6]

Moynihan also was well respected by his fellow senators for his analytical prowess and verbal elegance. One senator recalled he had "not known a more brilliant and more erudite Senator than [Moynihan]." Another termed him "a visionary" and added that he was one of the most "forward-thinking persons I have had the privilege to meet." Others used the terms "towering intellect," "a font of ideas," and "one of the great minds of America's 20th century."[7]

John East

The most powerful politician in North Carolina through the 1970s and 1980s was Senator Jesse Helms, an archconservative who influenced Ronald Reagan, the Republican Party, and the conservative movement. The other senator from North Carolina, however, was a Democrat named Robert B. Morgan. Although conservative, Morgan was not conservative enough for Jesse Helms. Helms recruited John East, a political science professor from East Carolina University, to run against Morgan and provided significant financial support for East to make a viable race. East narrowly won and joined Helms in the US Senate.[8]

East was chosen because he fit well within the ideological requirements of the conservative movement. As a political scientist, East had published frequently, but it was primarily in conservative academic journals such as *Modern Age*. He authored one article in a mainstream political science journal, *Western Political Quarterly* (now *Political Research Quarterly*).[9]

While teaching at East Carolina, he became heavily involved in electoral and party politics. He ran for the US House in 1966 and then for North Carolina secretary of state in 1968, losing both elections. He also served as a Republican National Committeeman from North Carolina. He already was known in electoral circles when Senator Helms urged him to run for the US Senate seat in 1980, which he subsequently won.[10]

East was a staunch conservative. He said of himself that he was "one of those rare creatures in academe, a conservative political science professor."[11] His Senate votes nearly always matched those of his mentor, Helms.

A year before the end of his first term, East announced he would not seek reelection due to ill health. He had contracted polio while serving in the US Marine Corps and spent the rest of his life confined to a wheelchair. Throughout 1985, he missed many Senate votes due to his health. He suffered from hypothyroidism, which can lead to depression.[12]

On June 30, 1986, he died of carbon monoxide poisoning in his garage. The reasons for his suicide are unknown. He had made plans to rejoin the Political Science Department at East Carolina. His mentor, Jesse Helms, had recommended to President Reagan that East be appointed a federal judge, but East told Helms he wanted to return to academe. At the time he died, he had been reviewing page proofs of a book of essays.[13]

Paul Wellstone

In 1990, a little-known political science professor defeated a two-term incumbent senator in Minnesota. Paul Wellstone, an associate professor at Carlton College in Northfield, was propelled from anonymity onto the national stage.[14] He would remain on that stage as a forceful proponent of progressive policy positions until his untimely death in an airplane crash during his reelection bid in 2002.

Wellstone's emphasis in graduate school was American politics with a specialization in race and poverty. These research interests stimulated his activism. To complete his dissertation on Black militants, he interviewed low-income Black Americans about their attitudes toward government generally and the police specifically. He considered this research project to be life-changing, since it broadened his perspective on how public policy affected ordinary citizens' lives. He organized protests while in graduate school, including one involving university cafeteria workers.[15]

From 1969 to his election to the US Senate, Wellstone taught political science at Carleton. But Wellstone's scholarship record was skimpy. He wrote only one scholarly article in his first two years. His first book, published by the University of Minnesota Press, documented his organizing efforts with poor people in a southern Minnesota county. The book only lightly addressed political science literature.[16] His research did not contain public policy recommendations for public policy officials. When the president of Carleton told him that he should include policy recommendations for decision-makers, Wellstone replied that his policy research wasn't for politicians; it was intended to help empower poor people to solve their problems.[17]

Wellstone was nearly terminated after four years when his department chair offered him only a one-year contract and then dismissal. He had incurred the wrath of the college administration when he attacked the chairman of the board of trustees for managing a "criminal corporation." His department voted unanimously not to rehire him.[18] Fifteen hundred students (out of sixteen hundred on campus) rallied in Wellstone's defense and the administration agreed to suspend the decision and conduct a review by two external scholars—Peter Bachrach at Temple and Ira Katznelson at Columbia. The two scholars interviewed faculty and students, reviewed his scholarship, and examined his community service. Both gave positive evaluations of Wellstone's work and recommended he be tenured. Due to Bachrach and Katznelson's review, Wellstone received early tenure.[19] The fact that the external review included Wellstone's community service was an indication that the two prominent scholars considered that facet of Wellstone's record to be significant enough to overcome the paucity of scholarship.

Wellstone continued his activism for the next sixteen years. He became involved in strikes and labor disputes. He worked with Minnesota farmers. He became a leader in the Democratic-Farmer-Labor Party in Minnesota. His activism also strengthened his contacts throughout the state.

Yet, Wellstone did not abandon scholarship. Instead, he intermingled scholarship with activism. He coauthored *Powerline: The First Battle of America's Energy War*, which narrated the story of Minnesota farmers fighting a powerful utility company that wanted to stretch a high-voltage power line across their farms. Wellstone not only wrote about the incident but also proffered advice to the farmers about how to organize their protests.[20]

At first, Wellstone eschewed electoral politics. Ironically, during his life he ran for office four times—once for state auditor and three times for the US

Senate. The state auditor campaign was an odd one because Wellstone had no experience in accounting or auditing. He admitted he did not do well reading tables and statistics. Clearly, he was unqualified for the job. But his passion to serve was overwhelming.

The job of being a US senator was closer to his interests and skills. But he was facing long odds when he ran in 1990 against Rudy Boschwitz, the incumbent who was a wealthy businessman and already had built a significant war chest to ward off potential challengers. Plus, Boschwitz enjoyed a 70 percent approval rating. Fortunately for Wellstone, stronger challengers were scared off by Boschwitz's money. However, Wellstone turned Boschwitz's wealth back on him, claiming the GOP incumbent represented elites while Wellstone would work for ordinary Minnesotans. To blunt Boschwitz's financial advantage, Wellstone used humor. His ads featured him introducing himself and saying that since he didn't have $6 million for his campaign, he would have to talk fast in the commercial. It was a fast-paced ad that drew the news media's attention and suddenly increased his name recognition.[21]

With his election to a six-year term, Wellstone left Carleton. He would not return. While campaigning for a third term in 2002, Wellstone, his wife, his daughter, and three staff members were killed in a small airplane crash in rural Minnesota. Former vice president Walter Mondale took Wellstone's place on the ballot. However, with the election less than two weeks away, Mondale had no time to mount a campaign. He narrowly lost to St. Paul mayor Norm Coleman.

The story of Paul Wellstone is instructive, because all the barriers to activism that face other people also confronted him. One was the reality of time. He later related that when he was a student, he was reluctant to get involved because he did not believe he had time for political activism. He was a full-time student, a star of the wrestling team, and worked full-time. In addition, he became a father while an undergraduate.[22] Yet, he joined protests, advised farmers, supported strikes, organized demonstrations, worked in a political party, and became a candidate while still teaching and raising a family.

Another obstacle was the initial lack of support from his institution. His department chair attempted to fire him. Carleton College backed down only when students demonstrated in his behalf. It was fitting that the very students he had taken to rallies, taught how to organize politically, and motivated to action would do so to save his job.

It was no surprise that students supported him. They appreciated his passion, his dedication to teaching them practical politics, and his own example. Repeatedly, he received teaching awards. Much of that may have been due to his position as a role model. One of his former students became his campaign manager for the first US Senate campaign.

Yet another stumbling block to activism is the paradigm among political scientists that one should remain an observer and not employ political science specifically for public good. Paul Wellstone was different in the sense that he said he was committed to using his "skills as a political scientist to empower people and to step forward with people in justice struggles."[23]

Wellstone left the academic world to, as he said, "use this position of power to make a difference."[24] Yet, he attributed his willingness to do so to students. He met students with negative perceptions of politics and politicians. He wanted to change that perception by becoming one of those politicians and using politics to improve the lives of ordinary people.

Jack Layton

As a young man, Jack Layton did not seem destined to become the leader of the New Democratic Party (NDP), the left-wing alternative to the Liberal and Progressive Conservative parties in Canada. His father became a member of Parliament representing the center-right Progressive Conservatives. Layton grew up in an upper-class family and neighborhood in Hudson, Quebec. His family belonged to an exclusive English-oriented yacht club, where he spent time swimming and sailing.[25]

But his first act of social defiance was as a junior commodore of the club, the head of the youth wing, when he invited French-speaking lower-class youth to a club dance without notifying the club board. His objective was to lessen the social inequality in the city. The board chastised him the next day, and he and the other youth club members disbanded themselves in protest.[26]

As an undergraduate, he was active in a left-wing political group opposing gentrification. He also was heavily influenced by Charles Taylor, who was a rising star in political philosophy at the time but also was an ardent supporter of the NDP. As a graduate student, he studied under James Laxer, who co-founded a youth group within the NDP that urged the party not to "waffle" on key issues.[27]

But his first career was as an academic. He received an MA from York University and sought a teaching position while working on a doctorate, which he received a decade later. He taught at Ryerson University (then known as Polytechnic Institute) and then York and Toronto. Yet, he also became integrated into a group of activists in Toronto city politics. He lobbied for rent control programs and fair transit fares and advocated for community policing.[28]

Layton was not a scholar. He published rarely in journals or academic books. His two books—both for general audiences—were written after he became a full-time politician.[29] And after nearly ten years as an academic, he was recruited by a left-wing former mayor to run for the Toronto City Council.

He was elected and would serve for more than a decade. In 1990, he became deputy mayor of Toronto but lost the election as mayor the following year. He also lost two subsequent two elections as the NDP candidate for the Canadian Federal Parliament, although he was reelected to the city council.

However, in 2003, he was elected as leader of the NDP and was elected four times for Parliament after that. In the last election in which he ran, his party became the second-largest parliamentary party, making Layton the leader of the Official Opposition. It was the first time an NDP leader had served in that role.[30] Layton became personally popular and was highly successful in revamping his party's image from one of a nascent third party to a successful major party through his performances in leader debates.

Unfortunately, Layton did not serve long. Within a few weeks of the election, he announced he was taking a temporary leave to fight cancer. However, within a month he was dead.

David Price

With a father who was a high school principal and a mother who was a teacher, it was not surprising that David Price became a teacher himself. He graduated from the University of North Carolina in 1961 and then continued his studies at Yale, earning first a divinity degree and then a doctoral degree in political science.[31]

Price became an expert on political parties and Congress, authoring several books and articles. He taught at Duke University in political science and public policy from 1973 until 1986. That year, he ran for Congress and, in his Democratic-leaning district, was elected. But he lost in the 1994 Republican surge. He returned to Duke but then was elected again in 1996. He retained a position at the Sanford School of Public Policy even while in Congress.

Unlike Wellstone, Price continued to publish in political science while in Congress. He wrote *The Congressional Experience*, a firsthand account of congressional politics and processes. In addition, he contributed a book chapter to a volume in honor of David Mayhew that explained increasing polarization and competitiveness as forces producing congressional dysfunction. And he wrote articles in *PS: Political Science & Politics*.[32]

Price was a longtime member serving on the House Appropriations Committee. He was the chair of the Subcommittee on Transportation, Housing and Urban Development, and Related Agencies. He also served on the House Budget Committee. Given his academic interests, it was no surprise he was invested in the House Democracy Partnership and at one time served as the commission's chair. The commission works to develop effective and independent legislatures through training and mentoring of legislatures in nations across the globe. One of Price's major policy objectives was improving election law. He became a forceful advocate of legislation that requires candidates to identify themselves in their advertisements.[33]

Price also became a voice of warning for the nation. Having served in Congress for more than thirty years, Price had a rare institutional memory and an appreciation for a time when Congress was a more collegial, productive body. He has warned that Congress "is an institution that's really damaged by partisanship and extremists."[34]

Price retired from Congress in 2022 after thirty-four years of service. He speculated that he might return to teaching. However, he urged others to continue to work on issues of importance to Americans, such as education, housing, and transportation. Wearing his professor hat, Price advised students who were contemplating a career in politics to be engaged politically but not to think that serving in elective office is the only way to serve: "Pay attention and be involved, including on a local level. Be aware of opportunities. Run for office yourself but do not put all your eggs in that basket."[35]

Ted Morton

Ted Morton did not intend to become involved in electoral politics or government service. A native of Wyoming, he earned a doctorate in political economy from the University of Toronto and was offered an assistant professor position at the University of Calgary. In his American politics course, he offered students a comparison with the Canadian political system and began to advocate for a reformation of the Canadian Senate toward the US model. In Canada, senators are appointed by the prime minister, not elected. Morton began to write op-eds urging election of senators, comparing the success of western oil-producing states in the United States in promoting their interests through an elected senate.[36]

His commentaries attracted the attention of the founder of a new political party—the Reform Party—and he became involved in the party after he obtained Canadian citizenship. He was encouraged to run for the Canadian Senate under a novel law passed by the Alberta Provincial Assembly. The law required an election of nominees whose names were then forwarded to the prime minister. However, the individuals were known only as "senators in waiting" because the prime minister was under no obligation to appoint them. Some prime ministers did, but others did not. Morton waited for six years but was not appointed.

However, he did become more involved in the Reform Party. In 2001, he served as the director of policy and research for the party for nine months but did not take a leave of absence to fulfill the role. His schedule was grueling: He spent Tuesday through Thursday in Ottawa and taught his classes on Mondays and Fridays.

Throughout the 1990s and into the early 2000s, with the exception of 2001, Morton's service was not full time. He was involved in Reform Party politics but was an active teacher and scholar. During this period, he authored and edited several books and journal articles. He wrote on the Canadian Charter and constitutional law.

After that service, he decided to concentrate on Alberta politics. He joined the Progressive Conservative Party of Alberta and ran for and was elected to the Alberta Legislative Assembly, where he served for eight years. While serving as an MLA, he was appointed to three ministerial positions—minister of sustainable resources development, minister of finance, and minister of energy. He ran for party leader (which would have made him premier) on two occasions but lost both times.[37]

His government service became full time during this eight-year period and he took an unpaid leave of absence. The University of Calgary provided this opportunity for individuals who are in public service. Morton said he is grateful for that policy that allows faculty to retain their positions, although without pay, while they are engaged in public service such as serving in elective or appointive office with government or political parties. "We academics often have types of expertise and policy knowledge that most politicians lack," Ted explains.[38]

His political career affected his teaching and scholarship. When he returned to the classroom, Morton used his government experience to develop a new course, Alberta Energy Politics. Also, he related the lessons he had learned from his government experience in his classes on constitutional law as well as American politics. In terms of scholarship, his research became more policy-oriented and less theoretical. He wrote on the federal carbon tax, the provincial budget, and referenda, among other topics. He is currently professor emeritus at the University of Calgary.

EXECUTIVE

Henry Kissinger

The most influential political scientist in US foreign policy, and the most notorious, was Henry Kissinger. Not only was Kissinger a prolific and prominent scholar in international relations, but he also held the highest government post occupied by an American political scientist—secretary of state—since Woodrow Wilson. And he won the Nobel Peace Prize for his work in extricating the United States from the Vietnam War.

At the age of fifteen, Kissinger emigrated to the United States from Nazi Germany. He served in the US Army in World War II and after the war attended Harvard. He was a student in the Government Department, graduating in 1950. He earned a PhD there in 1954 and then joined the faculty. He was at Harvard briefly before he joined the staff of the Council on Foreign Relations. However, he returned to the Harvard faculty in 1957 and remained until 1971. Even when he resigned, however, he was promised that he would not lose his tenured chair.[39]

Kissinger spent thirteen years in academe before leaving to serve as national security advisor in the Nixon administration. But the surprise is he did not leave earlier. He was a cynic toward academe. In a candid exchange with Richard Nixon caught on the Oval Office taping system, Kissinger told Nixon that "academic life is a depressing period." When Nixon asked how it was depressing, he continued by disparaging his fellow academics: "Well, first of all, because you're spending your life with a group of teenagers, Mr. President. And it is, after all, instead of helping the teenagers grow up they become almost as irresponsible as the people . . . with whom they meet with day in and day out."[40]

Kissinger added that academe was "an insecure making profession." He exempted himself and Arthur Schlesinger Jr., who he described as "top people." But the others were insecure because an academic "goes through ten years of maddening insecurity before he ever gets tenured." He told Nixon that "in academic life you are entirely dependent on the personal recommendation of some egomaniac. Nobody knows how good you are."[41] Kissinger was fond of repeating a phrase penned by Wallace Stanley Sayre, a Columbia University public administration professor, that "the reason academic politics are so bitter is that so little is at stake."[42]

Not surprisingly, even from his first arrival on the Harvard faculty, Kissinger was not the typical professor. For one thing, he quickly became a public intellectual. He wrote for the *New Republic* and *Foreign Affairs.* His books were closely read by policy makers as well as academics. For many years, he was a close foreign policy advisor to New York governor Nelson Rockefeller, particularly during his three unsuccessful presidential campaigns. However, he also advised the Kennedy and Johnson administrations, as well as the Hubert Humphrey campaign in 1968. He worked at the Rockefeller Brothers Fund and became a consultant to the Foreign Policy Research Institute at the University of Pennsylvania and the Joint Chiefs of Staff.[43]

During the 1968 presidential campaign, and while serving the Johnson administration, Kissinger was accused by journalist Seymour Hersch of leaking secret information about the Vietnam Peace talks to Richard Nixon, thus cementing his allegiance to Nixon (although two of Kissinger's biographers discount the charge).[44] After Nixon's election, Kissinger took a leave from Harvard to become national security advisor in the White House. But he was no ordinary national security advisor, because Nixon centered foreign policy making in the White House. He became the president's chief diplomat, pre-empting the role of Secretary of State William Rodgers. He negotiated the US withdrawal from Vietnam and was awarded the Nobel Peace Prize. He made a secret trip to Beijing to orchestrate the historic visit of Nixon to China in 1972. He also was instrumental in the arms control talks with the Soviet Union that led to détente between the superpowers. Kissinger was known for being manipulative, secretive, and ambitious, as well as cultivating the press to hone his personal image as a celebrity diplomat.

When he became secretary of state in 1973—first for Nixon and then for Gerald Ford—he was one of the most powerful occupants of that role in its history, particularly with a president (Ford) who knew relatively little about foreign policy. Kissinger was a key player in resolving Middle East conflicts. He became famous for his shuttle diplomacy, as well as his penchant for catering to the press to gain positive personal coverage.[45]

Throughout his career, Kissinger was known for his embrace of realpolitik. He was viewed as a cold realist who was willing to deal with the world as it was rather than engage in a moralistic foreign policy that he considered un-workable. As a result, he became associated with US acceptance of undesirable foreign leaders such as the Shah Reza Pahlavi, Augusto Pinochet, and Leonid Brezhnev. Kissinger became one of the most controversial US foreign policy leaders of the twentieth century.

Unlike others described in this book who returned to full-time academic life after their roles as practitioners, Kissinger never did. He did teach part-time at Georgetown University for a brief period. Instead, he created a con-sulting firm, Kissinger Associates, that drew clients from the rich and powerful across the globe.

Jeane Kirkpatrick

The transition from academic to public servant was abrupt for Jeane Kirk-patrick. She was teaching political science courses at Georgetown University when, in December 1980, she got a call from Ronald Reagan asking her to join his administration as the US ambassador to the United Nations.[46] She had met Reagan earlier that year when he asked to talk to her about a con-troversial article she had written differentiating US government response to left-wing dictatorships versus right-wing ones. The article, in the conserva-tive journal *Commentary*, was titled "Dictatorships & Double Standards" and piqued Reagan's interest because it strongly criticized the Carter administra-tion's foreign policy approach of championing the rise of left-wing regimes that were supported by Communist mentors while supporting the overthrow of right-wing dictators who, although oppressive, nevertheless served US national security interests.[47]

However, Kirkpatrick had worked at times outside academe prior to earning a PhD from Columbia University. She was hired by the Department of State's Office of Intelligence Research, where she met her future husband, Evron Kirkpatrick. After their marriage, she moved to the Economic Cooperation Administration. Then, she took a job at the Human Resources Research Organization. In each setting, however, her role was to conduct research for the various organizations, presaging her work in academe. She also assisted her husband in his work for the Democratic National Committee and senator and later vice president Hubert Humphrey. She wrote speeches for and advised Humphrey's campaigns, including his presidential bid in 1968.[48]

Once she joined academe full time, she devoted herself primarily to teaching and traditional political science research. During the thirteen years prior to her UN appointment, she wrote books and articles on gender and politics, political elites, and Peronism in Argentina. But she also became increasingly vocal as a public intellectual, as evidenced by the essay that led to her appointment. She became a frequent contributor to conservative opinion journals.

She served in the Reagan administration for four years but then returned to Georgetown. She had negotiated her return four years earlier when she left for public service in government. And she remained there for another seventeen years until she finally retired at the age of seventy-six. She had one brief foray into active diplomacy in 2003 when she was asked by President George W. Bush to convince Arab foreign ministers not to oppose the Iraq War.[49] After meeting with them in Geneva, Switzerland, she successfully muted their opposition. She spent most of those years following her government service continuing to seek to influence public policy through a syndicated column, congressional testimony, speeches, and essays in opinion magazines. She did not return to traditional scholarship.[50] She died in 2006 at the age of eighty.

Madeleine Albright

The first female US secretary of state was a Georgetown University professor whose father, a Czech diplomat, emigrated to the United States from Czechoslovakia with his family after Communists took over the government.[51] Madeleine Albright had a dramatic life. Her family moved to London to escape Nazism prior to World War II. But then they returned after the war to rebuild Czechoslovakia. But the Communist takeover was opposed by her father, Josef Kerbel, and he resigned and moved his family to Denver, where he became a professor of international relations at the University of Denver. Her father had a profound influence on her and stimulated her interest in global affairs. She graduated from the University of Denver in political science and then received a master's degree from Columbia University.

Albright worked on the staff of Senator Edmund Muskie (D-Maine) before joining the National Security Council staff under Jimmy Carter. She received a PhD while on Muskie's staff and after Carter's term ended in 1981 became a fellow at the Center for Strategic and International Studies and then worked as a faculty member at Georgetown University's School of Foreign Service.

Albright was not a scholar. In fact, her position as a faculty member was as a professor of practice. However, she was active at Georgetown in directing the school's program for women in politics. She also created a leadership seminar, much like the one conducted at Harvard by Henry Kissinger.

While at Georgetown, she kept involved in practical politics as well. She advised Democratic presidential and vice presidential candidates. She also served as president of the Center for National Policy, a Washington, DC, foreign-policy think tank.

She became a foreign policy advisor to then-candidate Bill Clinton during the 1992 presidential campaign. When Clinton won, he brought Albright into his administration, appointing her as US ambassador to the United Nations. During her tenure as the United States' chief delegate at the UN, she quarreled with Secretary General Boutros Boutros-Ghali over the involvement of the United States in UN peacekeeping efforts. The Clinton administration pulled back from UN missions after US troops were killed in Somalia and was absent in efforts to end the genocide in Rwanda in 1994. Albright later admitted she regretted that inaction.

In 1997, she became the first female secretary of state. She favored expansion of NATO to former Warsaw Pact nations and supported the bombing of military targets in Iraq in 1998 to halt Iraq's weapons of mass destruction program. She was a tenacious advocate of Clinton administration foreign policies and was praised for her diplomatic skills.

After her public service, she taught at Georgetown University but also ran her own consulting firm. She was awarded the Presidential Medal of Freedom by Barack Obama in 2012. She passed away in 2022.[52]

Ralph Bunche

During his life, Ralph Bunche was one of the most influential and respected Black intellectuals of his day. He wrote extensively on race relations, arguing that social, political, and economic factors were root causes of racism and rejecting calls for Black separatism. He also served as an international diplomat with the United Nations for twenty-five years. He won the Nobel Peace Prize in 1950 for his work in mediating the Israeli-Palestinian conflict. He was the first

Black person to win a Nobel prize. He also served as a UN official mediating subsequent conflicts in the Congo, Cyprus, and Syria. Ralph Bunche was the most prominent Black international figure of his day.

But Bunche's original career goal was to be a university professor of political science. After receiving a master's degree in political science from Harvard, Bunche was recruited to create a new political science department at Howard University. He hired two other professors and began to seek department resources and increased salaries. Given the small size of the department, it is not surprising he taught a wide array of courses, such as political thought, constitutional law, municipal administration, European politics, and international affairs, to name a few. He was appointed assistant to Howard's president and became a leading figure in Howard University administration.[53]

Yet, he continued his doctoral work and, in 1934, became the first Black American awarded a doctorate in political science in the United States. His dissertation on French colonialism in Africa predicted his future diplomatic efforts regarding decolonization. After receiving his doctorate, he continued to teach at Howard until World War II.

But even during his tenure at Howard, Bunche was actively engaged in nonacademic activism. He helped form the National Negro Congress, an organization designed to oppose racial discrimination. Shortly thereafter, he distanced himself from the organization when it became dominated by Communist Party officials.[54] He was involved in protests of racial discrimination policies during the 1940s and became a leader in the NAACP. Along with other NAACP leaders, he planned a march on Washington in 1941 that would have involved several thousand Black Americans protesting racial discrimination in the defense industry. The march was canceled after President Franklin Roosevelt signed an executive order banning such discrimination.[55]

Two months before Pearl Harbor, Bunche went to work with the Office of Strategic Services (OSS) as an African specialist. Two years later, he was transferred to the State Department. He was involved in drafting the charter of the United Nations, served as a member of the first US delegation to the UN, and then joined the new body in the Trusteeship Council, the organization responsible for overseeing territories under the mandate of the League of Nations. That included Palestine. In 1948, he successfully negotiated a truce and eventually an armistice between the Israelis and the Palestinians that lasted until 1956. He also established the role of UN peacekeeping forces in resolving global conflicts.[56]

Following the Nobel Peace Prize, Bunche became a celebrity. His picture appeared on the cover of *Ebony* magazine. He was asked to lecture across the country and given honorary degrees. He was mentioned as a potential candidate for the US Senate in New York or even a vice presidential candidate. Since he declared himself unaffiliated with any political party, he was sought by both Republicans and Democrats. Ambassadorships were explored as well. At one point, even before the Nobel prize, he was offered the job as assistant secretary of state but publicly declined it because he did not want to live in segregated Washington, DC.[57]

After World War II, Bunche intended to return to Howard. He also received offers from other universities, including Harvard, Stanford, and the University of Chicago. However, he remained at his post as under-secretary-general for special political affairs through the remainder of his life. He died in 1971 after long bouts of ill health. At his death, he was memorialized on the editorial pages of the *New York Times*.

Yet, Bunche is largely forgotten today. One of his biographers noted that anonymity may be attributed to his success as a negotiator: "Bunche's fame derived from his skill as a troubleshooter. By its nature, troubleshooting is most successful when the conflict that is its target is prevented or minimized. Therefore, Bunche's most successful actions were those the public was likely to hear the least about."[58] But from what contemporaries related about Bunche, being famous was not important to him anyway.

Stephane Dion

Stephane Dion was one of only three leaders of the Liberal Party in Canada who did not become prime minister. But he also had the distinction of being the only major party leader in Canadian history to have been a university political science professor prior to pursuing a political career. His professional beginnings were in academe, but, thanks to his opposition to Quebec separatism, he became a politician after a dozen years as an academic.[59]

Dion taught at the University of Montreal with a specialty in Canadian politics. He wrote on secessionism, partisan effects on public policy, and bureaucrats. He was a prolific scholar. His work was published in various venues, such as the *British Journal of Political Science, Polity, Comparative Political Studies*, the *Canadian Journal of Political Science*, and the *American Journal of Political Science*. He sought to explain to non-Canadian scholars the appeal of Quebec separatism at a time when separatist sentiment was at a fever pitch and the prospect of a separate Quebec was high.[60]

It was Dion's writings and speeches against separatism that caught the attention of then prime minister Jean Chretien. The need for Canadian unity prompted Chretien to appoint a political neophyte to his cabinet as minister of intergovernmental affairs. Dion had established his reputation as a scholar of Canadian politics, not as a politician. However, Dion also appreciated the need to speak to a broader audience, which attracted Chretien at a moment when he needed intellectual ballast for his effort to maintain Canadian unity in the face of Quebec nationalistic sentiment. Dion's ability to support both Quebec's distinctive culture and Canadian unity aided the federal government in disarming Quebec separatism. He explained that he was "Quebecois and Canadian at the same time, and I do not want to choose between those two identities."[61]

Later, Dion admitted he had no intention of entering practical politics and considered the university to be "my only professional universe." He was not expected to serve for long in an administration but was widely thought to be intent on shortly returning to teaching.[62] But he did not. He retained his scholarly approach but remained in practical politics. Dion was elected to the House of Commons following his cabinet appointment in 1996, and, reflecting his academic career, during his maiden speech Dion quoted Tocqueville, Rousseau, and Montesquieu in his call for caution regarding potential succession by Quebec.[63]

His work on Quebec nationalism gained him support from the Liberal Party, even though he was considered by some to be a "sort of wooden" intellectual narrowly focused on Quebec.[64] After ten years in Parliament (seven as minister of intergovernmental affairs and two as minister of environment, where he championed the Kyoto Protocol on climate change) he ran for Liberal leader. He was a longshot at first but eventually won the party's support for the job.

But his tenure as leader was brief. He was criticized for his strong French accent and his difficulty with English. Another problem was his image as a poor leader. He became pedantic when a broadcast reporter asked him a simple question about what he would do differently with the economy. He addressed the nation in a poorly made video. Dion was unable to gain broad public support. His party lost by-elections and then the next federal election, diminishing Dion's standing. He resigned as party leader but retained his seat in the House of Commons.[65] But seven years later, Dion was appointed minister of foreign affairs in the Justin Trudeau cabinet and later became Canada's special envoy to the European Union and ambassador to Germany.

Stephane Dion brought a political scientist's perspective to his work in government. Unfortunately, the negative stereotypes about academics also followed him into practical politics. However, he was able to turn his scholarly expertise on federalism into service to his country in helping prevent separation at a crucial moment in its history.

Condoleezza Rice
The best-known political scientist in the United States undoubtedly is Condoleezza Rice. She regularly appeared on Gallup's "most admired woman" survey,

even long after she left office.[66] She broke new ground as the first Black woman serving as White House national security advisor and then secretary of state.

However, her goal as an undergraduate student at the University of Denver was to become a political science professor. She was on a fast track to that end. She was a college freshman at fifteen and graduated four years later. She was hired by the Political Science Department at Stanford University at twenty-six and then began her career as an assistant professor. She taught courses on civil-military relations and Soviet foreign policy and published her dissertation with Princeton University Press. She won teaching awards and became known as a lecturer capable of teaching with few notes.[67]

A traditional academic career did not unfold. While still a junior faculty member at Stanford, she accepted a Council on Foreign Relations fellowship with the Joint Chiefs of Staff. There, she met Colin Powell, who became a mentor. After eight years at Stanford, she was appointed to the staff of the National Security Council as director of Soviet and East Europe in the George H. W. Bush administration.[68]

Stanford was accommodating to her. She received three leaves of absence within four years. But she was still bound by policies on the length of a leave of absence. She was told by Stanford administration that she must return after two years or lose her tenured position. In 1991, she resigned her post at the White House and returned to her role as an associate professor in the Political Science Department. However, two years later, the new Stanford president, Gerhard Casper, appointed her the university's provost. The choice was surprising because she was still an associate professor, which should have disqualified her. But she was immediately promoted to fill that requirement. She served there until 1999, when she took a leave to serve as foreign policy advisor to then presidential candidate George W. Bush.[69]

After Bush's election, she was appointed his national security advisor, a role she held for four years. She worked with Bush in the wake of 9/11, the war in Iraq, and the controversial "war on terror" that included torture of prisoners by US operatives. Rice became highly loyal to George W. Bush and, not surprisingly, became an advocate associated with controversial policies. She was criticized for not adequately informing Bush about the pros and cons of the Iraqi War. She also became associated with the controversial measures in the war on terror, such as torture.[70]

That loyalty served her well as the president asked her to replace Colin Powell, who had become isolated within the administration, as secretary of state at the beginning of Bush's second term. Rice would be only the second woman to serve as secretary of state, and she served among two strong-willed men—Donald Rumsfeld, secretary of defense, and Dick Cheney, vice president. Ultimately, she played a role in the ouster of Rumsfeld in 2006.

As secretary of state, her "first" status and her own publicity efforts made her a "rock star" and prompted speculation she would run for president or vice president at the end of Bush's second term. Yet, Rice failed in her main priority—resolving conflict in the Middle East related to the Palestinian state.

After her stint as secretary of state, Rice returned to academe. She became a full professor in Stanford's Political Science Department. In 2020, she became director of the Hoover Institution.

Tijjani Muhammad-Bande

On September 17, 2019, Tijjani Muhammad-Bande became president of the General Assembly of the United Nations. The position was not the first diplomatic post for Muhammad-Bande. He was vice president of the UN General Assembly, director-general of the National Institute for Policy and Strategic Studies and, prior to that, director-general of the African Center for Administration Training and Research for Development.

However, prior to his governmental appointments, he was a political science professor. He received an MA in political science from Boston University and a PhD in political science from the University of Toronto. He taught at the Usmanu Danfodiyo University in Sokoto, Nigeria, where he became a full professor. He later served as vice chancellor at the university.[71]

As General Assembly president, Muhammad-Bande wanted to make progress in eradicating poverty, addressing climate change, and promoting public education. He convened a meeting of policy makers, educators, and leaders of civil society organizations to achieve more cooperation across nations on raising education levels around the world. He also emphasized financial accountability and transparency to stem the illegal flow of money across the world. However, a major problem during his tenure was the world's handling of the COVID-19 pandemic.[72]

Muhammad-Bande has been a scholar of African politics since graduate school. His dissertation studied the role of history and community in the future of African governance. He has researched civil service in Africa but then became the administrator of programs designed to train African civil servants.[73]

Muhammad-Bande is still in government service. As of this writing, he is Nigeria's Permanent Representative to the United Nations, a post he has held since 2017. He is still active in seeking to find solutions to the problems he has identified throughout his career as both an academic and a diplomat.

Donna Shalala

When the results came in on November 6, 2018, it was clear that voters in Florida's twenty-seventh US House district had elected the second-oldest freshman representative to Congress in the nation's history. Donna Shalala's election to

Congress at seventy-seven years old was the culmination of a remarkable career as an academic, an administrator, and a public servant. Her expertise is urban politics, local government financing, and education policy.

After earning a PhD from the Maxwell School of Citizenship and Public Affairs (Syracuse), Shalala taught at the City University of New York, Columbia University, and the University of Wisconsin. While teaching in New York City, she was appointed to the Municipal Assistance Corporation, a body that had been formed to bring New York out of its severe fiscal woes. She was highly praised for her two-year stint as a director and treasurer of the corporation.[74]

She returned to academe in 1980 and spent the next thirteen years as the president of Hunter College and then chancellor of the University of Wisconsin-Madison. Then, she was appointed secretary of health and human services in the Clinton administration. At the time, one of her friends joked: "If Bill Clinton has been running for President since he was 2, Donna has been running for Cabinet Secretary since she was 3." She was praised for being an effective administrator. For her part, she explained, "Being able to do good is fun. Being able to make things better is sheer fun for me."[75]

Following her service as secretary of health and human services in the Clinton administration, she returned to educational administration as president of the University of Miami.[76] Even after retiring from the University of Miami, she continued her service as the head of the Clinton Foundation, a post she held for two years. Simultaneously, she was a faculty member in the Political Science Department at the University of Miami.

Then, she decided to run for Congress, which was a game-changer for Miami politics because she was so well known as a civic leader in Miami-Dade County.[77] Her congressional service was short-lived, however. After only one term, she was defeated for reelection in 2020. Shalala's revolving door from academe to government provides an example of a political scientist who valued public service but also kept one foot firmly in the world of academe.

LESSONS LEARNED

These vignettes of public officials who began their careers as academics are designed to help current political scientists understand the impact some political scientists have had in the sphere of civic engagement beyond the university. For some, even when they have left academe full-time, they still held a desire to return. Indeed, some did return, even briefly. Others have left behind academe after their public service and never returned. Still others, such as David Price, retained ties to the university and continued to publish.

It does appear that the tendency toward practical politics began early in most cases. Those who became practical politicians typically began their careers in both applied and academic jobs, sometimes rotating between the two. Condoleezza Rice, Henry Kissinger, and Jeane Kirkpatrick are examples. However, their early careers were not entirely applied. Most still lived in the academic world—teaching at a university and publishing in academic journals.

Yet, even those who were solidly in academe had ties to practitioners that made the transition possible. The examples given above suggest that academics specializing in international relations are more easily drawn into national government. Once again, Henry Kissinger, Jeane Kirkpatrick, and Condoleezza Rice are examples. Yet, there are examples of others who are oriented toward domestic politics. Clearly, Ted Morton, Donna Shalala, and Stephane Dion, none of whom were international relations experts, were recruited to government positions unrelated to foreign policy.

Policy expertise mattered in some cases. Stephane Dion became a government minister because of his involvement in the issue of Quebec separatism. In other cases, such as Jack Layton, David Price, Paul Wellstone, and John East, they simply ran for office and won. Had they not won, they may have continued a career in academics. Admittedly, some, such as Jack Layton and Paul Wellstone, may have continued to pursue a political career until they did win.

Regardless of the origins of their involvement, these political science professors provide examples of individuals who chose to apply their expertise in practical politics. They demonstrate that academics can be influential in government roles and make a difference on a full-time basis (at least for a time) in public policy at various levels. These are the most prominent because they transitioned to government. Few political scientists, however, will chose this path. The vignettes in the next chapter show what is a more common path.

2. Engagement as an Academic

Leaving academe to become a full-time practitioner is not the only way for a political scientist to be civically engaged. In fact, it is a rare way to do so. Most political scientists will avoid that kind of involvement. Instead, the vast majority who are civically engaged will limit their involvement to local volunteerism that can be pursued on a part-time basis while full-time employment is retained.

This chapter provides examples of academics who do (or did) just that. They are civically engaged but do so primarily on a part-time basis. Some may take temporary leaves for full-time service. Or they may be paid for their part-time service, but it is only a supplemental salary as a school board member or city councilor. And those salaries often pale in comparison to the time spent doing the job. People in such positions, particularly in local government, often calculate that, given the hours they expend on their particular role, they are being paid at the level of the minimum wage.

The descriptions of civically engaged political scientists below fall into four categories. The first includes examples of those elected to public office and demonstrates how they balance elective office with their full-time faculty position. The second category features a couple of examples of political scientists who have run for major elective office but were not elected. Their stories address how these political scientists ran electoral campaigns while continuing their full-time teaching jobs. The third presents the cases of two political scientists who served in national appointive office while on leaves from their respective universities. And the fourth category presents examples of four political scientists whose civic engagement is directed at the nonprofit sector—founding and/or leading 501(c)3 organizations targeting a particular issue.

ELECTIVE OFFICE

Kristi Andersen

A long-serving member of the Cazenovia New York Town Board (sixteen years), Kristi Andersen also was a member of the Syracuse University Political Science Department faculty for twelve years of that time. She is now an emeritus professor, but she has been a longtime community activist. In addition to

22

her service on the town board, she served on the New York State Democratic Committee, the Library Board of Trustees, the board of a local child care center, and as a Girl Scout leader.[1]

She ran for the town board in 2005 at the request of Democratic Party officials who felt that the time was ripe to elect Democrats and particularly women. She ran with two other candidates—one woman and one man. They conducted an extensive door-to-door campaign and appeared at local events, such as high school athletic competitions and farmers markets. Her campaign staff consisted of a campaign manager and heads of various committees. She posted yard signs, raised funds, conducted phone banks, and sought local publicity. The campaign's first move was to obtain a list of registered voters from the county elections board and then create a database of supporters that grew in size through the campaign.

According to Anderson, her goal was to get 950 votes. The slate identified 922 supporters, who were contacted in a get-out-the-vote effort. Ultimately, she received 1,109 votes in the election.[2]

Anderson's community service dovetailed with her position at Syracuse. She has lectured about local government to various groups and has been active in a program sponsored by Syracuse's Maxwell School of Citizenship and Public Affairs that helps support military veterans who are interested in running for elective office. Before she retired, she taught in the Citizenship and Civic Engagement program at Maxwell.

After being elected to the town board and serving for a short time, Anderson decided to share her experiences and observations with other political scientists. She wrote an article published in *PS: Political Science and Politics* on her run for office.[3] She urges others, particularly those teaching American politics, to consider becoming more engaged: "Detailed exposure to daily governmental issues (FOIA requests, dog control issues, dealing with state agencies, grant-writing, budgeting, open meeting laws and on and on) would provide a useful perspective for anyone teaching American politics."[4]

Julia Hellwege

Julia Hellwege is an assistant professor of political science at the University of South Dakota, but she also serves on the city council of Vermillion, South Dakota. She came to USD in 2016 after completing a PhD at the University of New Mexico. Her research interests include Latino politics, gender politics, pedagogy, and research methods. She has published in *Political Science Quarterly*, *PS: Political Science & Politics*, and *American Politics Research*. She has been awarded the Emerging Scholar Award by the APSA Latino Caucus and was given a university teaching award by the University of South Dakota.

But she also had the seed of practical politics planted in her brain long before she came to South Dakota. When she was a child, she worked on her father's successful mayoral campaign in Colorado. In graduate school in New Mexico, she helped organize the local "Ready to Run" program initiated by the Center for American Women and Politics at Rutgers.

In 2018, a city council vacancy occurred in her ward in Vermillion. She had no intention of running for it until a friend urged her to do so, explaining that typically few candidates filed for the post. Hellwege was reluctant because she was eight months pregnant and an untenured faculty member barely starting her professional career.

But she decided that she would do it, using the old cliché "if not me, then who?" She gathered the necessary petition signatures to file, but it turned out she was the only one who did so. She had the uncommon experience of being unopposed in her first race for public office.

Hellwege was fortunate that her department and university were supportive of her involvement. She relates that she was "often lauded for my involvement both in annual evaluations and in general conversation." Her university has "worked hard to integrate the university with the community. . . . Part of how we reach this goal is by encouraging our university faculty and staff to engage in the community."[5] The University of South Dakota's guidelines for tenure and promotion, as well as annual reviews, include encouragement to become involved in public service. According to Hellwege, the service "counts" particularly when it is associated with the faculty member's discipline.

It helped that she was not alone among her colleagues in her commitment to civic engagement. Another faculty member served on the local school board and yet another was on the city's planning commission. Plus, the most influential political scientist at the University of South Dakota was William O. (Doc) Farber, who had chaired the department for thirty-eight years and also served as the director of the state's Legislative Research Council, as a member of the South Dakota Constitutional Revision Commission and the Local Government Study Commission, and for ten years as chair of the city's planning commission.[6]

Hellwege says her involvement affects her teaching. For instance, she uses examples from her city council role in practically every course she teaches. She teaches a survey course in political science, as well as Women and Politics, The Politics of Inequality, The Legislative Process, and Campaigns and Democracy. She feels she serves as a role model that allows students to have "an accessible case study whom they can ask questions of and get the 'real world' application they so often crave." She relates that service is particularly important when "many of our students often feel disconnected from the political process."[7]

According to Hellwege, the "town and gown" tension that exists in many college towns also occurs in Vermillion. The involvement of faculty in public service is intended to alleviate some of that conflict. Hellwege relates she has experienced that local anxiety over the relations with the university. She explains that at times she is frustrated with other government leaders who do not engage in strategic thinking. But she admits that sometimes those same councilors can be exasperated with her for being "elitist." She warns that being a political scientist in such a setting can be lonely and isolating because of the differences in outlook, training, and perspective but that she gets along well with her fellow city councilors. Seeing an academic wanting to serve the community in and out of the classroom and seeking to find common ground with nonacademics undoubtedly helps to ease those "town and gown" frictions that so often arise between a university and its home community.

Karen Pooley

Some academics began in government and then moved into academe, bringing with them an interest in applied politics. Karen Pooley received a PhD in city planning from the University of Pennsylvania in 2007 but began her career in government rather than academia. She worked for New York City in the Department of Housing Preservation and Development and then for the Redevelopment Authority of Allentown, Pennsylvania. She joined the faculty of the Department of Political Science at Lehigh University in 2016 as a professor of practice.

Before joining the Lehigh faculty, she ran for the school board and won. She ran for reelection four years later, won again, and still serves on the board. Plus, she serves as an advocate for the Southside Community neighborhood.

Her service on the school board and for her community intertwines with her teaching interests. She teaches courses on the politics of public education, housing and community development, and city planning. She uses her connection to the community to involve students in community projects. For example, during one semester her students worked with a local developer on the creation of a local public market, particularly to address food injustice issues.[8]

She says her involvement also improves her teaching. According to Pooley, her practical involvement helps her know the players in policy arenas and allows her to see what is happening "on the ground." That knowledge sometimes precedes what she reads in academic papers. Also, she is able to include stories of the policy-making process that illustrate the concepts she is presenting.

Pooley urges political scientists to look beyond full-time positions for making an impact. "Public boards and committees," she explains, "can be less of a time commitment but just as good of a look into how these systems work, who the players are, what the pressures on those players are, how decisions get made, etc."

Thomas Volgy

Community involvement can be costly in some cases. Thomas Volgy, a political science professor at the University of Arizona, served for ten years on the Tucson City Council before running for mayor. He served one four-year term as mayor and then lost his bid for reelection. Volgy relates that while he was doing double duty at the university and the city government, he worked seven days a week and did not take a vacation during fourteen years of service.

Even though the mayoral position paid only a part-time salary, Volgy was required by the university to become a part-time employee. He laments that his mayoral service cost him half of his income during that period. The cost was even higher because he was not given the normal round of annual pay increases while mayor. As a result, he did not catch up with other full professors who had not served.

Yet, that regret has not soured him on government service as an academic. He called the experience "the most exciting and frustrating thing I had ever done in my life" but affirmed that the ability to have "an impact on one's community and country is terribly gratifying."[9]

John Portz

Academics may find it difficult to find the entry point to government, particularly since the academic world and government have become increasingly distinct from each other. But John Portz, a political scientist at Northeastern University, simply volunteered. When he started teaching at Northeastern, after finishing his doctorate at the University of Wisconsin, he moved to Watertown, a small city in Massachusetts. When the city announced the creation of a Blue Ribbon Panel on Economic Development, Portz contacted the city manager and offered to serve on the panel. Portz's dissertation was on local economic development. And he taught courses in state and local government, urban politics, and public policy. He was a natural for the panel, and he knew it. The city manager not only appointed him to the committee but also made him the chair. As a consequence of that service, he later became involved in other community activities, including service on a committee charged with repurposing a federal arsenal available for sale.

Seven years after moving to Watertown, Portz decided to run for the city council. He lost. But a year and a half later, he was appointed to the council when a council member died and left a vacancy. He was elected to a full two-year term that fall and three more times after that. However, his service to Watertown did not end there. He then ran for the local school board and served there for many years, including six as the chair of the board.

He worked full-time at Northeastern while engaging in part-time service for his community. He relates that he spent an average of ten to fifteen hours a week on city or school board business. Yet, his involvement impacted his teaching, where he integrates his experiences as examples as part of his lectures on state and local government and public policy. Also, Portz involved graduate students in his first foray into local politics, the Blue Ribbon Panel on Economic Development. They provided research support for the panel.

Government service also dovetailed with his research. His dissertation meshed well with his role on the blue ribbon panel. Then, his government service suggested threads of research for him to pursue. He conducted studies of education governance and leadership and public service. He coauthored *Leader-Managers in the Public Sector: Managing for Results* with department colleague and former Massachusetts governor Michael Dukakis, which included interviews of government leaders but also drew from his own experience on a city council and a school board. He currently is working on a book about educational accountability.

Portz's length of service is remarkable. He used his skill set as a political scientist to benefit his community for nearly twenty-five years. And it started simply by one act of volunteerism—contacting the city manager and offering to serve on a panel.

Damon Cann

Another political scientist who made a difference in a small city is Damon Cann, political science professor at Utah State University (USU). Cann lives in North Logan, Utah, which has a population of less than twelve thousand. In his case, as is often true of those who run for office, others urged him to run for the city council. A city council member encouraged Cann because of his "common sense and level-headedness" and because he would not come on the council with an agenda. As he relates, "I think they assumed that because I was a political scientist that I would be interested, not recognizing that it is relatively rare for political scientists to seek elective office."[10]

He ran and won that election. Four years later, he ran again and won. Two years later, he decided to run for mayor, a position he held for one four-year term before deciding to step down.

In Cann's case, his university was supportive. He says the university counted his elective service under the general category of "service" and recognized him for what he did, even though the university is not located in the city where Cann serves. He explains that the university has been "very patient and given me a lot of flexibility when daytime city obligations come up."[11]

Cann had been at USU for only three years and was untenured when he ran for the city council. His tenure and promotion cases did "count" his service in elective office. He was not punished for that work and instead was rewarded for it as "service." However, his elective service did not make his file successful or unsuccessful, because other components—teaching and scholarship—counted more. But the fact that he was credited for the service was helpful to him.

Cann explains that his political involvement has shaped the way he teaches. As example, even though he had spent years teaching American politics, he had never thought about what makes a good lawn sign or an effective mailer before he ran for the city council. Since he now has applied experience in campaigning, he requires students in his Parties & Elections class to prepare "real-world" materials within campaign simulations conducted within the course. There is still a strong theoretical element to his classes, but as he explains, "I've found that students appreciate the opportunity to apply the principles they are learning even in a simulated environment."[12]

His students benefited from the fact that he has been able to form networks through his role in the world of applied politics. He has been instrumental in securing internships for students because of the contacts he has made. Those connections have made him a better advocate for his students in the world of practical politics. Cann also concludes that students "take me a lot more seriously when they learn that I've actually been involved in the practice of the subject matter in addition to the study of it."[13]

His research interests within American politics also have been affected by his political role. He has examined how ideology shapes local government officials, which has led to conference presentations and a journal article.[14] Additionally, one of his graduate students chose the topic for a master's degree. And his interest in this line of research is ongoing.

For Cann, a decade in public office was a highly positive experience in two ways. He sums up the effects of his political involvement: "I feel like I was a better mayor for having been a political scientist, but I also feel like I'm a better political scientist for having been a mayor."

Glen Duerr
Glen Duerr's involvement happened incrementally. He served on a committee that reviewed the charter of the city of Beavercreek, Ohio. A suburb of Dayton,

Beavercreek has about forty-seven thousand residents. The committee's recommendations became ballot measures and, according to Duerr, helped him feel that he was making an impact in his community. After several years of raising young children, he served again—this time on the Board of Zoning Appeals.

He also was active in various clubs, his church, and his HOA. That activity connected him to many different people in a variety of settings. He said people from those varied circles began to urge him to run for office. He decided to make a run for the city council in 2019.

He barely lost his first election, coming in less than one-third of one percent of the vote behind the third candidate in an election for three available seats. But in May 2020, a vacancy occurred on the city council. Duerr was appointed to the position. So, when he ran again in 2021, he was better known as an incumbent. He was able to take second place for three available seats and begin a full four-year term in 2021.

Duerr says he gets support for his public service from his institution, Cedarville University. He already had tenure when he first ran for office, but his full professor review included discussion of his city council service, which he considered a "net positive." He also said his colleagues—in his department and in other parts of the university—supported his campaign. As well, he received positive feedback from both the university president and the academic vice president regarding his public service.[15]

Cedarville University is primarily a teaching institution, and Duerr focuses his attention on teaching. His teaching is not directly related to his service, since his courses are on foreign policy and international relations; he does not teach courses in local government. However, he says he has been able to fold his experiences into the content of some of his courses. He explains: "On certain topics, like democracy, my lectures have more depth and practical experience now. I am able to provide very practical insights to go alongside the overarching philosophy behind democracy."[16]

Duerr admits that his scholarship has diminished somewhat since his service began on the city council. He already had published three books before his full professor review, although all were on comparative politics and had no relation to American local government. However, he plans to write about his experiences as a candidate and a city council member when his service is over.

Shane Nordyke
Shane Nordyke teaches at the University of South Dakota and also serves on the Vermillion School Board. Her interest in public service began with her own family. As a mother of two school-age children, she had concerns about some

policies of the school district. Since she held a PhD in public policy, taught public policy, and directed the university's Government Research Bureau and the Chiesman Center for Democracy, she thought she could contribute to the school district's policy-making processes.[17]

The first time she ran, she lost. But she ran again and won. At the time of writing, she is still in her first term, but she says her service has been beneficial. The university has profited because her service strengthens ties between the local community and the university. In addition, she has integrated her experiences on the school board through examples in the courses she teaches on public policy. She said she has become known as an elected official on campus and has been asked to speak to student groups about running for office and serving on a school board.

Her research focus has been applied government research, and she also teaches a course on that topic. She is able to connect her school board experience to the applied research class, particularly since students are working on projects that directly relate to state and local agencies and, therefore, the issues she is addressing as a school board member as well. Her own research agenda is being influenced by her service. She says she expects her policy-oriented research to move toward the education issues she is facing as a school board member.

Tari Renner

Tari Renner has been a member of the Political Science Department at Illinois Wesleyan University for nearly thirty years, including a dozen years as department chair. But during that period, he has run for office seven times and won five of those elections. He has served in four different government offices while simultaneously teaching full-time.

Renner's first run for office occurred while he was still department chair. He was elected to the county board in 1998 and then reelected four years later. In 2004, he decided to run for Congress but lost that election. After being reelected to the county board two years later, he decided to run for mayor of Bloomington, Illinois. The election was the closest in the city's history; only fifteen votes separated the two candidates. But Renner came up short. After resigning from the county board, he was appointed to the county's planning commission. Four years after his narrow defeat, he ran again for mayor. This time, he won, and four years later he was reelected. After his second term, he stepped down as mayor in 2021.[18]

Renner's university ties were continually reinforced during his political career. According to Renner and his campaign manager, the campus community was a major factor in his election as mayor in 2013. Current or former students of Renner constituted his campaign management team. A major target of the campaign was getting out the student vote. However, he used a separate organization from his campaign to recruit and mobilize voters because, he admits, he was "a bit concerned that [he] would be accused of exploiting students."[19]

Renner explains that his teaching was enriched by his public service, including his multiple candidacies. Not surprisingly, his classes included examples of his many campaigns. Additionally, he provided the campus community with analyses of his political involvement, explaining why he won or lost campaigns. That was not surprising in one sense, because Renner also frequently analyzed politics and government for local media.[20]

While serving in elective office, Renner continued to publish book chapters and articles on parties and elections as well as local government. In fact, his public service informed his scholarship since much of his research dealt with issues of governance he was personally addressing at the local government level.

Renner believes another beneficiary of his service, particularly as an academic, was the community. When he served on the county board, he tried to bring a "bigger analytical picture" to the county. Also, he wanted to encourage board members to use, analyze, and question the data they were given.[21]

Illinois Wesleyan University was accommodating to his service. When he was elected as mayor, he was told that he was not expected to serve on committees, apply for grants, or publish books or articles. That approach was reassuring and proved that the university valued his service to the community. He suggests other colleges and universities "should follow a version of the IWU model."[22]

CAMPAIGNING FOR OFFICE

Jennifer Lawless
Other political scientists have set their sights on state or national involvement. One example is Jennifer Lawless, currently at the University of Virginia. Lawless is a prominent scholar on women and politics. Her work has been published in the *American Journal of Political Science*, *Political Research Quarterly*, and the *Journal of Politics*, along with other journals.

In addition, she has engaged in practical politics through her service on boards of nonprofits. She has been on the boards of the Women's Fund of Rhode Island, Planned Parenthood of Rhode Island, the New Politics Leadership Academy, and Emerge America. She has advised various women's organizations on political engagement.[23]

Her most intensive involvement was her run for Congress in the second congressional district of Rhode Island in 2006. At the time, she was an assistant professor of political science at Brown University. As is usually the case for academics, Lawless could not afford to take a leave of absence to run for Congress. Nor was her university supportive of her decision to run for Congress. During the campaign for the Democratic Party nomination, she relates that on weekdays she spent eight hours a day on campus and then, from midafternoon, was campaigning. On weekends, she devoted all of her time to campaigning.[24]

Lawless lost her bid for the Democratic nomination for Congress. But she says the experience was "the most important thing I've ever done" and she views it as "100 percent positive." She was able to gain greater empathy for people who want government to work for them because they are struggling in various ways. She sees practical politics as giving her a much better understanding of how politics works, which includes the ability to determine whether political science's assumptions are correct.[25]

She has authored or coauthored books on political ambition and the problems women encounter in running for office.[26] That work is enriched by her personal experience. When she discusses the challenges women face in running for office, she writes with a firsthand comprehension of what that means for a candidate. She faced the obstacles to involvement herself in attempting to raise money, gain endorsements, and carve out time for campaigning.

Not only did she gain experience as a person and a professor, she explains, but so did her students. She has been able to develop a "more innovative and creative pedagogy" because of her experience. She can discuss electoral politics with her students with a "more solid foundation." In addition, her political involvement has enabled her to tap into a network of experts who become class speakers and help students acquire internships. "I would otherwise not have developed those relationships," she concludes.[27]

Michael Munger
Another political scientist who is intensely involved in electoral politics is Michael Munger. Munger ran for governor of North Carolina as the Libertarian Party candidate in 2008 and again for the North Carolina House of Representatives in 2020 and 2022.[28] He has been a powerful force in North Carolina to build the Libertarian Party. He was the first third-party candidate to be invited to participate in a gubernatorial televised debate.[29]

Munger says he got involved in practical politics because he realized such involvement could allow him to reach more people as a public intellectual. "In graduate school, I wrote an op ed that was published by the *New York Times* on trade policy," he explains. "More people read that, in one day, than have cumulatively read all of my academic work, combined." In addition, he can speak to large audiences as a candidate. While running for governor in 2008, he participated in four televised debates and was able to make his arguments to a broad audience.[30]

As a candidate for the state legislature, Munger integrated his academic experience with potential service in the state legislature, touting his long tenure directing a public administration program at Duke that had trained many of the city and county government officials throughout the state. He argued he could serve as an effective liaison between those local government officials and the state legislature.[31]

His teaching and scholarship have not been negatively affected by his civic engagement. He has received teaching awards at Duke and has authored many books and journal articles in publications such as the *American Political Science Review*, the *American Journal of Political Science*, *Social Science Quarterly*, and the *Journal of Politics* throughout his career.

APPOINTIVE OFFICE

Ian Brodie

Ian Brodie was a junior faculty member at the University of Western Ontario when one of his graduate school professors became the campaign manager for a candidate for the leadership of the Canadian Alliance party. Brodie volunteered for the campaign. Later, he was offered a job in the office of the leader of the Parliamentary Opposition in the Canadian Parliament. However, Brodie claims that he was hired only because the new leader's chief of staff wanted Ian's wife, Vida, to serve on the opposition leader's staff. "Everyone involved knows she was a more valuable member of [Stephen] Harper's Team than I ever was."[32]

Even before serving on Harper's staff—both in opposition and later in government—Brodie emerged from a fecund atmosphere promoting the intersection of academe and practical politics at the University of Calgary. The Political Science Department included Tom Flanagan, future chief of staff to the prime minister and widely known as the Karl Rove of Canadian politics, and Ted Morton, who later would serve as provincial finance minister in Alberta. Along with Barry Cooper and Rainer Knopff, these professors were known as the "Calgary School," a group of political scientists who became involved in public policy and public service in order to advocate for their conservative political positions. When I was a Fulbright scholar at the University of Calgary, I was assigned the office that had just been vacated by Preston Manning, the founder of the Reform Party of Canada. That party eventually led to the demise of the Progressive Conservative Party that had served as the main opposition to the Liberals for over half a century.

Brodie served for a time as the executive director of the newly formed Conservative Party, the successor of the Canadian Alliance. His mandate was to build a new party that united former Reform Party members as well as those who had long considered themselves Progressive Conservatives and would be able to win after more than a decade of conservative factionalism and Liberal Party rule. Brodie helped the party prepare for its win the next year. Then, he was asked to serve as the chief of staff of Harper, leader of the opposition. When Harper became prime minister, Brodie became his first chief of staff and served in the position for two years.[33]

After his full-time government service, he returned to academe; he currently teaches at the University of Calgary in the Political Science Department. But he still does both government, public, and party work while retaining his full-time academic position. In 2020, he spent six months once again working for the leader of the opposition in Ottawa. He serves as the director of the Institute for Research on Public Policy, a national public-policy think tank, and was a cochair of the Alberta Premier's Advisory Council on Public Service.

Brodie believes his practical political role has complemented his academic role: "There is . . . no question that my rich involvement in public service has immeasurably enriched my scholarship and my teaching, and probably my university service work as well. So, on the whole, I consider it a win-win." He says his involvement has made him "a better political scientist and a better person."[34]

Not surprisingly, the University of Calgary administration has been supportive of his political involvement. But he does not feel the discipline generally is supportive, particularly of partisans. He feels political scientists don't understand why people become involved in political parties and don't like political parties and that, therefore, "most political scientists detest partisans."[35]

Brodie also sees a problem in being a conservative in a more liberal profession. He contends that the bias against partisanship "is a real constraint on doing work that has a partisan tinge to it, especially if the party you're working for isn't on the left side of the political spectrum."[36] Tolerance for a particular type of involvement can depend on where one works. For private, conservative religious schools, conservative involvement could be viewed as a plus. That may not be the case at many secular institutions.

John DiIulio Jr.
As a professor of political science at Princeton University and then the University of Pennsylvania, John DiIulio Jr. was well known for his scholarly work

and public commentary on crime prevention and juvenile delinquency. But he also wrote commentaries on religion and public policy. In the 1990s, he coauthored work with prominent conservatives such as James Q. Wilson, with whom he coauthored an American government text, and William Bennett, the Reagan administration's secretary of education, although he also advised Vice President Al Gore.

Dilulio coined the phrase "super-predators" to describe youth who were reckless and violent. He predicted that youth violence would increase dramatically in the twenty-first century. His ideas were accepted by policy makers who passed legislation toughening penalties for crimes. However, the term became controversial as critics argued it was applied primarily to young Black men. It even entered into a 2020 presidential candidate debate when President Donald Trump accused former vice president Joe Biden of using the term to describe Black youth. Dilulio later said he regretted coining the phrase.[37]

He was attacked by one critic as a "headline-seeking criminologist" and was dismissed by another who wrote: "No single person has been more closely associated with unsound crime analysis and punitive imprisonment policies than John Dilulio." A more charitable commentator described him as "an academic with a pamphleteer's rhetoric."[38]

His writings on the role of religion in American democracy and, particularly, the effects of the faith-based communities in reducing crime caught the interest of George W. Bush.[39] As an evangelical himself, Bush wanted to show that the private sector, particularly the faith sector, could be more effective than government aid programs in preventing crime. Therefore, government should give financial support to faith-based community organizations to reduce crime and solve social problems.

Dilulio was asked to create a new federal office designed to integrate faith-based organizations into government efforts to combat crime. Initially, he committed no more than two years to the job before returning to his academic post at the University of Pennsylvania. Yet, in August 2001, after only six months on the job, Dilulio resigned his post. He was caught up in partisan politics when his attempts at a consensus approach on the office's work were blunted by ideological conservatives and a White House determined to satisfy the religious right rather than work with Democrats.[40]

His resignation after such a short tenure and his return to the University of Pennsylvania was a blow to the administration, because his faith-based program was considered a signature policy initiative for George W. Bush. But Dilulio remained committed to the effort. When Barack Obama was elected in 2008, Dilulio advised him on the creation of a similar faith-based initiative to the Bush administration's efforts and praised his first choice of a director.[41]

NONPROFIT LEADERSHIP

Noelle Brigden

Politics is a natural form of civic engagement for political scientists. But it is not the only avenue for involvement. Some political scientists have chosen nonprofit formation as a civic outlet. Noelle Brigden teaches political science at Marquette University. But she also maintains a nonprofit corporation in her spare time. Her nonprofit runs a community gym in a neighborhood outside San Salvador. The gym provides personal empowerment in a traumatic environment through powerlifting instruction and training.[42]

She also is involved in another nonprofit, Restorative Justice in Movement. It works with Marquette to inspire women of color whose family members have been incarcerated. The nonprofit uses physical activities to build community and empower women.[43]

Her interest in these nonprofits came from a personal experience. When she was much younger, she shattered a vertebra. When she began to do fieldwork in El Salvador, her old injury flared back up. She began to lift weights to strengthen her body and overcome her physical insecurities. Eventually, she taught others how to use fitness rituals to overcome personal trauma, particularly due to violence in their environments.[44]

However, her nonprofit work now affects her teaching and research. She says she brings "more 'real world' understanding of the politics of NGOS and the lived ethics of fieldwork into the classroom." And she says her students enjoy the examples she can provide from her own personal experiences.

Keith Whittington

Keith Whittington's academic work dovetails neatly with his civic engagement. His full-time job is teaching constitutional law courses in the Politics Department at Princeton. But his public engagement also concentrates on the First Amendment. He is the chair of the Academic Freedom Alliance. The group, which consists of about two hundred scholars, is dedicated to preserving freedom of speech for college educators. The group has drawn supporters from both liberal and conservative camps within academe and intends to offer public and legal support to professors who are unfairly targeted, according to the group, for their speech.[45]

Whittington also belongs to Checks and Balances, a group of conservative and libertarian lawyers who opposed abuses of power by the Trump administration.[46] He serves on the academic board of advisors for the Bill of Rights Institute, a conservative group that disseminates educational material and offers programs for teachers, and on the board of directors for the Foundation for

Individual Rights in Education, which is a legal advocacy group that challenges university administrative actions that threaten academic free speech.

These civic activities attracted Whittington because they were related to his scholarly work. He has written broadly in political science journals such as *Polity*, *Publius*, and the *Journal of Politics*, as well as various law reviews on judicial review, judicial supremacy, presidential impeachment, and judicial selection. He has authored textbooks on constitutional law.

But his scholarly work has intersected with his public engagement, as he has researched and written more recently on academic free speech. In 2019, he published a book with Princeton University Press arguing for the necessity of higher education institutions supporting academic free speech.[47] As he explains: "In the Trump years, I became more focused on trying to do more public-facing work, from public speaking to writing for a public audience. My scholarly work seemed directly relevant to issues that were confronting the public these days."[48]

Whittington acknowledges that his new focus means "there are specific research projects that I'll never wind up doing because they get crowded out." But that doesn't mean he will not produce research; it only means his new research projects may not cover the same topics he has dealt with before. Similarly, at this point in his career he avoids as much as possible the heavy university administrative responsibilities that he carried previously.

Teaching is another facet of Whittington's career that has been influenced by his civic interests. The flexibility of teaching allows him to connect his teaching directly with his public advocacy. He designed a class related specifically to Trump-era constitutional issues, admitting, "I doubt I would have thought to do such a course at an earlier stage of my career."[49]

Public involvement has had an effect on how he has approached his writing. He has pondered how to speak about complicated issues in a way that is accessible to a general audience beyond scholars. That engagement also has led him to think about how he can apply his "abstract expertise to timely problems."[50]

Marc Howard

In 1990, Marc Howard's high school friend Marty Tankleff was convicted of murdering his parents. Tankleff insisted he was not guilty of the crime. After Howard visited Tankleff in prison, he became determined to help overturn his friend's conviction. He assisted Tankleff's lawyers with appeals, wrote an amicus brief, and penned op-eds protesting Tankleff's unjust incarceration for a crime he did not commit.

After seventeen years in prison, those appeals succeeded. New York state reinvestigated the case and concluded there was not sufficient evidence that

Tankleff was guilty. That experienced changed Howard's life. He was a political science professor at Georgetown University, but he decided to get a law degree as well and to work on behalf of others who had been wrongly convicted.

In 2016, he founded the Georgetown University Prisons and Justice Initiative. The project has several components. One element is a course where students investigate and document inmate cases to assist in their exoneration. Another is a program designed to help inmates gain college degrees from Georgetown. Inmates in Maryland are able to take three for-credit courses a semester that count toward the completion of a bachelor's degree in liberal arts. Two other programs help formerly incarcerated men and women transition to employment through a one-year program leading to a certificate in business and entrepreneurship or one in paralegal studies.[51]

The prison class program includes financial aid as well as access to library resources at Georgetown. These programs have made Georgetown University unique in its attention to incarcerated individuals seeking to reenter their lives outside of prison. Other institutions have contacted the initiative to investigate how they can establish similar programs.[52]

In 2020, Howard also founded the Frederick Douglass Project for Justice. The objective of this program is to change public perceptions about prison life by facilitating conversations between people in and out of prison through prison visits. The project hopes that such meetings will allow people to "learn from each other, form powerful human connections, and transform both their own lives and society at large."[53]

Howard's public service also has transformed his academic career. His teaching and research had centered on comparative politics, but it is now dedicated to criminal justice and prison reform. He admits his scholarship has slowed with so much time devoted to managing these initiatives.[54] But he has integrated students into his programs in an uncommon way. His guest speakers included formerly incarcerated individuals and he takes his students to prison. He provides them with the opportunity to become involved in real-world[55] applications with real-world consequences—that is, the potential exoneration of wrongly incarcerated individuals. As of early 2022, his students had contributed to the release from prison of three individuals.

His scholarship has not disappeared, however. He authored *Unusually Cruel: Prisons, Punishment, and the Real American Exceptionalism* with Oxford University Press. The book offers a comparative perspective of corrections systems, highlighting the "exceptionalism" of the United States' approach to incarceration.[56]

When extensive time is devoted to this form of community service, the reaction from the administration might be expected to be negative. Howard says for him the opposite is true: "The reaction has been overwhelmingly positive—from the university president and senior leadership to my faculty colleagues to the staff all across the campus. . . . I also consider myself lucky to work at a Jesuit institution that deeply values and supports the notion of service to others and helping the needy."[57]

Howard had already earned tenure and full professor before his initiation of these projects; whether his involvement would have affected his reviews remains a question. He does not believe universities should prioritize his form of community service to the degree that it could overcome a weak research profile, but he does think that political scientists "should be willing and able to follow their passions into practical involvement if the situation calls for it." That means faculty should not be professionally punished for engaging in it but rather supported by the institution.[58]

David Szakonyi
Corruption is a common feature of developed countries, but the investigations of corrupt practices by government officials and their cronies typically have been conducted independently without coordination. David Szakonyi, an assistant professor at George Washington University specializing in political economy, clientelism, and Russian politics, decided to do something about that. In 2020, he cofounded the Anti-Corruption Data Collective (ACDC) with journalist Frederik Obermaier, who was involved in the revelations called the Panama Papers and the Paradise Papers, and Zoe Reiter, an anti-corruption advocate who has worked to help law enforcement agencies capture organize crime figures.

ACDC brings together journalists, academics, programmers, and activists in collaboration to identify and expose corruption, as well as lobby for policy change. The collective offers data expertise to ongoing investigations to assist in the identification of corruption flows that often cross national boundaries.

Even though the collective has been in existence for only a few years, it has played a significant role in exposing corruption. In 2021, ACDC worked with the *Texas Observer*, a news magazine covering Texas politics, to discover that banks in the United States rarely faced penalties for participating in money-laundering activities. The same year, it uncovered opaqueness in the investment fund industry in Luxembourg that was allowing some investors to avoid paying taxes and to engage in money laundering. The ACDC's report, in conjunction with Transparency International, led European Commission leaders to promise to "strengthen the rules at our disposal on tax avoidance and evasion."[59] One of its earliest investigations targeted the trajectories of government loans given through the Paycheck Protection Program, which is designed to assist small businesses with COVID-19 relief. The collective found seventy-five businesses that did not exist prior to the COVID pandemic but received at least $150,000 in federal loans.[60]

Szakonyi says his involvement with ACDC has a huge impact on his scholarship. Because of ACDC, he has produced three working papers and has plans for six more. His own research interests have been transformed through new data sets and a new group of new coauthors similarly interested in anti-corruption research. Also, one goal of ACDC is to encourage other academics to pursue lines of research through the data sets they are creating. He believes this has made him a better scholar.[61]

In addition, he now has opportunities to reach an audience beyond political scientists. And he can help other academics see their research publicized broadly. ACDC wants to "make sure the [journal] articles are accompanied by journalistic treatment and policy recommendations so that the lessons learned get heard by the right stakeholders." Szakonyi also is pleased that his new academic work is useful to policy makers, since it addresses timely and significant policy issues.

He expects to develop a new course on corruption. However, even within his existing courses, he feels his teaching has been improved by his association with ACDC: "I've got a much more developed and firsthand understanding of the most current and cutting-edge issues in money and politics. I try to integrate these perspectives and provide much richer color to my class lectures and discussion."

LESSONS LEARNED

For the political scientist who seeks to become involved civically, the task may seem a bit daunting. As I mentioned earlier, there is little or no professional encouragement to do so. In fact, there is discouragement professionally, since the study of political science can be conducted without proximity to those who actually practice politics.

But another issue is the fact that political scientists rarely travel in the same circles as professional politicians. Even when contact ensues, there may be suspicion on both sides: Intellectuals may view politicians as not terribly bright or analytical, while politicians may consider intellectuals to be aloof and condescending at worst and clueless about practical politics at best.

Still another obstacle is the perception that practical politics is a waste of time. Nothing can be accomplished anyway, so why participate, as the logic goes. That attitude is stunning coming from those who teach students about government. What is the point of teaching if it is to tell students who are majoring in political science and plan on careers in government that there is no real value in doing so?

There are ways out of this conundrum. They all require a willingness on the part of political scientists to view practical involvement in positive terms, an acceptance of practical politicians as they are and not as some clone of academics, and a sense of duty to the community that transcends the classroom and even the university campus.

For those who are interested in taking the steps but wonder how, here are some suggestions to facilitate initial involvement. I have drawn them from the vignettes offered in this chapter.

Look for Needs

One recommendation is to look around for something that needs to be done. It could be at any level—local, state, national, or global. It could be expertise in policy-making processes or a specific policy area, such as education, planning, or national security. David Szakonyi saw a need for a database on corruption that could be accessible to policy makers, journalists, and academics. The solution to that problem dovetailed with his research interests and skills. Similarly, John Portz saw a need he could fill when he heard of the creation of a new city commission on economic development. With his research expertise, he felt he could be helpful, so he contacted the city manager and expressed interest in serving on that particular commission.

But the need may not match specifically a political scientist's research or teaching specialties. The academic brings general analysis and research skills, as well as communication abilities. As a consequence of his friend's incarceration, Marc Howard realized that there were many incarcerated individuals who needed an advocate—someone interested in their case and willing to assist them in their struggles with the legal system. Criminal justice reform was not his research interest. Yet, he retooled to play a role in meeting that need. Such retooling is not essential to be civically engaged. Rather, political scientists can offer contributions that stem from critical reasoning, knowledge of political processes, and a desire to contribute.

Express Interest to Others

Telling someone else of your interest in participating can be the impetus for that person or someone they know to involve you. A colleague of mine told me that another faculty member had expressed interest in running for office. I approached that faculty member and discussed the possibility of running. Ultimately, she decided not to. However, once her profile was raised, she was on the short list for a gubernatorial candidate looking for a lieutenant governor candidate for his ticket. Later, she spoke at a party event. She became more integrated into the party merely because she told a colleague she was interested in being involved.

The reality is that such expressions may have to be made more than once and at different times in order to be successful. I sought to get involved in a political party organization in my county and provided my name to the county chair on more than one occasion. It took several attempts before I was successful. The party was disorganized, lacked a mechanism for integrating volunteers, and, even worse, was exclusive. Hence, I concluded that there was a significant need for my involvement to help break down those barriers for others.

Say Yes: Respond Positively to Recruitment by Others

One of the most common ways to engage is to respond to recruitment. These recruitment opportunities come because others see us in a way we may not see ourselves—as a candidate, a commission member, a city councilor, a state legislator, a member of a nonprofit board, a leader of a nonprofit, and so on. Academics are viewed by others as smart people who can analyze problems and elevate the public policy–making process. Also, academics usually lack a particular personal agenda. Unlike business professionals who may benefit economically from the experience, academics rarely gain an economic benefit from practical involvement. In fact, recruiters usually are unaware that academics are not rewarded by the university or the discipline for involvement.

At times, the recruitment is formal and official. Party leaders or current or former governmental, community, or nonprofit leaders may target certain political scientists for encouragement to participate. Kristi Andersen was recruited by Democratic Party leaders. The town had a 2–1 Republican registration and had experienced low voter turnout because municipal elections largely went uncontested. She was encouraged by the previous successful election of a town leader who campaigned on a platform of planned growth. Democrats were hopeful they could elect a slate of town elected officials and turn Cazenovia blue. She responded to their call for involvement and was elected, along with another candidate on the slate.[62] Similarly, Damon Cann was approached by others to run for city council. A current city council member recruited him because they thought he would be a good council member.

At other times, the encouragement is not "official" but comes from friends and neighbors who believe the political scientist will represent them well or serve as an effective leader. That happened to Julia Hellwege, who was approached by a friend to consider running. The solicitation may be unofficial, but it also may be indicative of how "ordinary citizens" might respond to a run for office by the academic.

Sometimes the "call to serve" comes at unexpected and even unusual times, as Hellwege learned. She was a new junior faculty member and she was pregnant when a friend suggested she run for the city council. She had plenty of reasons for not heeding that advice. Instead, she volunteered by running for the office and, due to the absence of competition, was automatically elected and given the opportunity to serve.

3. Civic Engagement Leadership

Now I turn to my own civic engagement, which occurred in tandem with my political science career. This chapter will discuss a form of engagement that clearly dovetailed with my academic position: leadership of a university civic engagement program. I begin with that form of engagement not because it came first but primarily to demonstrate that political scientists can integrate civic engagement into actual service within (and not just apart from) the academic institution.

The national trends in political science that I discussed earlier were affecting my own undergraduate-only department. Increasingly, the emphasis of our curriculum was on training social scientists. More methods courses were required. And, not surprisingly, our approach to students too often was to create clones of ourselves—individuals headed toward a graduate education in social science, preferably a PhD. We knew the vast majority of our students were not PhD bound. But, sometimes, our greatest interest was in those who were. Since we lacked graduate students, they became our research and teaching assistants. Those were the students we seemed to associate with the most.

I was not opposed to guiding a few extremely bright students toward a doctoral program in political science. But I felt it was vital that we concentrate our efforts primarily on the vast majority of students who would not become like us. Rather, they would go to law school or get an MBA or work in government or in the private sector using the liberal arts skills that we helped them develop.

Something lacking in our curriculum, as was true nationally in political science, was attention to the training of good citizens. I wondered about the role I could play in reorienting political science—or at least political science at BYU. For many years, I contemplated the creation of a center that would join political science with practical politics. My desire was for a center that would serve students by teaching them practical skills of citizenship.

BYU lacked that kind of center. It did have a center that studied elections, but the emphasis, again, was on research. Other universities, even in Utah, had such centers. But BYU, as a private university, was perceived as separate from state-oriented politics. Nor was there a desire on the part of the administration to become involved in national politics.

CREATING AN ENTITY FOR CIVIC ENGAGEMENT

The idea of a center for political involvement languished in my mind until an event happened that changed my role at BYU and gave me the opportunity to move closer to my wish. In 2011, a new dean, Ben Ogles, arrived at the College of Family, Home, and Social Sciences. The college is an untypical combination of social science departments—political science, economics, psychology, sociology, social work, anthropology, and history—and a school of family life. Unlike previous deans, Dean Ogles was the product of a national search that brought in someone who had not worked at BYU before. After many years at Ohio University, he brought new ideas for administering the college.

However, he said he wanted to know what the faculty, staff, and students wanted. So, in his inaugural address as dean he announced he would be forming a futures committee. This committee's mission would be to examine existing processes and policies, survey the various stakeholders of the college—students, faculty, staff, and alumni—and then propose to him possible reforms. The mandate was broad and the task challenging.

That's why I went to Dean Ogles and volunteered to serve on the committee. Then, I did something more audacious. I volunteered to chair the committee. He was surprised at the offer, but, after checking with my department chair, agreed to appoint me. Even though I jumped at the opportunity he was creating to make things better for so many people throughout the college, I admit that my offer had a strong tinge of self-interest. One element of self-interest was the fact that I hate lengthy, unproductive meetings. These are particularly common in academic settings, where there seems to be an enormous amount of time available to discuss minutiae. I did not want to sit through such meetings, and I felt that, as the committee chair, I would be able to move things along quickly. As it turned out, we did move quickly. While the dean indicated at the outset that he expected our process would take eighteen months, we produced a set of recommendations in half that time.

I had another self-interested motivation as well. That was a desire to use this process to create the kind of center for civic and political engagement that I felt needed to exist but that I had not yet found a way to bring about. I knew that as a member of the committee I would have the opportunity to propose such a center and that as the chair I would have even more clout to bring it about.

The committee began meeting in January 2012. I became immersed in the many aspects of this committee's mandate, including tenure and promotion processes, role of staff, treatment of female faculty and staff, student advising, graduate placement, and so on. At the same time, I kept thinking about how to raise this proposal. One thought was to add a couple of questions about citizenship to the surveys we were promulgating to faculty, staff, students, and alumni.

The alumni surveys were particularly telling and helpful in making the argument for a civic engagement center. One question we asked was how much they were engaged civically in their communities, including whether they participated in such activities as writing to public officials, serving on community boards and commissions, attending community meetings, and so on. To my surprise, particularly since these were the alumni of a social sciences college, only a quarter said they had ever done these things. Another question was whether alumni felt they had role models for engagement while they were at BYU. Few answered positively. Some wrote comments saying they wished there had been such role models among the faculty.

I used these questions to develop a proposal for a center for civic engagement and passed it on to the other committee members. They were not enthusiastic. But they were willing to include the proposal in our set of recommendations simply to accommodate me. That was enough for it to move forward to the dean. I knew if I could get it out of that committee, I could work to convince the dean that this was a worthwhile proposal for his consideration.

The committee produced twenty-five recommendations regarding various aspects of the college's functions. These included proposed changes in the tenure and promotion process, the implementation of awards to recognize faculty accomplishments, the creation of a new administrative/staff advisory council, the formation of a college technology services advisory board, and many others. Among that list was a recommendation of a center for public engagement that would "educate students . . . on the value of public engagement and service."

Those recommendations were passed on to the dean, who then presented them to the faculty and staff. To our surprise, he made no changes to the recommendations when presenting them to the faculty and staff. Critical responses from others targeted many of the recommendations, but not this one, which meant the dean was ready to go ahead with the one recommendation I was most interested in.

However, I needed to make a critical decision at that point. My goal was a center dedicated to political engagement. But I quickly realized that I needed to broaden my scope to cover civic engagement and not just political engagement. That meant a center would address forms of civic engagement that were not political in nature. For example, that included involvement in nonprofits that were not necessarily political.

Of course, my perspective was that even civic engagement broadly was political. Nonprofits often deal with policy of some sort—government grants, lobbying for certain policy objectives, interacting with government agencies and elected officials, and the like. It was difficult to distinguish between a political nonprofit and nonpolitical nonprofit, although I knew the difference between a 501c3 that could not play an explicitly political role and a 501c4 that could.

I also knew that I could foster political engagement through this center in a way that I could not otherwise, even if it was named "civic engagement" and included forms of engagement beyond politics. That mission was not insignificant at that time. Increasingly, young people were turning away from political engagement. And if they were engaged, it took place in ways that were not explicitly political. I saw an acute need to educate students on the value of political engagement and how to do it.

In my mind, I could discuss civic engagement broadly through this new center—including working with nonprofits and encouraging students to become engaged in less political ways. That effort would assist students who sought to become civically engaged in that way. At the same time, I could direct the politically oriented students as well. And perhaps I could help those less political students to see political involvement more positively, particularly if I equipped them with the skills to operate within the political system.

So, when the dean asked me if this center would address political engagement or civic engagement more broadly, I answered that my focus would be on the latter. I made it clear that political engagement would be an important segment of the curriculum and focus but not the sole one. He accepted that answer and moved forward.

After getting approval from the central administration, Dean Ogles met and began to discuss how this particular recommendation would be implemented. The only caveat was the use of the term "center." The central administration felt there were too many centers on campus already. They wanted to use the term "office." I did not object since the difference in nomenclature did not bother me. The functions would be the same regardless of whether it was called an office, a center, or an institute. He suggested a faculty advisory committee be appointed to draw up a plan for this new office. We brainstormed on possible committee members, and he extended the appointments after consultation with department chairs.

The new faculty advisory committee for the Office of Civic Engagement Leadership was drawn from various departments in the college. My hope was to include a representative from every department. However, the administrators in a couple of departments had no real interest or there was no logical faculty member to appoint. But, thankfully, most of the departments were represented.

Broad representation was critical to me. Since this was a new unit in the college that needed to gain a foothold in college support, I wanted the office to acquire advocates in every department of the college. The failure to get representatives in all departments ultimately hurt the office, because faculty in one of the departments originally not represented became somewhat unsupportive later on. However, in another department, a representative was found later and became an active supporter of the office among his faculty.

Fortunately, the dean found faculty within various departments who, for the most part, were committed to making the new office a success. Each had a record of civic engagement within their fields. Some had extensive relations with community partners. Some already taught courses that could be incorporated into the new program. Others published journal articles on topics related to civic engagement.

Another important element of this committee was continuity. Fortunately, some remained on the committee for several terms. They provided the stability to the new program that was essential for it to become an integral part of the college's operations.

Where to house the new office was never an issue. The dean and I agreed that it should not exist within a particular department. Rather, it should be a college-level unit. At such a level, it would be a service program for the whole college and not just a single department. As a college entity, it would have access to college resources for publicity and funding. I would not have to report to a chair who would then report to the dean. I would not be subject to a department's budget.

My preference was that this Office of Civic Engagement would be a university-wide unit serving the whole community. However, I knew that the office would have to prove itself at the college level before that was possible. Moreover, I knew I could acquire much of that role by my own outreach beyond our college, which I did.

The faculty advisory committee began meeting immediately and began brainstorming the direction of this new office. The committee agreed on some key points of its mission. It would be a resource for the college and even the university in terms of fostering an interest and means of participation in civic engagement for students, as well as faculty and staff, both directly and indirectly. Direct participation would come primarily in the form of classes and events. Indirect participation would be through work with faculty. In other words, the office would help faculty to incorporate civic engagement components into their teaching.

CREATING A MINOR

An early question was whether the new office would administer some academic program. The idea of a certificate seemed to fit best with the tenor of the office. A certificate fit more neatly into the professional world. People often receive certificates for particular job skill training. They are recognized far more in nonacademic settings than academic ones. Yet, BYU already had certificate programs in some areas. The business school sponsored a certificate in nonprofit management as well as global management. Foreign language departments offered language certificates. We thought the administration would be supportive of another one, particularly since it was a highly practical program and would cater to practitioners' preference for certificates.

But we were wrong. The vice president for academic affairs responded that they felt the university had too many certificate programs already. The dean suggested we pursue a minor instead. We felt a certificate would be more useful to our graduates, but this was not a "hill to die on" for us.

Now we turned our attention to the development of a minor. What would it look like? What requirements would it include? What new courses would be needed? What existing courses in various departments could be included?

To answer these questions, I began to do research on other civic engagement programs throughout the country to determine how they were structured. Not surprisingly, I found that the approach to civic engagement varied widely across the nation. Some were solely community outreach programs, offering an opportunity for students to gain a community experience with a soup kitchen, day care center, or domestic violence service center. Others were more academic, with required courses geared toward a certificate, minor, or even a major. Some offered their own courses while others designated service-learning courses throughout the university.

I proposed a hybrid model that incorporated elements of existing programs. The minor should include a mixture of core and elective courses. The core courses initially consisted of a one credit introduction to civic engagement. That course would be open to any interested student across the university and not just within the college. It would help students see what civic engagement was and the multiplicity of forms it could take. It would also seek to empower them—help them understand that they could make a difference.

I knew that few students who took this course would go on to minor in civic engagement leadership. For many, it was just a one-hour course to fulfill elective requirements with an intriguing title. That heightened its importance to me. This would be their single exposure in an academic setting.

Originally, the course had two main components. The first was the use of case studies of people who succeeded in reshaping their communities through civic involvement. Students read about people who lobbied for preservation of heritage sites and for more state support for solar power and about a sportswriter who established a nonprofit to buy mosquito nets for African children, among other case studies. We reviewed each case study and examined how the effort started and what elements affected its success. We also discussed their own suggestions—both in groups and as individuals—for needed change and analyzed how they would go about effecting that change.

The second was a set of guest speakers who served as in-person examples of individuals who had made a difference in divergent settings—nonprofits, government, political campaigns, and community engagement. The speakers were drawn largely from local community partners. Many served on the office's external advisory board. They knew their role and played it well. Not only did they offer living examples of the messages we were conveying in the course, but they also explicitly encouraged students to become involved in their organizations or at least to become more involved generally.

Then, I added a third component—group projects. The students did not actually complete the projects, but they did design them and present them to the rest of the class. These were projects they created in their assigned group. I was impressed with their innovativeness and hoped that these projects might be implemented at some future time now that the seed had been planted.

In addition, there was another requirement that I instituted from the beginning. Students were expected to volunteer for a nonprofit organization, government agency or unit, or a political party or candidate campaign and then report on their experience. These volunteer opportunities had to be off-campus. That additional caveat was intended to take students off the campus and into the local community. I gave them a list of possible nonprofits to work with during the semester. During the fall semester, when general elections occurred, I added local candidates and political party contacts.

The volunteer requirement seemed a given. Again, I knew that relatively few students would become minors. For the others, this might be one of the few times during their undergraduate careers when they interacted with the local community.

To be clear, it was not the case that my students were unfamiliar with service. The vast majority had served in various responsibilities within the church, as befit a religious university. And many had served missions of up to two years for the church in various parts of the world on a volunteer basis. However, service in the way I was offering was less familiar to them. As I had learned from the alumni survey we conducted, the vast majority of alumni had not been involved in the governance of their own community. My volunteer requirement was a means to encourage future involvement in community affairs.

And many students responded in the way I hoped. Some reported that they became so engaged in the service they provided that they went beyond the required hours. Others reported that they planned to continue to work with that organization beyond the semester.

Initially, the core also consisted of a capstone seminar. One objective of the senior-oriented seminar was designed to expose students to more sophisticated readings about civic engagement. Unfortunately, there were not many texts to rely on. Some were dedicated to how to teach civic engagement, but they were not appropriate for students. The field of civic engagement was still new, and the literature specific to the field was not well developed.

A second objective was the completion of a senior-level civic engagement project. The project was undertaken individually, although students were encouraged to practice leadership by involving fellow students (outside the class) as well as people in the community in the project. The students were required to propose the project, design it, and implement it. Preferably all of that took place during the course of the semester. Some students took incompletes and finished the project in the next semester. And again, my emphasis was on projects that occurred off campus and in conjunction with external community partners.

Moreover, the projects needed to be sustainable. In other words, the project had to outlast their involvement with the organization. I did not want a one-time project that did not change the organization over the long run. It took some time for me to enforce this provision. Initially, I approved projects that I regretted later. That was not because they were failures but because I did not push the student hard enough in the direction of sustainability. For example, in one of the first of these classes, I approved a diaper drive by a student who wanted to help the Utah Diaper Bank. She succeeded in recruiting various groups and organizations to help her collect diapers. In that sense, she demonstrated leadership in the effort. And the endeavor changed her. She was one of those students who had never undertaken such a project before and was unsure what to do and how to do it. She was pleased with herself when she exceeded by several multiples the goal she had set for diapers, however she did not really change the organization in the long run. But the next time a student wanted to do something similar, I pushed her further. She not only undertook the diaper campaign but then wrote a guide for future volunteers seeking to do the same. The organization could distribute these guides for individuals wanting to run their own diaper campaigns in the future.

Some students took to the assignment naturally. They were excited about the prospect of creating a project and implementing it. Others faced it with trepidation. They had never been asked to design something brand-new and then carry it out themselves.

The projects were as varied as the students. Several students created volunteer programs for organizations and then implemented them by writing training materials, preparing the first sessions, and then turning the materials and the sessions over to the organization they worked with. One student worked with a homeless shelter to initiate skills classes for women in the shelter. The student surveyed the women to discover what they wanted to learn, found individuals in the community to teach the classes, scheduled them on a weekly basis, and then turned the classes over to a staff member who agreed to coordinate them. Another student approached a local Hispanic center and learned that many low-income parents were struggling to help their children with their homework because they themselves lacked computer skills. She designed classes for parents that taught them how to use computers and the Internet to equip them with the skills to help their children.

A major project, one that took much longer than the semester, was the creation of a carnival for children as part of a cancer fundraising 5k run named after a late university president who had died of cancer. The student noticed that many parents were bringing their children to watch the events but the children had nothing to do. She worked with the fundraiser organizers to expand the event, approached local businesses to provide games and rides for the children, and then coordinated the carnival on the day of the event. The carnival not only raised more funds but also increased attendance at the cancer fundraiser. The organizers of the fundraiser wanted to make the carnival an annual event.

One student initiated a bicycle summit on campus. He recruited local police, bicycle shops, and bicycle repair people to participate. Students learned about bicycle repair (and got their bicycles repaired for free), were given tips about bike safety, and were informed about bicycle paths and trails in the area. The student also learned about bureaucracies. Initially, no administrator would grant him permission to hold this summit. After going in circles with reluctant administrators, he finally wrote an email to the president of the university. The response from the president was positive and the administrators then allowed the bike summit to go forward. In fact, the university picked up the idea itself and made it an annual event. The student gleaned valuable insights into how to handle a bureaucracy.

Even though students were learning a lot and having experiences that would reshape their commitment toward and skills in civic engagement leadership, I noticed quickly that I was stuffing too much into these two courses. Moreover, there was too little preparation within the first course for the second course. And students were reflecting their concerns in student reviews. They were responding that these courses were taking much more time than the typical courses with those credit hour designations. At the same time, they remarked that they were learning a lot, but they felt that the courses should carry more credit hours to match the time they were devoting to the course.

Clearly, a third course was needed. I proposed to the faculty advisory committee and then to the college and university curriculum committees a mid-level course that concentrated on group projects. I felt that a middle course would better transition students between the introductory and senior-level courses. Students would learn to do a project in cooperation with other students before they did their own in the capstone course. This course would be for minors, although any student could sign up for it. However, nearly all were minors.

I took the group project design requirement out of the first course and one of the readings in the capstone and then created a course where students would be given an array of potential group projects they could choose from. These were already arranged with external community partners. This course was intended to help students become familiar with the task of working with an external community partner. Hopefully, these relationships would be useful as they chose individual projects for the capstone seminar.

Of course, our minor consisted of more than two or three core courses. The electives would connect the core courses to the students' majors, minors, or specific academic interests. The faculty advisory committee and I began to review the university's catalog for courses with appropriate civic engagement–related courses. For example, several urban planning minor courses were designed to teach students to operate in governmental settings where they worked extensively with the general public on municipal or county planning. In these courses, students actually created city plans and worked with local governments on real-world projects that included citizen input. We included those courses because they neatly fit within the minor's emphasis on assisting policy makers in their efforts to work with an engaged public.

Political science, understandably, was a major source of electives. These included electives in campaigns and elections, state and local government, and political participation. However, we also drew from courses in social work, sociology, psychology, and history. These courses all included applied work that involved students in working with external community partners (nonprofits or government agencies). The history courses studied civic engagement historically, specifically, revolutionary and liberation movements.

Then, we moved beyond the departments in our college to others across the university. We approached the Communications Department because its faculty taught courses in public relations and social media that related to public opinion campaigns for government or nonprofits. Similarly, we drew from the Public Health Department two courses that addressed public health campaigns.

The addition of these courses broadened the minor's appeal, since more students could understand the implications of their civic engagement courses in their particular field of interest. We allowed students to double count some of the major courses as civic engagement minor electives and eased their integration into the minor. As well, forming relationships across the university helped further the minor's profile and utility across various departments and colleges.

We also instituted a civic engagement internship course, which was an elective and not a requirement. Students created their own internships—either locally or outside the area (even outside the country)—and then applied to use the experience for internship credit. We also recognized various majors' internship course if the specific internship correlated with civic engagement. However, the specific civic engagement internship credit allowed students in majors where there was no internship course to pursue their own internship under our auspices.

It was important to me that our program stand out. Our intent was not just to encourage students in their civic engagement. Rather, we wanted them to become leaders. We wanted our students not only to be engaged personally but also to become equipped to serve as leaders in motivating others to do so. We hoped they would become leaders in politics and government, community affairs, and/or nonprofit management. But even if they did not pursue a career related to civic engagement, we wanted them to be ready to be leaders in groups and movements, stimulating others to become engaged. To emphasize that point, I suggested we change our name from the Office of Civic Engagement to the Office of Civic Engagement Leadership.

INTERACTING WITH FACULTY

It occurred to me that civic engagement training did not need to be limited to the courses within the minor. In some other universities, courses had been designated as service-learning courses because there was some component within the syllabus requirements that corresponded with engagement. I concluded that the Office of Civic Engagement Leadership should encourage the inclusion of such components in courses across the university (particularly within the college) by faculty.

After some consideration, I proposed to the faculty advisory committee a faculty training session that would educate interested faculty about the value of civic engagement teaching segments and teach them how to adapt them to various disciplines. They were encouraging and even volunteered to help teach these sessions. Fortunately, the dean not only was supportive but also was willing to provide a research account stipend to participants who successfully completed the training.

The training consisted of three one-hour sessions over a lunch hour. However, there were additional assignments "out of class" such as the development of specific curriculum changes and small group interaction to review and critique those changes.

After a couple of years, I felt I still was not involving enough faculty in the program. There was a limit to how many people could serve on the faculty advisory committee. Yet, I wanted to expand the buy-in for the program across the college and the university and deepen the relationships with faculty beyond the training.

Working with the faculty advisory committee, I established a faculty affiliate program. The purpose was to draw more faculty into the program and help them realize that others were pursuing civic engagement-related research as well as using civic engagement techniques in their courses that could be useful to others. I hoped that these faculty would become advocates for civic engagement in their departments.

The affiliates came primarily from the faculty civic engagement curriculum training sessions. Each year, at the close of the sessions, I invited those faculty to affiliate with the office. Some did. Affiliates came from a range of departments, not all of them in our college. They were drawn from history, political science, sociology, humanities, social work, and philosophy, among others.

In my last couple of years directing the program, the university initiated experiential learning grants. Since our program was all about experiential learning, I applied for money to administer a grant program within civic engagement. The money was primarily for faculty working with students on various learning experiences outside the classroom. This included, for example, urban planning students traveling to communities to assist in regional planning or anthropology students learning ethnographic research methods to work in a local Hispanic community center.

REACHING THE WHOLE CAMPUS

As another effort to expand our reach, the office sponsored a series of events designed to increase interest in and dedication to becoming civically engaged. We knew widely publicized, and hopefully well attended, events would accomplish that objective, as well as raise the profile of the office. Clearly, there were students we could reach through events who would not become minors or even students in our classes.

One such type of event was an annual workshop. This day-long event featured several panel discussions as well as a keynote address by a prominent individual who had a record of civic engagement. Our first speaker was Elizabeth

Smart. She was well known nationally but also had been a BYU student and still lived nearby. Since her graduation, she had been active in lobbying governments regarding sexual predator legislation and formed a foundation to help sexual assault victims. Her address was attended by nearly four hundred people and helped students learn about her work and also become aware of the new office.

In addition to keynote speakers, panels held during the day featured government officials, leaders of nonprofits, and other community leaders who spoke on a variety of topics such as how to become involved in a nonprofit, how to communicate with elected officials, how to help refugees, and how to foster civility in public discourse. The faculty advisory committee spent several of our monthly meetings discussing what panel topics to include, who to invite, and who could make contact.

One year, our theme was becoming civically engaged to improve race relations. Our keynote speaker was David Garrow, a civil rights movement historian who recounted the activities of civil rights leaders to end Jim Crow laws. A highlight of the day was a panel featuring a local Black church choir singing hymns from the civil rights movement.

Another theme, in conjunction with the passage of the Nineteenth Amendment a century before, was the role of women in civic engagement. Our keynote speaker was the owner of a chain of movie theaters, car dealerships, and an NBA team. But her credentials for this role were centered on her community involvement. She had worked to end homelessness, improve health care, boost financial support for public education, and achieve electoral reform. She served our purpose in providing a model both of a successful businesswoman and of an engaged citizen who was giving back to her community. Additionally, we had panels on women leading nonprofits, running for office, and changing government.

I found that the vast majority of individuals were more than willing to take a couple of hours out of their schedules to speak to students about their organizations and careers or offer tips on how to become involved civically. And students were delighted by the opportunity to pose questions and mingle with the panelists after the workshop. These workshops were the highlight of the year for the office.

Research Conference

Since our office operated in a university setting and we wanted to integrate what students were learning in the classroom with their practical interests and involvement, we instituted an annual research conference to promote faculty and student enthusiasm for civic engagement research. We purposely stressed the interdisciplinary nature of civic engagement by inviting academic researchers who crossed discipline lines. Some were political scientists, but others included sociologists, education researchers, communication scholars, and psychologists. Our themes varied.

Most of the panels during the daylong conference featured a noted researcher who would present her or his research and then receive comments from a couple of BYU faculty and students. Participants included, for example, Joseph Kahne (education, Mills College), David Campbell (political science, Notre Dame), Letitia Bode (communications, Georgetown), and Ben Lough (sociology, Illinois). In addition, a prominent academic served as our keynote speaker for the conference. Over various years, these included scholars such as Peter Levine (philosophy, Tufts University), Richard Bushman (history, Columbia), and Bryan Johnson (religious studies, Baylor).

One panel in the day was reserved for four or five students to present their research. Students chosen for this experience were recommended by faculty or had previously presented at a college-wide poster session. Students came from a variety of disciplines—Family Life, Anthropology, Urban Planning, political science, and so on. The external scholars who had presented earlier in the day became the discussants for these student paper presentations.

To further promote student interest in civic engagement research, annually we hosted a lecture by an academic. These included, for example, Sam Wineburg (Stanford), who presented on how students can be more savvy evaluators of the civic-related information they receive online; Jennifer Stromer-Galley (Syracuse), who discussed the role of social media in the 2016 presidential election; and Diana Owen (Georgetown), who discussed youth civic engagement and social media.

These research-oriented events served our purpose of demonstrating that civic engagement was not just a practitioners' activity. Scholars could orient their research to answer important questions related to civic engagement, and that work could be done across disciplines. They also raised the profile of the Office within the university as faculty were invited to the panels, lectures, and luncheons to mingle with external scholars and learn more about the work of the Office of Civic Engagement Leadership.

Lectures and Panel Discussions

We sought to hold two to three events during a semester. In addition to the workshop and research conference, we sponsored various lectures and panel discussions. Most featured practitioners in government, nonprofits, or other community work. For example, we invited a bank president who had spearheaded various initiatives on homelessness, education funding, and health-care access; the head of a nonprofit that sponsored discussion sessions between Democrats and Republicans to increase understanding across partisan lines; and the head of the local branch of the NAACP to discuss her organization's work and its goals for the future in improving race relations in Utah. A frequent speaker who drew a large audience was a Black Baptist minister from Salt Lake City and former civil rights movement marcher who inspired students to make a difference in their communities, particularly by thinking beyond themselves and in broader, community-oriented terms.

Since students lived in Provo and complained frequently about housing, traffic, and parking issues, twice we invited the mayor to meet with students and address their concerns. He graciously accepted our invitations. As we hoped, he encouraged students to get off the campus and become involved in the governance of the city.

Recognitions

Within a short time of our creation as an office, I suggested to the faculty advisory committee that we initiate a set of awards to recognize those who had made significant contributions in some area of civic engagement. These awards would signal our awareness of the work of individuals who are making a difference. And we would be helping students see that they, too, could be instrumental in furthering a civic cause that was bigger than themselves.

We established a citizen award as well as a student award, although we sometimes gave more than one of each in a year. The faculty advisory committee suggested the recipients of the student award, while our external advisory board did the same for the citizen award. We gave these awards at a luncheon during the annual workshop.

For example, we recognized a student who had been instrumental in making Provo safer for bicycle use, another student who coordinated a voter registration drive, and yet another who formed a nonprofit to advocate for pedestrians. Citizens we recognized included an education activist who had been active in lobbying for educational awareness of the special needs of children with autism, another community activist who led a homeless assistance organization, and a high school principal who had developed a suicide prevention program.

INTERACTING WITH COMMUNITY PARTNERS

Since a civic engagement program, by design, unites the university, particularly its students, with the larger community, I wanted to better understand how that could best be accomplished. Within a couple of months of the creation of the office, I invited a dozen leaders of local nonprofit community organizations, government officers, and political party representatives to lunch to pick their brains on this topic. These were individuals who had worked with the university's various departments and programs in the past. Before I sent my future students in this program out into the community to engage in individual or group projects, or even merely to volunteer, I wanted to know how these individuals felt about our students and what they would like to see in experiential learning projects they were going to be involved in.

Their one-time cooperation was extraordinarily useful in designing individual and group projects and educating students on how best to work with community partners. However, the experience convinced me that my goals could not be achieved without an ongoing relationship between our office and these community partners. They would be an ongoing source of advice.

Again, with the help of the faculty advisory committee (some of whom had better contacts with community partners than I did), I created an external advisory board and began to ask representatives from external community partners to serve. I was pleasantly surprised that nearly all agreed. These included leaders of the United Way, Habitat for Humanity, Community Action Services, the Governor's Office on Volunteerism, the Utah Nonprofits Association, the Provo Mayor's Office, and so on. The board initially met quarterly and then moved to a semi-annual schedule. The vast majority of the dozen or so members took their responsibilities seriously by attending the meetings and giving advice on the operation of the program.

During our meetings, I posed various issues for their counsel. These included internship programs, implementation of group projects, placement of students after graduation, and the like. In addition, I kept them abreast of changes in the program, as well as reports on past and upcoming events of the office. During the meetings, I introduced them to students in the program so they could hear directly about their experiences in the various courses, as well as what projects they were designing and completing.

These community partner representatives became a valuable resource for internships, student projects, and placement. And many attended and even participated in the events of the program, particularly serving on panels. They volunteered to speak in classes, which most of them did at some point. I found that they were happiest when they were able to interact with students directly.

APSA SECTION

In 2019, I attended the annual meeting of the American Political Science Association in Washington, DC. One of the panels was on the status of civic engagement in the discipline. The panelists urged members of the audience to develop curricula and encourage research in civic engagement. I posed a question to the panelists but also to the audience of about thirty people: Why isn't there a section of the APSA dedicated to civic engagement? They responded that it was a good idea but that it would take some time to create such a section.

After the session, I went up to two people I knew in attendance—Peter Levine, a political philosophy professor at Tufts University and a former head of the Center for Information & Research on Civic Learning and Engagement (CIRCLE), and Elizabeth Bennion, a political science professor at Indiana University–South Bend who had cowritten a book on teaching civic engagement—and posed the same question. Rogers Smith, who was closing his one-year term as president of APSA, joined the conversation and echoed the need for such a section and explained a little bit about how to create one. The general sentiment was that it was a cumbersome process to form new sections and perhaps one could be created sometime in the future. But I responded: Why not now? And I promised to look into the details of the process.

Not long after the conference was over, I explored the organization's website and spoke with a staff member who supervised sections. She provided information about how to create a section. She also expressed great interest in having such a section as part of APSA. Clearly, she wanted this to happen and was pleased that someone was pursuing the idea. APSA staff themselves cannot create sections. It must be an organic effort that comes from the members.

At that point, I circled back to Peter Levine and Elizabeth Bennion and explained the process. We needed to offer a proposal to the APSA for the creation of the section that included discussion of its mission and uniqueness compared to other existing sections. A set of bylaws and proposed section officers was required as well. In addition, the proposal needed to be accompanied by a petition signed by at least two hundred current members of the American Political Science Association.

That last requirement worried us. Could we attract two hundred people to sign the petition to create this new section? We drafted a brief proposal for the section and then sent it to APSA, asking if they would publicize it for members and give them the opportunity to join. In addition, we created a spreadsheet that allowed APSA members to add their names if they wished to join us in petitioning for the creation of this new section. Then, we sent emails to APSA members we could think of who might be interested in joining us.

We did not have to wait long for the response. It was overwhelming. When we submitted the petition less than a week after the emails went out to APSA members, we had 304 signatures on the petition. Clearly, this was a popular step—perhaps one that many people realized was long overdue. That was extremely heartening for us.

We submitted the petition to APSA on November 19, 2019. Their board approved the new section in February 2020. Now, we were on our way. We drew up our section bylaws, drawing heavily on the models of other recent sections. We solicited volunteers for positions. Several people volunteered to serve in a variety of capacities. Elizabeth and I agreed to be the temporary cochairs while Peter Levine would be the vice chair. Verlan Lewis (University of Colorado Colorado Springs) volunteered to be secretary and Malliga Och (Idaho State University) as the treasurer. Jeffrey Kraus (Wagner College) became the first program chair. APSA gave us two panels for the 2020 annual meeting, where we advertised the section using the themes of civic engagement in teaching and civic engagement in research.

The 2020 APSA annual meeting, like so many other events in the age of COVID-19, was held virtually. However, there was good attendance at our two panels from people who wanted to learn about the subject but also about this new section we had created. Similarly, our business meeting and reception were well attended. We opened the meeting up for a brainstorming session and received various ideas about how to move forward, as well as offers to help to do so.

When we came to the point of electing permanent officers, Peter and Verlan asked to be excused from further service due to other professional commitments. But Jeffrey stepped up to be the secretary, and Carah Whaley (James Madison University) agreed to be the vice chair. Soon thereafter we put out a call for volunteers for four committees—civic education, awards, publications, and mentoring. About thirty people volunteered to serve on one committee or the other. Some signed up for any we chose to place them in. We were pleased about the broad-based interest in serving in this new section.

As our first year progressed, we began to organize the committees. They began to meet on their own and take actions in their respective areas. For example, the awards committee created four awards to recognize future members of the section. One was an established leader award that acknowledged the achievements of someone who had an outstanding and sustained leadership role in civic engagement. Another recognized an outstanding civic engagement project. A third was dedicated to the best APSA paper of the year, while the fourth honors an emerging scholar. Those awards were accepted by the section membership at the 2021 business meeting.

The mentoring committee initiated a series of virtual "happy hours" where members could talk to each other informally about their work—hopefully giving junior members an opportunity to chat casually with more senior faculty. Also, they solicited interest in being a mentor to a particular junior faculty member or graduate student and did the same with potential mentees. Then, they paired them. Mentoring is a critical function of a section because it allows junior colleagues to gain insights about the discipline and the subfield, as well as academic life, beyond their own department. It is a form of civic engagement.

The committee on publications began to investigate the prospect of a journal for the section. Additionally, they initiated an edited volume on civic engagement. They negotiated with *PS*, the APSA journal, to include a spotlight on civic engagement for its January 2022 issue. And they created a web and social media presence and a monthly newsletter. They, as well, were active in building this new section.

It was my pleasure to watch this activity, that is, to see a new section emerge and then be embraced by those who wanted to see it fill a much-needed niche. The core of active members gave promise that the section would have a fruitful future and become an important asset to the American Political Science Association. The APSA's increased interest in civic engagement, even before the formation of the section, suggested that the organization would take special interest in this section. (The fact that the president of APSA attended the section's annual business meeting in 2021 was one sign of that interest.)

The section bylaws included staggered terms for the two cochairs so there would be continuity. I took the one-year term while Elizabeth took the two-year term. As a result, I stepped down as cochair of the section and left it in highly capable hands. When I did so, the section had several hundred members. It was not in danger of losing its status as a section by falling below two hundred members. Nor was it going to be a moribund section where members might need to be coerced into volunteering. It had a bright future as a force in the discipline in assisting teachers of civic engagement, stimulating research, and recognizing and therefore encouraging civic engagement within and beyond academe.

LESSONS LEARNED

People in positions of authority have the opportunity to do much good. They have the power to create, encourage, and direct resources. My dean had the ability to do that with his support for the initiation of an Office of Civic Engagement Leadership. And he did so. And when he allowed me to be the chair of the futures committee, he gave me the power to suggest this new administrative unit as part of a set of reforms. I could have done it separately, but inclusion in a package of reforms was the ideal approach, since a new dean was soliciting suggestions for change.

That does not mean a position of authority is a requisite for getting things done. Most of what can be accomplished by an academic can be done without holding some administrative position. This includes stimulating civic engagement among students in a class or serving in the community in some way.

In fact, the danger of holding a position is that it can become the objective, rather than the good that can be done. Too many administrators hold the office but do not use it. They manage some administrative unit, but they do not lead. In particular, they do not innovate, create, and build. Nor do they encourage others to do the same. Rather, they value the position for its status and possibilities for future advancement.

That segues into another lesson. Timing is important. A new administrator was anxious to make a difference during his term as dean. But he was not coming into the job with a preset agenda regarding specific alterations. Rather, he wanted the impetus for change to be organic—originating from the faculty and staff. I saw this as a prime opportunity to make a change I had contemplated for years but for which the timing had not been right. The new college administration, and the new dean's approach, became the ideal time to make the push.

This does not mean that change must wait for the perfect alignment of the stars. It becomes necessary to take action to take advantage of good timing, as I did in volunteering to direct his new committee. And sometimes it is necessary to create the right climate for acceptance of change. In my case, by demonstrating through the survey results that there was a need for this kind of unprecedented effort by the college, I was able to convince the rest of the committee and the dean that a center for civic engagement was necessary.

Another lesson I learned was that my interests in political engagement in both academic and applied settings could be married through the creation of a unit dedicated to stimulating civic engagement. As later chapters will show, I did engage in activities unrelated to the university—before and after the creation of the Office of Civic Engagement Leadership. However, I was looking for something I could do within the university. This type of service allowed me to receive "job" credit for my civic engagement work. I could count this activity toward service but also toward teaching, since I was offering courses.

It also would have been possible to mesh my research with my administrative and teaching work. Since I already had other research agendas underway, I did not really do that. Yet, I could have created a trifecta around civic engagement—service, teaching, and research.

It is not necessary to create a new administrative unit to merge civic engagement with other academic duties. Few political scientists will ever do that. But there are certainly less time-consuming, administrative opportunities available. Introducing civic engagement components in existing courses is one such opportunity. Another is the introduction of new courses more closely associated with civic engagement. Association with an existing university or college center or institute in a volunteer capacity could also satisfy a need for civic engagement service within the university.

4. Utah Debate Commission

On an October evening in 2012, I tuned in to the Utah Gubernatorial Debate being hosted by two public television stations in Utah. The Republican (the incumbent governor) and the Democrat outlined their positions on a host of issues affecting the state. As I sat there watching the debate, two thoughts struck me.

One was that this was a highly informative debate. We were hearing about how these two candidates would handle the state's challenges over the next four years in areas such as public education, higher education, transportation, health care, relations with the federal government, taxes, and so on. Any voter who was tuning in would be able to glean important insights about what their vote choice would mean for the future of the state.

But the second thought was that few people were in fact tuning in, since public television viewership typically pales in comparison to commercial stations. I flipped the channels and saw that the commercial television stations were showing entertainment programming, not the debate. And none of them was hosting or showing any other candidate debates, with the exception of one close congressional district race in Utah that year.

To me, that was a tragic combination—an opportunity to learn about how future leaders would govern the state was missed by the vast majority of voters. The same also applied to the US Senate race going on that year. Similarly, that debate was aired only on public television and was not carried by any of the commercial, and much better viewed, television stations.

While contemplating what could be done about this, I thought about another set of debates going on that fall—the presidential candidate debates. The Commission on Presidential Debates (CPD) was sponsoring four debates—three between the presidential candidates and one debate for vice presidential candidates. These debates had become fixtures in presidential elections since their inception in 1987.

Prior to the CPD, presidential general election debates had been sponsored by the League of Women Voters or specific media organizations. The first general election presidential debates occurred in 1960, when John F. Kennedy and Richard Nixon met. However, it was not until 1976 that an incumbent agreed to debate his opponent and debates became routine features of presidential general election campaigns.[1]

The two major parties took over the debate process from the League of

Women Voters in 1987. The chairs of the two major parties met together to form an independent, bipartisan organization that would organize and host general election debates and offer the feed to television stations. The Commission on Presidential Debates created an institutional structure for general election debates that was almost uniformly well received and had earned the trust of tens of millions of Americans who tuned in to learn about the candidates.

Until 2020, no major party presidential candidate had declined an invitation to participate in the CPD's debates. That year, however, the CPD announced its second debate would be virtual because President Donald Trump had contracted COVID-19 and former vice president Joe Biden refused to debate him in person. After the announcement, Trump announced he would not participate in a virtual debate. In response, the CPD canceled the debate, although it did hold the other scheduled debates that year.[2]

Throughout the history of the CPD, media outlets have viewed the debates as an opportunity to cover a vital event in the course of a presidential general election campaign. And voters still tune in for the debates. In 2020, 73 million viewers watched the first presidential debate, which was the third-highest audience total in the past fifty years.[3]

CREATING A DEBATE COMMISSION

As I considered this situation—Utah had a poor debate system, while the CPD had created an effective one—I wondered what could be done about it. I pondered whether it would be possible to replicate the CPD example at the state level. Why not create a state debate commission—the Utah Debate Commission—that would serve the same functions as the Commission on Presidential Debates, but at the state level?

I began to wonder whether I was the first to have such an idea. Rarely is that the case in life. And it was not true in this case either. As I researched, I found that another state had already created such a commission. The Indiana Debate Commission had been formed in 2007 and had operated in general elections since that time. That state debate commission had been formed by broadcasters, and their board consisted primarily of representatives of various media organizations in the state.

I thought it might be best to go beyond the media to create a more stable and inclusive commission. Media outlets were essential. But there were other stakeholders who should be represented as well. I believed there should be three main groups in a state debate commission.

One, of course, was the media. Television stations, particularly, were important since they would be broadcasting the debates. Their needs as broadcasters had to be considered to make sure they were committed to airing these debates. Public television stations should be part of that group, but, even more importantly, commercial television stations had to be included. Print media outlets were important as well in terms of publicizing the commission and its debates. They also could be valuable in placing pressure on candidates who were reluctant to participate, particularly incumbents. A united front of newspaper editorials criticizing a candidate for failure to participate would be a powerful disincentive for the hesitant candidate.

Another group consisted of the higher educational institutions in the state. In Utah, two of the state's universities—the University of Utah and Brigham Young University—had provided the venues for the debates. Both had worked with their respective public television stations to offer studio facilities and live audiences. Moreover, students had been integral to the BYU operation, arranging the debates and asking questions.

I felt that connection should continue for three reasons. First was the pedagogical value to students. The Utah Debate Commission could provide an opportunity for students around the state to be involved in the logistics of debate hosting, participate in the audience, and ask questions of the candidates. Second, the universities would provide geographical diversity for debates. In the past, the debates had been held only in Salt Lake City and Provo. Including all the universities and colleges would mean debates held throughout the state. These would involve citizens across the state and even address regional issues important to that particular part of the state. But a third reason was legitimacy. The involvement of all the universities in the state would give the commission immediate credibility with the media, as well as with the general public.

The third group were the politicians. A debate commission would be a new entity for the state. Politicians might feel threatened by it. They might refuse to participate in an untested process. If that happened en masse, the debate commission concept would fail.

However, if senior politicos—people they respected within their own parties—served on the board, then candidates and party leaders might give the commission credence. Candidates might be reluctant to decline an invitation if a senior politico from his or her own party was encouraging them to participate.

Senior politicos also had name recognition that guaranteed coverage of the commission's activities. The first cochairs of the Commission on Presidential Debates were the chairs of the national party commissions at the time—Paul Kirk and Frank Fahrenkopf Jr. And the honorary chairs included former US presidents. Like the Commission on Presidential Debates, I wanted to get well-known individuals on the board early on to signal to the media and the public that the commission was a serious entity.

But where to start? I wrote up a proposal of a commission outlining my ideas about how it should be structured. I wrote that the commission should be multi-partisan, set candidate thresholds that would provide a meaningful exchange rather than have a half-dozen candidates who get four minutes each, rotate debate venues around the state, and schedule three debates for each race. The last point was ambitious and, as I discovered, not feasible. I said the debate commission would form partnerships with television stations to facilitate live television coverage of the debates. I knew live coverage would heighten the interest, since the event was occurring in real time and viewers would be watching as the events occurred. I also urged that the debate schedule be announced well in advance of the selection of a party nominee. That was intended to institutionalize the commission's actions and create the environment a nominee would step into rather than allowing them to create it themselves.

My proposal suggested the commission have two cochairs—one from each major party. In that respect I was mimicking the CPD. These cochairs would be the senior politicos who would give the UDC legitimacy and encourage participation by candidates of the two major parties. I also suggested a broad-based board that did not include current political officeholders and that had at least one representative from a minor party and one known to be unaffiliated.

I began to circulate my two-page proposal to a few people I knew at the University of Utah and Utah State University. Then, I expanded to other academics—directors of institutes and chairs of political science departments in the state. The response was typical for a new venture: good idea but it will take time to carry out.

One of my concerns was how Republicans would react to the proposal. One of the institute directors also was a Republican Party operative who had worked closely with Mitt Romney during his 2008 and 2012 presidential runs. I asked him if he could broach the idea with Republican politicos he knew to gauge the reaction. To my delight, he reported they were supportive because it would change their debate participation in a way they felt was more favorable to them. One of the draws of a debate commission would be the live televised debate carried across multiple television stations that would have extensive public reach. The incumbents said they preferred participating in such a debate instead of the dozen or so non-televised debates they were expected to attend during a typical campaign. Of course, the intent of the debate commission was not to displace these other debates. However, I recognized that such an outcome was likely because they would become less essential.

I decided the best way to push the idea was to hold a meeting of these academics at a central location to discuss the idea further, flesh it out, and emerge with a recommendation for moving forward. The meeting was arranged for June 11, 2013, at the Hinckley Institute of Politics at the University of Utah. Representatives from the University of Utah, Utah State University, Weber State University, Southern Utah University, Utah Valley University, and BYU (me) attended. After a couple of hours of discussion, we decided to move forward with the idea by calling another meeting for August and inviting people from the other two groups—the media and politicos—to participate.

During those two months, I made quite a few phone calls to introduce the concept to various broadcast station general managers and news directors, as well as newspaper editors. The response was nearly uniformly positive. Only two were not. One was a lobbyist who represented an organization that had sponsored candidates' debates in the past. He was opposed because he felt the UDC was robbing various specialty groups of the opportunity to hold debates regarding their particular issue interests. The other, however, was more serious. It was the news director at the University of Utah public television station who had been instrumental in organizing past candidate debates. He was extremely reluctant to see a commission come in and take over the debate process. I urged him not to think of this commission in those terms. The commission would not have a monopoly on debates. It would simply assure that a debate in a particular race would be widely viewed beyond one or two public broadcasting stations. Later, he was offered the role as moderator for several of the debates, which, as I predicted, were shown not just on his station but across most or all of the commercial television stations in the state.

The most enthusiastic person I contacted was the editor of one of the major newspapers. Since that newspaper was owned by the same company that also owned one of the most-watched television stations in the state, he was influential in the decision-making for the station as well. In our conversation, not only did he support the idea but he also promised that the television station would carry all of the debates. That promise subsequently was carried out and encouraged the other stations to follow suit. That act was a significant boost for the not-yet-formed Utah Debate Commission.

From the beginning, I knew it was important to have the right individuals for the two cochairs. They must be people well-known among politicos so they could offer that instant legitimacy and play critical roles in convincing candidates to participate. These people would need to be willing to take the initiative from the start.

The choice for the Republican cochair was obvious—Olene Walker, the first female governor of Utah. She had been lieutenant governor for nearly eleven years when she became governor after the resignation of Michael Leavitt to become head of the Environmental Protection Agency in the George W. Bush administration. When I called and made the request, she immediately accepted. She explained that she had been a debater in college and was convinced of the value of candidate debates.

The other cochair I chose was Scott Howell, the former minority leader in the Utah Senate. Howell was a prominent Democrat who twice was the Democratic Party nominee for the US Senate against Senator Orrin Hatch. He was well respected by various wings of the Democratic Party even though he was a more moderate Democrat. Howell also accepted quickly.

On August 13, about twenty people met in a third-floor conference room of the City and County Building in downtown Salt Lake City. They included representatives of each of the television stations, editors of the two Salt Lake newspapers, academics from each of the six universities in the state, and political leaders. The concept was presented formally to them. A discussion ensued that focused primarily on how such an organization would elevate candidate communication and voter information, as well as the general level of public discourse by hosting civil, informative debates in contrast to a growing candidate reliance on negative advertising.

The group decided to begin the process of formally incorporating as the Utah Debate Commission. The two cochairs were nominated and elected. Then, the group formed an executive committee with the responsibility for implementing that incorporation, securing seed funding, and drawing up a set of bylaws and a mission statement for the new organization. The executive committee included the two cochairs, the enthusiastic newspaper editor, and myself. Finally, the group established a regular bimonthly meeting schedule to plan for the 2014 election season.

The executive committee wrote a mission statement declaring the purpose and functions of the Utah Debate Commission. In addition, it wrote the bylaws that set out the policies of the new organization. The bylaws designated two groups as permanent members of the board—media organizations and universities—while other members of the board, such as political, community, or business leaders, were temporary and rotated on and off. The media organizations designated representatives, who normally were the news directors or editors, as did the six universities. (Within a couple of years, the academic institution representation was expanded to include two colleges in the state.) Memoranda of agreement were signed with the universities that committed them to cooperate with the commission and provide the venues for debates.

Late in the fall of that year, the executive committee decided to hire a part-time executive director. Most of the work of organization was falling on my shoulders. I wrote the drafts of the mission statement and the bylaws. I had contacted nearly all the people who became involved. But I knew that was the price to pay for getting a new organization off the ground. Yet, I also knew that I could not continue to do most everything, particularly as the UDC moved to actual production of debates.

We put out a job advertisement and received several serious applications. At one executive committee meeting, Governor Walker asked how we would feel if her daughter applied for the position. Her daughter had been the first director of the Walker Institute of Politics at Weber State University and had a law degree from the University of Utah. Governor Walker offered to resign if we hired her daughter.

Her daughter, Nena Slighting, did apply and was hired. One advantage she had over others we interviewed was her willingness to grow with us. She understood that she needed to fundraise (something she had already done for her mother's institute) and that we could not guarantee her salary. She would have to fundraise it. Plus, she had an even-handed personality that would make her capable of dealing with the pressures from various corners—the media, the candidates, the parties, the universities, and the like.

Governor Walker did not resign immediately. However, she was in poor health and did resign after our first election season. Sadly, she died shortly thereafter.

Nena Slighting began to organize the fall debates immediately. She applied for 501c3 status, helped create committees, began working with universities on locations, hired a producer, and so on. She also identified potential donors and raised enough money to fund the first season of debates. It was wonderful to have a partner in this enterprise who was as dedicated to the realization of a state debate commission as I was.

RUNNING DEBATES

On February 24, 2014, the newly created Utah Debate Commission was announced in a press conference on the steps of the Utah Capitol building. The organizers, led by the two cochairs, explained what the Utah Debate Commission was, why it was needed, and how it would work. At the same time, the schedule for fall debates was announced including dates and locations. There would be four debates of congressional candidates to cover the four congressional districts in the state. As well, there would be an attorney general debate. Utah elects its state-level officials in presidential election years, a fact that was considered a plus for the commission since the first year would not include a state-level race debate. Additionally, there was no US Senate seat open that year, which meant the commission could concentrate on congressional districts. However, a special election provision exists in the case of a vacancy and the subsequent appointment of a replacement. The previous year, the state's attorney general had resigned under accusations of corruption. That triggered the special election.

Unfortunately, the challenges for the Utah Debate Commission were just beginning. While most incumbents had signaled a willingness to participate in the debates, one—the newly appointed attorney general—was undecided. The chair of the Republican Party was encouraging the attorney general not to participate. Also, the chair was demanding that one of the members of the commission's board be a Republican of his choice.

In addition to the two partisans who were the cochairs, four other partisans had been appointed to the board already. However, these partisans had been selected by the board, not by the parties. The GOP chair wanted his own person on the board. The board, and particularly the executive committee, wrestled with this problem for some time and disagreed strongly about what the outcome should be. Eventually, a compromise was worked out. The bylaws were changed to allow a major party state chair to select a representative. However, the GOP chair agreed that one of the two Republicans already on the board would be his representative. When that state party chair lost his bid for reelection, that bylaw was removed.

The challenge to the role of the UDC continued. In early 2016, after the debate schedule had been announced, the governor's office called to explain to Nena Slighting that the governor would be unavailable on that date for the debate. The debate was scheduled for six months away. The governor was attempting to see whether he could bend the debate schedule. Ironically, the strongest proponent of not changing the schedule was one of the Republican partisans on the board. The executive committee decided they would not change the schedule to accommodate the governor. In response, the governor's office told the UDC that the governor would attend. The commission had met the first challenge by an incumbent—and won.

The threshold for candidate participation had been set at 10 percent in a poll commissioned by the UDC in late August. This decision also had been subject to much debate. Some board members advocated a lower threshold. The news director at the public television station objected to such a threshold because he had set a lower one for his own debates. He felt the UDC was being inclusionary and would be subject to lawsuits by third-party candidates. However, a majority of the board disagreed, arguing that a lower threshold would lead to too many candidates on the debate stage at one time and that some of those candidates would be candidates in name only. Plus, the proponents of this position pointed out that the Commission on Presidential Debates had set a higher threshold—15 percent—and had won legal challenges. The compromise decided by the board was continuation of the 10 percent threshold with a consideration for the margin of error. With a margin of error at approximately 4 percent, that meant the real threshold was 6 percent.

After the invitations had been sent to candidates that fall, several candidates for governor and US senator from minor parties objected. They contended they should be included because they were legal candidates on the ballot. When they were rebuffed by the commission, they staged a joint protest at a gubernatorial debate held in Logan. The protest attracted press attention, which was the point, but did not result in pressure on the UDC to include them then or in the future.

Later that year, the UDC would face another decision—whether to hold a debate with one candidate. The Democratic candidate for attorney general had not communicated to the executive director before the debate that he would not be participating; instead, she was notified indirectly on the morning of the debate. Instead, he was withdrawing from the race. His withdrawal raised the question of whether the debate should continue with only one candidate. The policy adopted at the inception of the commission was that a candidate could not veto a debate by not participating. The debate would go on with only one candidate.

Now, the UDC executive committee faced the decision of whether to apply the policy. Again, after some discussion that morning, the decision was made to abide by the bylaws and hold the debate regardless. This was my position. I presented the problem of precedent. If the UDC changed its position at this point, it would not be credible in the future when claiming it actually would give the whole time to one candidate if the other failed to show.

Of course, the debate was not a debate. The moderator asked questions of the Republican candidate. Ironically, that candidate was the incumbent attorney general who had publicly wavered on whether he would participate in the special election debate. Only one television station aired the debate, which the board understood.

The following year, the issue of threshold would arise again. The UDC switched polling firms for a special congressional election in 2017. The new firm committed a serious polling error—mixing its samples. Then, it weighted respondents, which raised suspicions about the accuracy of its results when they were reported. The candidate for the United Utah Party, who had barely missed the threshold, challenged the poll and asked for it to be redone.

After initial resistance, the poll was redone without the error or weighting.

In the new poll, the UUP candidate crossed the threshold of 6 percent and became the first nonmajor party candidate to qualify for a Utah Debate Commission debate. The episode was publicly damaging to the commission. The board created a committee of scholars to oversee the polling in the future.

The UDC poll was a unique feature for debate commissions. A UDC commissioned survey was chosen as the means for determining thresholds because there were no other polls done at that time of year. Typically, media-commissioned polls were conducted before a primary election and immediately afterward, and then again in October. But at the time the UDC had to make decisions about who would participate in debates held as early as mid-September, a poll did not exist. Moreover, media-commissioned polls sometimes focused on certain competitive races and not others. The UDC needed a survey that would include all the races where debates would be held. However, the poll was not inexpensive, and it became a major expense each election year.

Another issue was the selection of moderators. Our policies placed the moderator decision squarely in the hands of the UDC. That meant the board had to exercise great care in the selection of moderators. We wanted the moderators to have a reputation for impartiality. They should be respected by the general public as well as by the elites in Utah politics.

Another wrinkle in the moderator choice was the competition among television stations. When the stations had conducted their own debates, they used their star reporters or anchors as moderators in order to showcase them. However, if most or all of the stations were carrying the same event, any moderator from a particular station would be "showcased" on another station. That was unacceptable to the television station general managers and news directors. One of the first decisions, then, was to remove from consideration any current television news anchor or reporter.

Fortunately, there were two individuals who already were highly regarded as debate moderators. One was the public station news director who initially opposed the commission. Our promise that he would be a moderator for a debate each election cycle eased his concerns about the commission. And, for the first two cycles before he retired, he effectively moderated debates for the UDC. The other was David Magleby, a BYU professor who had moderated candidate debates in Utah for three decades. He graciously agreed to be a moderator with the UDC.

Other moderators were drawn from talk radio hosts (who were not in competition with television news programs), college professors, and former news anchors. They were vetted to assure they were not viewed as partisans who would face objections from one campaign or another. On the whole, the moderators performed ably and, due to the careful scrutiny by the board, avoided criticism of bias.

One unintended byproduct of the commission was cooperation among people who generally compete with each other. Every couple of months, news directors gathered together in the meetings of the Utah Debate Commission and worked together to produce professional quality, substantive candidate debates for the citizens of the state of Utah. Watching them cooperate to this end, instead of simply competing with each other, was satisfying.

In June 2017, I stepped away from the UDC Board because of my involvement in the United Utah Party. During the subsequent years, the UDC expanded its board and changed members as some individuals rotated off. Additionally, media organizations and academic institutions switched out representatives. The UDC also added primary election debates. Within a few years, the UDC had become an institution in the state. It was the main debate forum in Utah. Few candidates turned down an invitation to debate. The threshold remained intact, although two other minor party candidates—another from the UUP and a Libertarian—qualified for debates in 2018 and 2020, respectively.

The UDC has solved several problems in electoral communication. It has placed someone other than the candidates and parties in control of debates. (Not surprisingly, both have vested interests in tilting the process in their direction.) It has given candidates a forum for expressing their views. And it has offered a substantive source of information for voters about candidates that, thanks to broadcasters, is widely available to them and includes the major party candidates as well as other candidates who have a base of support within the electorate. And it has allowed broadcast media outlets to fulfill their public service obligations without having to do all the work themselves.

I am pleased to have been a part of the creation of this commission. One former member of the board remarked that he hoped the Utah Debate Commission would still be around in fifty years. That is my hope as well. It was a privilege to meet with people who came from various backgrounds—media, academe, politics, business—and were dedicated to serving the public.

LESSONS LEARNED

One lesson is the difference between merely having ideas and making them a reality. The former is easy, while the latter requires commitment to the idea. I have been in many meetings when someone presents an idea for the organization to implement. They are good ideas—worthy of consideration, development, and action. But they accomplish nothing unless someone is willing to work to make them happen. Ideally, that someone should be the same someone who proposed the idea. Yet, often that person is more comfortable proposing than working.

The response to my idea of a state debate commission was positive by nearly everyone I spoke with. However, few wanted to spend time on a project that was not already underway and, essentially, guaranteed to be a success. As a consequence, I had to do the work necessary to take the idea far enough along to be picked up by others. I had to make phone calls, send emails, draft proposals, find meeting venues, and apply for legal recognition. I had to work hard to bring the idea to fruition. I could not rely on others to pick up an idea and run with it. That rarely happens.

Another lesson was the importance of understanding others' perspectives and appealing to them in order to gain their cooperation. For example, politicians were not immediately drawn to the idea of a state debate commission for the same reasons I was. To me, this organization would serve the interests of good government. But politicians who would be the candidates in the debate were more interested in how participation would serve them. To them, such an idea had merit because it simplified their lives. Rather than running all over the state doing a dozen debates before various groups, they could reach the whole state in a live televised debate sponsored by the Utah Debate Commission.

Still another lesson was the power of one individual to make a difference. In this case, that wasn't just me. Rather, it was those who joined me early on. I was grateful for those who signed on to this idea quickly. They were willing to take a gamble that this would work and offered critical support that convinced others to participate. A few years ago, I watched a lecturer show a video of a man on a beach who began dancing unabashedly among the beachgoers. He does that for a couple of minutes before another man gets up and starts dancing next to him. Then, others get up as well, and suddenly there is a crowd dancing. The first man was the influencer, but so was the second one who decided to join the lone figure on the beach. Similarly, those who are willing to join a movement at its inception are the risk-takers who change the world as well.

5. Service to a Major Party

As someone who came of age during the Watergate scandal, I am leery of partisan politics. I see its value in presenting and advocating for particular ideologies and issue positions, as well as engaging voters. However, I am personally uncomfortable with the extremism that has characterized the major parties in recent years. Nevertheless, as long as Americans grow up identifying with a political party, partisans vote along party lines, and the ballot is organized by party, those who seek to make a difference beyond the municipal level must come to terms with the power of political parties. That means identifying with a political party and working within its framework to affect who runs for office, how they do so, and what they accomplish within office.

My first encounter with party politics was as a volunteer on the George McGovern campaign in 1972 as he sought to oust Richard Nixon from the White House. I felt the Vietnam War was a conflict we needed to exit and that Nixon was accomplishing the task far too slowly. The McGovern campaign in my small city in Georgia was a lost cause, as it was nationally. But we staffed a local storefront campaign headquarters with volunteers (primarily college students) and distributed literature, sought media coverage, and put out signs. I learned a valuable lesson about partisanship when the Democratic nominee for US Senate, Sam Nunn, distanced himself from the party's presidential candidate. McGovern never came to Georgia. He knew it was hopeless. But the Nunn campaign put up signs around the state reading "Nixon/Nunn."

The South was undergoing a significant voter realignment. After a century of Democratic dominance, George Wallace had captured most of the Deep South with an independent presidential campaign in 1968. He had returned to the Democratic Party by 1972 but then left the campaign after he was shot during the primaries. The end of Wallace's campaign was the final nail in the coffin of the Democratic Party in the South. That fall, voters in southern states en masse voted for the Republican Party nominee.

Our local campaign was in the middle of that re-sorting of voter preferences. Although our candidate was the Democratic Party nominee, he was anathema to most voters. McGovern did poorly in our town, as he did in the state. But, I was grateful for the experience of working on a campaign.

Even though I enjoyed the opportunity, ironically, I remained largely aloof from partisan politics for some time after that campaign. I was attending graduate school and then raising a family. It wasn't until the late 1990s that I began to reenter partisan politics. I received a phone call from a woman in my city who served on the school board and was active in Republican Party politics. She called to urge me to run for the state legislature. Then, others contacted me as well.

My state legislative district, like most of the state, was heavily Republican. I had not lived there long, but while I was there I had watched Democrats wage hopeless campaigns for elective office in my county. The situation created a quandary for people like me who wanted to be involved but didn't feel comfortable with the Republican Party. My only experience with the Republicans had been northeast Republicans I had encountered in New York and Connecticut, where we had lived for ten years before moving to Utah. Those Republicans were more moderate. One, for example, was Lowell Weicker, who served as a US senator and then the governor of Connecticut. He had a reputation as being one of the most liberal Republicans, although there had been several other moderate Republicans in the Northeast at the time, such as Rhode Island US senator John Chaffee, Maine US senator William Cohen, and New Jersey governor Christine Todd Whitman.

I had little experience with the Republicans in Utah. My first response to these requests to run was that I was too moderate for the Republican Party. Frankly, I didn't think I could make it through the party's convention with a centrist approach to political issues. With some of those urging me to run, I broached the idea of running as an independent. They discouraged me from that course. They said independents had a poor reputation in the state. They tended to be written off as weird.

My run is something I will discuss in chapter 7. Here, I will address my experience with party. I realized quickly that I was associating with people whose opinions were far to the right of my own. The convention system guaranteed that these people are the ones who would be the face of the Republican Party for me. Utah's caucus/convention system placed the activists in the forefront of the nomination process. At neighborhood caucuses, the voters (i.e., the more committed partisans) gathered in school classrooms and individual homes to elect delegates to the county and state conventions. Those elected tended to be the party activists. In most cases, they held strong commitments to the party or would not have been elected to represent the precinct's partisans in the first place.

This was an eye-opening opportunity for me to become integrally involved with the party's local activists, although it was only for a short period of time since the campaign lasted only about a month—the period between filing and the county convention. I will discuss the campaign later, but I can say in this chapter that the experience left me disenchanted with partisan politics.

For several years, I pondered what to do. The Republican Party was too far to the right. I had identified myself as a moderate who could see more than one point of view and felt that compromise was not a dirty word. Yet, I still viewed the Democratic Party as a lost cause.

At that point, I realized I had three options. One was to go back to the Republicans and become involved to moderate the Republican Party. The size of the party made penetration of that sort unlikely. As just mentioned, the Republican Party in my area was dominated by activists who were far to the right. Additionally, they had already identified me as a hostile force in their ability to keep the party pure.

The second option was to join with the Democrats in order to moderate that party. The Democratic Party in my county, given its miniscule size, was highly porous. I realized it would not take many people to turn the party in a different direction. Plus, the Republican Party saw no need to change, while the Democrats might be more open to change since they were losing.

The third option was to do nothing. Already, I was involved with city issues that were nonpartisan. I could have continued to focus on those issues. However, that option forced me to remain at the municipal level rather than the county or state level, since that was the only one that was nonpartisan.

THE COUNTY DEMOCRATIC PARTY

After much deliberation, I decided to take the second option and give the Democrats another try. In 2004, I attended the Democratic caucus. Since the Democratic Party in the county was so small, only one caucus was held. About one hundred people were there in the Provo City Council chambers. After the meeting, I met Vaughn Cook, the new county party chair, and volunteered to help. I was impressed that he was more moderate in tone and anxious for help. Moreover, the Democratic gubernatorial candidate that year was the son of a former Utah governor. He also conveyed an image as a more moderate Democrat. I decided once again to become involved.

I organized a voter ID program for the county party, secured a location for phone banking, and recruited students, professors, and other community members to make phone calls to survey voter preferences and then, later, to get those who were supporters out to vote. The gubernatorial candidate did better than most Democrats had in the recent past but still lost by a large margin.

For the next election cycle, Vaughn Cook urged me to run for Congress. BYU did not allow people to run for that kind of office, even if it was not a viable campaign, without taking an unpaid professional leave. I could not afford that kind of leave without a significant financial investment from others. I thought that such investment would be unlikely for a Democrat in Utah.

Instead, I volunteered to head the candidate recruitment committee. With several others, I helped the party identify potential candidates and lobby them to run. We concentrated on people who could relate to local voters more so than the usual more left-leaning Democrats the state party recruited to run as token candidates. None of our candidates won or even came close.

It was clear to me some things needed to be changed if the party was to do better. A major problem was that the candidates lacked the resources to succeed. The state party gave them little help. And sometimes that help was counter-productive because the campaign guidance they were given assumed they were running in Democratic-majority districts and counties. There was little interaction among the candidates that would have provided moral support. But a major problem was branding. The local candidates were branded as national Democrats rather than the generally more moderate candidates they were. The local party needed to establish its own separate brand, as Democrats had done in other more conservative states in the region, such as Montana, Arizona, and Wyoming.

After the 2006 election, Vaughn Cook told me he wanted to step down as party chair and urged me to succeed him. I debated for some months whether to become more involved. I knew I could easily go back to doing occasional work for the party and continue to watch it languish. Or I could give up on it completely. That seemed like the logical choice given how much work it would take to move the needle in Utah politics. And I also was well aware of what I would be getting myself into if I became the party chair. As a maintainer of the status quo, this position would not require much time and energy. But I had no intention of maintaining the status quo. I wanted to move that needle. That would take time that would equate to nearly a part-time job. Plus, there would be no pay.

Yet, I concluded I had an obligation to do more. I felt I had some expertise in this area. I had run before. I had been involved in campaigns. My own studies had familiarized me with the literature on parties, campaigns, and elections.

However, I made a determination that this new commitment would not impact my research. I did not want my involvement to affect my ability to do my full-time job, including writing, research, and publication. At the time, I was working on an edited volume that would come out the next year, as well as on a single author book that would be published in 2009. Since I was a full professor, I did not have to face reviews anymore. But I felt a duty not to let my work slide. Fortunately, it did not.

My family situation also made this time commitment possible. My youngest child was seventeen and heavily involved in high school activities. The demand for my time from my children was minimal at that time.

I decided to run for county party chair. Additionally, I asked others if they would run as well for the other positions—vice chair, secretary, and treasurer. But the old guard of the Democratic Party was not going to give up without a fight. The leading liberal within the party decided she would run for chair as well. And she recruited others who had dominated the party for years to run as well. There would now be two competing slates representing two directions for the party. One was the current direction, which was disconnection with the majority of voters (who were more center-right) and continual abysmal electoral performance. The other was a shift to the ideological center that would potentially win over unaffiliated and moderate Republican voters.[1]

Turnout for the county convention was larger than typical, as a real race was occurring for party office for the first time in a long while. Our team mobilized the vote and was able to prevail with two-thirds of the vote for me and near that number for the others on our slate. This was potentially a new day for the Democratic Party in the county.[2]

Rebranding

Now, the hard work began. We had an uphill battle to change the brand, recruit candidates, provide them with training and other support, raise money, and boost morale. The very fact that I was the new chair helped change the brand. BYU and Mormons were known as Republicans. The fact that a BYU professor was chair of the Democratic Party in the county, and not of the Republican, was a news story.

That helped, but we wanted to go further. One way was to create our own platform separate from the state and national platforms. There had been a county party platform in the past, but it was not as distinctive as it needed to be. We used it to reassure Utah County voters that we shared their views on issues such as abortion and the Second Amendment. But we also used it to distinguish ourselves from the Republicans on a critical issue for Utah County voters—the education of their children.

When news media picked up on the distinctions between us and the state and national platforms, we were pleased.[3] That coverage informed voters that we were not the same Democrats they had repeatedly voted against in the past. And, therefore, they should give us a second look.

We knew what Utah voters wanted because of polls done by various organizations, particularly the local newspapers. But we did not know what Utah County voters wanted. So, we began to hold focus groups and conduct public opinion surveys of Utah voters. That information helped us understand what was important to voters and how best to reach out to them.

From our research, we learned that voters would support Democratic candidates, but only if they felt comfortable with them. Religious affiliation was a powerful component in the assessment of candidates. They said they could support Democratic candidates if they were undeniably associated with the Church of Jesus Christ of Latter-day Saints. In other words, if they were local leaders in the church, voters would feel confident the candidates were people who shared their values.

This finding was not surprising. What did surprise us was how readily voters were providing a solution to our problem. The candidate needed to share their values and to openly display that.

Yet, the culture was not quite as overt as that sounds. Voters did not want a candidate to campaign primarily on their religious affiliation. That offended the sensibilities of the voters. That meant candidates had to send subtle messages to the voters—code words that communicated shared values but allowed the candidate to assert that they were not overtly using religion. For example, candidates could say they were "active in their church and community." That had particular meaning for Latter-day Saints, who made up the vast majority of voters in Utah County, because "active" is a term used to denote a faithful member, similar to the way "devout" would be used for another religious denomination. Or they might say they had served a mission for their church. The name of the church would be omitted. But the signal was sent that the candidate was an "active" member.

Republicans had been using the code words for many years. Democrats had been reluctant to do so. Partly this was because many Democrats were not "active" LDS Church members or they were not members at all. However, even for those who were, there had been a reluctance to hint, even slightly, any religious affiliation for fear of breaching the wall between church and state.

Our job was to convince our candidates who were active Latter-day Saints, and nearly all were, that they could discuss their religion. In fact, it was an explanation to the voters of who they were. We even had a group of our candidates meet with a top church leader at the church's headquarters in Salt Lake City who conveyed the same message—if church involvement has been a major part of your life, share that with the voters, he advised. Be authentic.

Another helpful finding was the ordering of issue priorities. As I said earlier, we found that public education was the number one issue for these voters. Utah County voters had larger-sized families and the education of their children was paramount in their minds. We also learned about other issue priorities. One was concern about rapid growth. The population of the county was growing precipitously. Utah County's population had increased by 40 percent between 1990 and 2000, and it would increase by another 40 percent by 2010.[4] Voters were concerned about preservation of their neighborhoods and their quality of life. At the same time, they wanted transportation corridors that would take them from one place to another readily. In addition, many were worried about crime in their communities.

These results were extraordinarily helpful. As we shared them with candidates, we discussed ways they could address these issues in candidate announcements, literature, and other messaging. The polls and focus groups also helped prevent hobbyhorse issues that candidates liked but voters were not interested in. One candidate, who was an ideal candidate because of his prior involvement in the community and his former high-ranking church position, was obsessed with environmental issues. However, the poll showed that the voters in the county ranked the environment as a low priority. He got the message and adjusted accordingly.

Another finding from our research was the highly negative perceptions of Democrats. Voters in our focus groups viewed Democrats as aliens who did not share local values and concerns. Amazingly, some of our focus group participants said they did not even know Democrats. Of course, they did. But the Democrats they knew were quiet about it because they were fearful of social approbation and ostracism if they publicly identified themselves.

This finding prompted us to initiate a public relations campaign to inform voters that Democrats were not aliens. In fact, they were their neighbors. We called it the "I am your neighbor" campaign. We ran ads in the local newspaper featuring local Democrats and making the point that they were just ordinary neighbors. The ads included a photograph of the person and their name as well as a little biography about them that showed their "fit" within the local community—mother of three children, Sunday School teacher, active in the PTA, and so on.

The ads were noticed by locals, as the people in the ads related that people came up to them and told them they had seen their photo in the paper. Obviously, most readers would not have known the individual personally, but they would get the message that there were Democrats and they were not alien people. Interestingly, three years later, the Church of Jesus Christ of Latter-day Saints launched a similar campaign called "I Am a Mormon" intended to show Mormons as ordinary people. The similarity and the timing made me wonder if our campaign hadn't inspired theirs.

We invested in the party's website to make it more attractive to young voters. In addition, we facilitated online donations, which was a novel move for a county party organization at the time. We also utilized YouTube as a place to release video messages, another unusual move at the time for a county party.[5]

Another tactic was a billboard campaign. We bought billboard space throughout the county with messages we hoped would be memorable. One, for example, addressed the tendency to vote straight Republican. At the time, Utah was one of the few states that allowed voters to cast a straight ticket without voting for individual candidates. In fact, the straight party button was the first thing voters saw when they entered the voting booth. Our billboards sought to make straight-ticket voters feel guilty about simply voting a straight ticket and leaving rather than going down the ballot to look at the names of the candidates. We hoped that if they did that, they would see the names of our candidates and vote for them. One billboard read "Friends Don't Let Friends Vote Straight Party." Another drew on Rene Descartes's famous line "I think therefore I am" with a twist: "I Think, Therefore I Will Vote the Person, not the Party."

We also sponsored events that reinforced our brand message as distinct from national Democrats. We sponsored an event on families that underscored the message that Republicans were not the only ones concerned about the welfare of families. We used the opportunity to talk about how policy—including education, health, social services, and other issues—impacts families.

In another move, we hosted a fundraising dinner where we honored the first female governor of Utah, who was a Republican.[6] Olene Walker had served as lieutenant governor for eleven years and then, when the governor resigned to take a position as EPA director, Walker succeeded him. She immediately solidified a reputation as a moderate, and the Republican convention delegates failed to nominate her for a full term. At that time, Walker had a 70 percent approval rating among Utahns.

We praised Walker for her bipartisanship and expressed our county party's willingness to do so, but from the other side of the aisle. The idea that Democrats would honor a Republican was novel, but it was the very message we wanted to convey to moderate Republican voters: We were not their typical political party constantly attacking those on the other side of the aisle.

Not surprisingly, our new branding angered the left-wing of the Democratic Party, both in our county and in Salt Lake. They called us "Republican-lite" and urged the state party chair to rein us in. Certainly, there would be no financial support from the state party, although we didn't expect any. They did send two college students to the county to advise our candidates on how to run. But they were urging candidates to run against our new brand. We asked them to support our approach or work with other candidates elsewhere. They left.

However, we felt the Utah Democratic Party engaged in self-defeating behavior that damaged us as well, particularly our attempts to rebrand the county party to attract moderate Republican voters. For example, in August 2008, the Utah Democratic Party began to issue statements attacking Mitt Romney. Romney had run for the GOP presidential nomination but had been beaten by John McCain and no longer was a candidate. He was under consideration for the vice presidential nomination, but McCain had not selected him (and ultimately would not).

The attack on Romney was encouraged by the Democratic National Committee and the Utah party had cooperated. But I thought it was gratuitous. And stupid. Romney had won 90 percent of the vote in the Utah GOP presidential primary earlier that year. He was widely popular in the state. Even many Latter-day Saint Democrats liked him. He was viewed as a moderate Republican who had passed a health care plan while governor of Massachusetts that became the model for Barack Obama's plan.

So, the county party put out a press release calling out the state party for attacking Romney.[7] We pointed out that it was unnecessary because he was not a candidate and that Romney was popular with many Utahns, particularly because he had reached nearly the pinnacle of American politics as a Latter-day Saint. Many Utahns who were Latter-day Saints were proud of that accomplishment, we noted. As well, we said that we liked some of what Romney had done in Massachusetts. The state party did not comment on our press release. But, privately, they were stunned. I hoped they got the message that we were not going to let them undo our rebranding effort by their slavish adherence to what the national party wanted. We also hoped voters got the message that we did not fit their image of the Democratic Party.

Our goal was to upset the Republicans as well! That's why we not only defended Mitt Romney but used Romney against the Republicans. While in Massachusetts, Romney had criticized Utah's one-party dominance. He had said: "I lived in a place that had a one-party state that was primarily Republican. I thought, 'Well, won't that be nice.' The answer is, 'No.'" We thought Republican voters should know that, particularly since the Utah Republican Party had distributed a mailer saying that Romney was endorsing the Republican ticket. We launched a robocall campaign using audio of Romney's statement and then we sent that message to sixty thousand households in the county.[8] Not surprisingly, the Republicans were livid and attacked us for being unethical and using Romney's statement without his permission. Clearly, they did not appreciate the fact that they had competition. Given how Romney became persona non grata to Utah Republicans after his votes as a US senator to impeach Donald Trump, we may have been somewhat prescient.[9]

Although we did not receive financial support from the state party, we did acquire significant local help. The invigoration of the Democratic Party in the county caught the attention of donors who sought a more moderate alternative to the Republican Party. The party itself raised nearly $200,000 over two election cycles. Additionally, the candidates were able to tap people in their community who had never donated to a Democrat before but were willing to support their friend or family member. Within the first month after filing, four of our eleven legislative candidates had out-raised their opponents.[10] The Republicans eventually caught up, but Democratic candidates were remarkably successful. Collectively, the thirteen legislative and county candidates raised close to $250,000. One state legislative candidate alone raised nearly $50,000. It was an unheard-of number for Democratic candidates in Utah County who had usually spent a few hundred dollars for filing fees and a few fliers and brochures.

Properly financed campaigns gave us the opportunity to run effective campaigns. While Democratic candidates typically had purchased one hundred signs and struggled to place them, our candidates bought five hundred signs. They paid workers to distribute literature. They advertised in the local newspaper and bought billboards, which Republicans had done regularly.

The party's fundraising allowed us to rent a three-room headquarters in the middle of downtown Provo, the largest and most centrally located city in the county.[11] The location became a visual reminder that the Democrats were a presence in the county. It also boosted the morale of the party supporters. Democrats had not had a physical party headquarters for a long time. It helped them feel good about donating money, giving time and energy, and talking to their friends and neighbors about candidates. We used the office for literature drop campaigns, leadership meetings, candidate training, and so on.

Candidate Recruitment

By the fall of the year preceding the general election, our leadership team began recruiting candidates. Not only did we want to place a candidate in every legislative district and county position (a goal we fell a little short of with a couple of vacancies), but we wanted candidates who people would know and feel comfortable voting for. My mantra was that we needed to recruit candidates who "belonged in government." These would be people with prior credentials that would attract voters.

Our team created lists of individuals who we might approach. We also asked local precinct chairs for lists. Unfortunately, many of them suggested the same people who had run before or people who were willing to place their names on a ballot for the cause but wouldn't really run a campaign. As willing as they were, these were not the people who we wanted to run again.

And then there were those who wanted to run for high office but had no credentials. A part of my job as a candidate recruiter was to discourage people who imagined they would be an effective candidate for the US Senate or Congress even though they had no name recognition, political experience, financial support, or knowledge of what was involved either in a campaign or in actual public service. Rather than discourage them from political involvement, I attempted to redirect them toward lesser offices or a role helping a candidate that would prepare them for a future run. Sometimes that worked. At other times, they were discouraged that they were not reinforced by me in their self-delusion and disappeared.

The process of identifying candidates involved brainstorming with people who were prominent in the community. It was snowballing. We would approach a few people to ask for names and then we would go to those people and ask for more names. We were not just looking for people who were registered Democrats. We knew that many people, even prominent ones, shared our centrist approach as opposed to Republican extremism. However, they had not registered as Democrats for the reasons stated above. In fact, some of our candidates were long-term Republicans. As was common in Utah County, many voters had registered as Republicans to vote in the Republican primary election, which was tantamount to the general election. Others had not considered registering as Democrats because it was highly socially unpopular to do so. But they also felt uncomfortable siding with a party that did not share their views on key social issues. Yet, they were more moderate on other issues, such as education financing and social welfare spending.

This approach piqued the interest of the news media. The fact that some long-time Republicans were switching to the Democrats was newsworthy.[12] But it led to criticism by the old guard of the local Democratic Party as well as activists in the state party. They wanted a candidate to have a long record of visible loyalty to the Democratic Party. Even more importantly, they wanted candidates who came from the left wing of the party.

Many were particularly upset at our approach of recruiting candidates who were active members of the Church of Jesus Christ of Latter-day Saints. Unfortunately, a strong element of the Democratic Party in Utah, and in Utah County, was hostile to Mormons. They were not much interested in appealing to Mormons (which they considered a lost cause), but their objective was to retain a social club that opposed the dominant religion. It was difficult to convince them that the Democratic Party had no future in Utah if it was known as the anti-Mormon party. The same would be true for an anti-Catholic party in Massachusetts or Rhode Island or an anti–Southern Baptist party in Mississippi.

After identifying potential candidates, we then formed a strategy to approach them. This include answering the following questions: What office should we encourage them to run for—Congress, state legislature, or county commissioner? What resources (money, volunteers, advertising) did we want to devote to their race and promise would be delivered to them? Who should make the pitch to them?

The common approach among Democratic Party leaders in the past had been a phone call to the individual asking if they would run. Again, that often happened during the filing period when Democrats were desperate to have a name on a ballot. I felt that method only reinforced failure. We needed to signal that we were serious about their candidacy and would support them if they decided to run.

Our approach was to have a friend contact them and ask them for a meeting with us. We did not disclose the reason. Then, I attended the meeting, along with another candidate who already was running, or a person they were close to, or a Democratic leader (such as a current or former state legislator). Then, we usually used a uniquely tailored slide presentation to explain what we wanted them to do, how they could do it, and what we would do for them. We emphasized the necessity of their candidacy to our overall strategy of bringing balance back to our county's politics. We also brought them a packet of information our research committee had prepared about the district and, if applicable, the incumbent they would be running against.

All of this was designed to convey the importance in our minds of what they were doing and the value of their respective candidacy to us. This was not an act of desperation on our part. It was a well-thought-out strategy that they could play a critical role in.

The first person we recruited was a former school superintendent. He was a long-time resident of the community, had served as a principal, and headed the school district for nine years before retiring and becoming a BYU professor. He was an ideal candidate.

A moderate Democratic state senator agreed to accompany me to make the pitch. She was able to explain what it was like to be a representative. Interestingly, his greatest concern was whether his Republican opponent would make an issue out of the fact that he had a son who was gay. His son did not hide his sexual orientation, but he had not broadcast it either. In 2007 in Utah, that was a valid question. We reassured him that would not happen and that, if it did, the effort would backfire. As it turned out, no mention was made of his son during the course of the campaign.

We started snowballing, using one candidate to help us recruit another.

The presence of someone who already had committed to run was a powerful incentive to the next candidate. They realized they would not be alone and that someone they respected would be out there in the public eye as well. For example, through the former school superintendent, we recruited a former university president who was well known among BYU faculty and students since he had once served as dean of the business school at BYU.[13]

The wife of the current dean, who was a prominent attorney in the county, also decided to run. Her candidacy incurred the wrath of the Republican leadership. When her husband became a candidate for the presidency of the local state university the next year, Republican state legislators contacted him and informed him that if he wanted to continue as a candidate for that job, he needed to appear before the Republican leadership and apologize for his wife running as a Democrat. He refused to do so and withdrew his candidacy.[14]

We were able to recruit some candidates who had run before. They included two former mayors, a former city council member, and a current school board member. This array of talent was impressive, and we touted their credentials to the press, the public, and prospective candidates. Other candidates had not served in elective office but had their own qualifications to be considered as people who "belong in government." They included the school superintendent and former university president mentioned above, a former city council member, and two former regional PTA presidents.

Yet, most of our candidates were novices at campaigning. None had run in a partisan race. One of the problems of past campaigns had been the tendency to leave candidates on their own when they did not know what they were doing. Or, perhaps worse, they were given bad advice about how to campaign outside traditional Democratic areas.

We initiated campaign training courses that ran for several months. In addition, we offered a course to their campaign managers that lasted several weeks. These candidate or campaign manager training sessions typically occurred early on a Saturday morning before candidates started their canvassing. The sessions involved topics such as fundraising, media relations, choosing a campaign manager, messaging, and so on. Some candidates took the training sessions seriously and attended most, if not all. Others did not. The one candidate who was a current school board member felt she knew enough about campaigning already. For the most part, however, these novice candidates who attended the training performed much better on election day than those who did not.

Candidates were urged to make splashy announcements of their candidacies to attract media attention. In the past, Democrats had filed at the last minute and only after intense lobbying from the party. There was little publicity surrounding their campaigns. They either did not know how to get press attention or didn't really want to. Most of our candidates held campaign launches and invited the press and supporters to attend. The former school superintendent held his announcement in a school classroom. The result was press coverage of these new candidates who did not fit the "alien" profile.

Party Organization

Candidate recruitment was only one part of the equation. We also needed to build an organization. We reached out to individuals to accept a draft to become a precinct chair or a legislative district chair in areas where we didn't have them, even on paper. We urged people to come to our conventions and divided into legislative districts to elect district and precinct officers in those districts. Past conventions had revolved around issue or demographic caucuses—women's caucus, labor caucus, education caucus, and the like. We felt it was more important to organize as legislative districts than caucuses, since that organization would offer candidates a support group. We held training sessions for people in these positions to help them do their jobs, such as supporting candidates, recruiting activists, putting up signs, and distributing literature.

Party organization at the local level is more theoretical than real. They are paper organizations that may come alive, if they do at all, only in the last few weeks of a campaign. Understandably, that is when most people become engaged in politics.

As a consequence, the organizations we hoped to build on behalf of candidates did not materialize in most cases. One reason was the general disengagement of Democrats. They had lost for so many years that failure seemed the likely outcome no matter what they did. Another problem was that the left wing of the party was unenthusiastic about our candidates because they perceived them as not liberal enough—not true Democrats in the purist sense.

Fortunately, many of the candidates had their own personal organizations they could rely on. These were family, friends, and neighbors who were willing to work on behalf of the candidate in performing the kinds of tasks we had hoped local party members would do. The combination of local Democrats who were willing to help and the personal networks offered varying levels of support to candidates.

Parties, like so much of electoral politics, have become professionalized. We became professionalized as well. Using the funds we raised, we hired a part-time executive director and a part-time executive assistant for one election cycle. We also hired phone bank workers who spent weeks in our headquarters identifying voters and then conducting GOTV drives. Fortunately, we had a supply of college students at the two local colleges who were looking for part-time employment.

RUNNING FOR STATE PARTY CHAIR

We did move the needle in Utah County politics—for a short time and in some ways. We gained significant media attention for our candidates and successfully sent the message to many voters that the brand was different. These were not the former Democratic candidates they were accustomed to. There was a lot of buzz in our community about these Utah County Democratic candidates. We were hearing that Republicans were wondering if we might cut into their base of support.

We did. None of our candidates beat their Republican opponents during the two cycles we ran in. But we made inroads. One candidate received 45 percent of the vote—the first time a Democrat had crossed that threshold since the early 1990s. Four of our candidates broke the 40 percent barrier. Three others were in the high 30s. Although still a long way from that elusive 50 percent plus one mark, clearly there were many voters who were casting a vote for a Democrat—probably for the first time in their lives. Our candidates far exceeded the vote totals of Democratic candidates at national and statewide levels. For example, in one district, our legislative candidate received 41 percent of the vote while Barack Obama received 16 percent. Clearly, voters were distinguishing between national and local Democrats, and many were willing to cross over from a Republican presidential and congressional candidate to a Democratic state legislative candidate.

However, we knew it was not possible to effect complete change in four years. The party label was still toxic. For example, one of our legislative candidates won 38 percent of the vote as a Democrat but the next year won 70 percent of the vote in a nonpartisan city council race. The party label was a heavy albatross around the necks of our candidates.

By 2011, I felt I had done all I could to "move the needle" and stepped down as chair. I also felt I needed to concentrate again on my scholarship and teaching. My view had been that service of this kind should be temporary and that responsibility should rotate across individuals. That is particularly true of those of us who do this on a part-time, voluntary basis. Being the chair of a county political party, particularly when the objective is not simply to occupy a position but to change people's minds, is exhausting. It took me some months to recover from that activity.

However, I quickly saw my efforts overturned, particularly at the state party level. A new state party chair was elected in 2011, just as I was leaving the county party post. He was determined to push the party to the left ideologically. He became a state senator who represented the most liberal district in the state and was largely ineffective in the senate due to his extreme ideological approach and bombastic style.

But in 2014, he resigned as chair. There would be an election at the party convention that year for his successor. I decided to run. My intent was not to win. I was not so naive as to think I could win. Even though I had reinvigorated the Democratic Party in Utah County, ran more candidates who attracted moderate voters, raised funds for them, began to shift the voters toward a more favorable image for the party, and saw candidates do much better than they had for years, I had no illusions that that would win the support of the majority of delegates who were more to the left than I was.

As I was thinking about this run, the former mayor of Salt Lake County was urged to run and agreed to do so. I knew him because I had advised him during his unsuccessful run for governor four years earlier. He was one of the most civil and gentle people I had met. And, clearly, he would win the race.

My objective was to raise the issue that had doomed Democrats in the state for the past half century—the relationship with voters who were members of the Church of Jesus Christ of Latter-day Saints. I would use the campaign as a platform to urge Democrats to find common cause with Latter-day Saints. My points were, first, that Democrats needed to adopt an ecumenical approach to social issues. In other words, they should not expect party activists or supporters to pass a litmus test on issues such as abortion or gay marriage. Rather, they should tout diversity within their ranks so that active LDS voters who felt differently about these issues than many Democrats would still feel comfortable within the Utah Democratic Party.

I then trumpeted my own credentials as someone who had worked to bring over many moderate voters to cast a ballot for a Democrat in Utah County. If the party wanted to initiate outreach to LDS voters, I was the best choice to do so. I had been doing that for four years in Utah County.

Yet, I knew that two-part message was anathema to many Democrats. They did not want to "dilute" the message to convert these voters. In fact, they were satisfied not having LDS voters in their coalition. That shift would make it more difficult for anti-Mormons to use the Democratic Party as their haven against the dominant religion in the state. That very religious-political cleavage is what I was attempting to bridge. I knew I could not do it in four years. I knew it could not be done in one party chair election. But I hoped to confront Democrats with the issue and publicize the fact that this situation was a primary contributor to Democratic failure and Republican success.

Fortunately, the campaign was short. I spent a month calling delegates, attending delegate meetings, and speaking at county conventions, reiterating that message. Some people were receptive to the message. Others did not even want to talk to me. I received one-third of the vote and graciously congratulated my opponent and offered to help him. He verbally accepted the offer but did not ask for help. Nor did he change the Democratic Party in any substantive way during his three-year tenure.

After that election, I worked with others to form a centrist Democratic PAC. Our goal was to recruit candidates who were more centrist and to apply pressure within the party. Unfortunately, the leftward shift of the party—both nationally and on the state level—made our efforts increasingly impractical. We supported two candidates in 2016—one for the US Senate and one for governor. The first candidate was a moderate Democrat who was a successful small businessman with strong ties to the LDS Church and deep Utah roots. His opponent was a grocery clerk who appealed to the left wing of the party. She won the low turnout primary with 60 percent, largely because she was the first major party nominee in a statewide race who was transgender. That fall, she won only a quarter of the vote.

The other candidate was another moderate Democratic small businessman with multigenerational roots in Utah. He won 20 percent of the vote at the state convention and did not even make it into the primary. The winner was relatively new to the state, was not LDS, and had been recruited by the left wing of the party. He also won only slightly more than a quarter of the general election vote.

It was a disheartening outcome and led several Democrats in our group to wonder when the party would alter its self-destructive tendencies in nominating candidates who satisfied party litmus tests but were repellant to Utah voters. To our dismay, state politics had become as polarized as national politics. The two major political parties were moving further away from each other and offering no comfort to more moderate voters who were disappointed by the unpalatable choice between left and right.

LESSONS LEARNED

The task of heading a political party was stressful. The multiple tasks of candidate recruitment, fundraising, party organization, messaging, and so on are demanding for any party chair. Managing the ideological factions within a political party organization requires diplomatic skills and a willingness to compromise to keep groups of members happy and allied with the party. For major party chairs, moderate and extremist factions vie for dominance.

But the stress is ratcheted up when the party is attempting to rebuild. I was constantly thinking about failure. Would we do no better than those in the past? Would candidates actually step up and run? Simultaneously, could we discourage those candidates who would damage our brand? Would people contribute money to a party that had a "loser" reputation, as was the case for the Democrats?

I learned a lot about branding or rebranding—transforming a negative image into a positive one. The Democratic Party was anathema to many voters in our county. Even those LDS Church members who did not hold such extreme views and could admit some good in the Democratic Party were wary of becoming Democrats—both on religious and on social grounds—or being publicly identified with the Democrats via yard signs, endorsements, donations, or even private conversations. For example, a neighbor of mine who placed a yard sign for one of our candidates was queried by his next-door neighbor who wondered if he realized the candidate he was promoting on his sign was a Democrat. His neighbor's question made him sheepish about the sign and he removed it. Candidates were constantly reporting such reluctance to buck the social/religious expectations of the area.

Becoming a Republican had been part of the socialization process so many members of the Church of Jesus Christ of Latter-day Saints had typically experienced. Several generations of young people had grown up since the 1970s with the belief that the Republican Party and the LDS Church were one in purpose. The church had primed the pump of political party affiliation by emphasizing and reemphasizing two key issues during that period: abortion and gay rights. In turn, it was no coincidence that Republican Party leaders in Utah were capitalizing on those issues to cement the linkage between their party and church members. We were working against that well-ingrained belief that Democrats were hostile to LDS views on these two key social issues. Moreover, we were fighting Democrats who were working hard to reinforce the Democrats' adherence to litmus tests on those two issues.

We were caught in the middle attempting to show that we were anomalies in the Democratic Party, carving out our own niche that might re-create electoral competition in our county. We knew that such electoral competition was critical to good governance. However, it would never happen with this wholesale rejection of one of the two major party alternatives by so many in the electorate. We hoped revising the brand for our particular area would stimulate electoral competition. It did. But the forces we were fighting against were too ingrained to be challenged successfully in a matter of a couple of elections. It was enormously difficult to convince voters to abandon their preconceptions, particularly when the message they were getting from the national and state party only reinforced those preconceptions. In this case, it was the preconception toward a party they had grown up believing could not be supported, regardless of who the candidates were.

The practical experience of governing a party, particularly party organizations starting in the hole in terms of image, was valuable for me in my teaching. Certainly, I could relate anecdotes that offered real-world perspectives to students. Plus, I had made contacts with real-world politicians that were helpful in hosting campus guests for lectures or panel discussions, scheduling guest speakers in class, arranging internships, and even helping students get employment post-graduation. But as I taught courses on media, political parties, and campaigns and elections, those experiences working with a political party organization helped me reinforce or challenge existing political science theories. It also communicated a powerful lesson to students—political parties matter, and as long as they do matter in a democratic political system, one should get involved with them.

6. Founding a New Minor Party

Given my frustrations with both major political parties, as early as 2011, I had explored the possibility of forming a third political party in Utah. I organized meetings attended by Democrats and some Republicans. Democrats were more interested because they were seeking an alternative to a Democratic Party in the state that was caught up in religious division. Moreover, Democrats in Utah had acquired a common flaw of perpetually losing major party organizations, that is, no longer willing to work to win.

But Republicans were not so anxious to abandon their party. The cost of doing so was greater, since Republicans punished fellow Republicans who even flirted with Democrats. They were not above essentially "excommunicating" Republicans who endorsed Democrats or who did not support the Republican Party platform. In that sense, Republicans were like Democrats. The difference was that, because Republicans controlled most of Utah's government—both at the state and the local levels—Republican retribution likely meant the end of a political career.

Plus, the Utah Republican Party was successful, unlike the Democrats. They were winning elections. Republicans could concentrate on their nomination process and win general elections almost by default. Their concern was centered on reshaping their own party's nominations. Prominent and wealthy Republicans sought to open up the caucus/convention system to allow more competition within the primaries. They were not interested in what happened in the general election, since they knew they would easily win in the vast majority of the local contests and in all statewide races.

My effort failed because I stopped trying. I knew it would not be successful unless Republicans were willing to join. Without them, there would be little support from moderate Republican activists and supporters. A new party would seem like nothing more than a rump of the Utah Democratic Party. I pulled back and focused instead on the new political action committee.

A WINDOW OF OPPORTUNITY

Then Donald Trump happened. When he entered the Republican presidential nomination contest in 2015, Republicans were lamenting the fact that Trump would turn the primaries into a circus. He would demean the process by his presence, and his rhetoric would hurt the party. But the idea that Trump actually would win the nomination was roundly dismissed.

When Trump won the GOP nomination, some Republicans began to shed their party membership. Utah Republicans who disliked Trump were encouraged by Mitt Romney's harsh repudiation of Trump in a speech at the University of Utah on March 3, 2016. Romney called Trump "a phony, a fraud" and said that Trump was "playing the American public for suckers." He also accused him of lacking "the temperament to be president."[1] As the most popular Mormon politician at the time, Romney's attack on Trump further complicated Utah voters' embrace of Trump.

A campaign by conservatives to find an independent candidate was launched in the spring but did not succeed until August, when former CIA officer Evan McMullin agreed to carry the group's banner. The division within the Republican Party placed Utah Republicans in a bind. While Utah voters had become staunchly Republican over the previous forty years or so, they now faced a quandary. Should they continue to vote for the Republican nominee whose personal life clashed sharply with the expectations of Utah voters and whose statements about minorities even prompted leaders of the Church of Jesus Christ of Latter-day Saints to repudiate Trump's immigration views (although not by name), or should they abandon the Republican Party and vote for McMullin, who was essentially a Republican but was not the Republican nominee?

At one point, McMullin led both Trump and Democratic nominee Hillary Clinton in Utah polls.[2] As is typical of voters toying with the idea of voting for a third-party or independent candidate, most came back to the Republican Party. Nevertheless, McMullin's 21 percent vote total, coupled with the Libertarian candidate's 4 percent, was a major repudiation of the nominees of both of the two major parties by Utah voters.

Now, the political environment had changed. Republicans who were not interested in 2011 were ready to leave their party. While some had done so by changing their party registration, others had simply rejected the Republican presidential nominee. Even when they had gone on to vote Republican at lower levels, the trust in the Republican Party had been broken by the nomination of Donald Trump.

In the fall of 2016, I met with a former Republican state legislator and two former Democratic candidates to discuss various options. One was to form a political action committee to attempt to moderate the Republican and Democratic nomination processes through support of centrist candidates. I felt that had already been tried. The polarizing forces within both parties had taken control. More moderate candidates would either defect to the poles to win their respective party nominations or do so once they had joined their party's legislative caucus to fend off more extremist candidates in their reelection bid. In sum, the extremist camps had taken over the two major parties so completely that they held the strongest sway in the party nomination processes. The fact that most candidates were selected at the conventions and were decided by a few hundred or a few thousand people made it simpler for the extremes to dominate the process. The primary route that had been added by legislation had opened up the nomination processes somewhat but not as much as had been expected.

Another idea was to use the initiative process to reform the electoral process. This included ending the straight party option on the ballot (which was removed by the legislature four years later), opening up the primaries beyond party registrants, limiting campaign finance, etc. The barrier for this reform was money. The legislature had made the initiative process complex, time-consuming, and expensive. In fact, Utah was known as one of the most initiative-unfriendly states in the nation with its signature requirements. Typically, initiatives in this less populated state still required the outlay of millions of dollars to pay signature gatherers and then wage a large-scale political campaign to educate voters and fight opponents. That idea was not rejected. In fact, it was viewed as a possible simultaneous activity with the third idea, which was the formation of a new political party.

Even with the McMullin vote that year, I was still unclear whether there would be voter interest in the formation of a third party, particularly one that was moderate. I designed a survey that was conducted in early November 2016 to gauge support. Just over six hundred Utah voters were polled. We asked if the respondents were happy with the existing two parties or would like to see another party. Fifty-one percent said they wanted another option, while only one-third responded they were satisfied with the two major parties. When we asked what kind of party those people would like to see, two-thirds said they wanted a moderate rather than a more conservative or more liberal party. Not surprisingly, the younger the respondent, the less satisfied they were with the two major parties and the more open they were to a third party.

These results, among others we found, suggested that there was generic support for a third moderate party. But perhaps even more heartening was the broad support among people under the age of forty-five. This finding suggested that the future pointed toward an upheaval of the two-party system.

We knew that diffuse support for a third party was not the same as specific support for a particular third-party candidate. There were many other factors at play in the determination of a voter as to whether to support a third-party candidate in a particular race. One was the attitude toward the incumbent (in most cases, the Republican). Another was knowledge of the party and of the candidate and a perception that the candidate was electorally viable.

Knowledge of the candidate and the party required money as well as organization. We knew that it was an uphill battle for moderates in politics. Moderates lack the passion of ideological extremists. Would moderate activists step forward to work tirelessly for a moderate candidate as the highly ideological activists do for their candidates? That was a question mark as we considered these survey results.

We concluded that we needed to gather more information before moving forward. We sponsored focus groups of unaffiliated and moderate Republican voters in suburban Salt Lake City. We considered this group to be the possible base for a new moderate party. A friend who had served as a focus group moderator volunteered to conduct the focus groups.

From these groups, we learned quite a bit about how voters perceived the two major parties—both nationally and in Utah. We explored more about how they might react to a third party and what they would like that third party to do on the political landscape. We even asked what qualities they thought would be most important in that third party, including what it should be named.

Our focus groups informed us that the survey finding was accurate. There was support for a moderate party. Voters were frustrated not only with their options but also with approaches of the two major parties. They were highly negative toward the Democratic Party, which did not surprise us. But the level of hostility toward the Republican Party did catch us off guard. They were particularly antagonistic toward the partisan bickering that characterized political discourse in the nation and in Utah. They wanted a political party that would bring these diverse elements together, a party that would unite us.

At the same time, we started to involve more people in our deliberations. We scheduled a series of "movers and shakers" meetings in several cities in and around Salt Lake City. Invitations largely were word-of-mouth rather than public. And they included former officeholders and candidates, interest group representatives, former campaign workers, and so on. The meetings included perhaps ten to twenty people gathered in a living room to hear the proposal of the formation of a new party and glean their reaction. The reaction varied. Some people signed on immediately. Others wished us well but did not want to join at the time. However, we were accomplishing our goal of gauging the reactions of potential activists.

From those meetings, we formed an executive committee who met via Zoom on a weekly basis to consider what to do next. In these meetings, we reviewed the findings from the surveys and the focus groups and the reactions from the "movers and shakers" meetings. We discussed whether to proceed with the formation of a new party. Understandably, there was still reluctance. We had a good sense of the difficulty of this task. It was not that forming a party was such a problem. But trying to make a difference in the political environment—that was a trickier proposition.

A POLITICAL EXPERIMENT

From the beginning, I viewed this as an experiment. I was familiar with the literature on third parties. By this point, I had taught courses on political parties for more than thirty years. The question was whether the conditions were ripe for change. Was the two-party loyalty waning sufficiently to justify a new party? Would there be enough people dissatisfied with the two major parties to consider a third-party candidate? Was there room in the middle for a new party?

One of the considerations was the political landscape in Utah, particularly. The emotional ties to the Republican Party had weakened due to Donald Trump. And, in 2016, many voters had taken that one step further by actually voting for someone other than Trump.

Moreover, Utah was not a competitive state. In actuality, it was not a two-party system. Rather, it was closer to a one-and-one-half or maybe even one-and-one-quarter system. Democrats were not competitive statewide or in three of the four congressional districts. One cause for failure in these districts was gerrymandering. However, gerrymandering could not account for the fact that Democrats were having a difficult time getting above one-third of the vote for statewide offices. In 2016, as mentioned earlier, in the two highest profile races—the US Senate and governor—the Democratic candidates did not crack 30 percent. Democrats held less than a quarter of the seats in the legislature, which was due partly to gerrymandering. But it also was due to the fact that the party rarely contested seats beyond its base in Salt Lake County. That meant running candidates who did not campaign or even leaving the Democratic column vacant in that race.

A third party, then, effectively could become the second party in the state, given the Democrats' abandonment of so much of the state's electoral contests. A new party could displace the Democrats outside of Salt Lake City as the competitor to the Republicans. That was an argument we were making in these "movers and shakers" meetings and that resonated with potential supporters.

I acknowledged that the experiment might not work. Viable candidates might not step forward. Third parties often attracted candidates from the fringe—seeking attention for themselves, pushing an unpopular issue, or following some other motivation unrelated to the success of the party. It could be that the candidates lack the necessary funding to communicate their message. Could we avoid that scenario? Perhaps activists would not step forward and work for candidates. The political environment might change and the dissatisfaction with the two major parties would dissipate. There were numerous factors that could determine whether this experiment would succeed. Another problem was time itself. Did we have the patience to build the party over the long run, or would interest wane if the party had not won elections in the first year or two?

We decided to move ahead with the registration of a new political party in Utah, which would be called the United Utah Party. That name came from focus group comments that the main function participants wanted a new party to perform was to unite people. We investigated how to register and decided first to form a political action committee that would allow us to raise money for signature gathering. Utah required two thousand signatures of voters who signed a petition saying they would join a new party. In April, we formed the political action committee and began to raise money for signature gatherers as well as to construct an organization for volunteer signature gathering.

Our expectation was that it would take a few months to gather the signatures and submit them to the state before the November deadline for application for a new party. But, in May, events intruded that altered our plans and accelerated our process of registration.

On May 19, the representative from the third congressional district, Jason Chaffetz, announced that he was resigning, effective June 30. He had just started his ninth term four months earlier, but the speculation was he had been offered a job as a commentator on Fox News and couldn't take it as long as he was in Congress. Another insider theory was that while Chaffetz had scored high visibility as an aggressive investigator of the Obama administration, he would play a decidedly smaller role as a member of Congress in a Trump presidency.

His resignation prompted the governor to call a special election. A special election for a congressional vacancy had not occurred in Utah since 1928. And the governor's actions in laying out the schedule for filling the vacancy incurred the wrath of the legislature, who felt they should have been consulted if not actually in control of the process.[3]

Our executive committee now debated how this special election affected us. One member of the group, Jim Bennett (the son of the late US senator Bob Bennett), urged us to contest the election and offered himself as a candidate. The problem was we were not yet officially registered as a political party. According to the governor's election schedule, the candidates needed to file by May 26 to compete. On May 19, we had not yet reached enough signatures.

We accelerated the process of gathering signatures by paying more for workers to finish the job. We planned to submit the signatures by May 25—the same day Jim Bennett would announce his candidacy. We hoped they would certify the signatures by May 26 and he would be able to run as the first candidate of the United Utah Party.

However, we needed to explain what the United Utah Party was before he announced his candidacy. We scheduled a news conference at a room in the Capitol building for May 22. With news cameras whirring and print reporters scribbling, the executive committee announced that we were forming this new political party in Utah called the United Utah Party. It would be a centrist party dedicated to reforming the political system and representing those who felt politically alienated by both of the major parties.[4]

The response depended on who was doing the responding. The press was fair but generally skeptical, as were political scientists quoted by the press. However, ordinary voters contacted us and thanked us for offering another alternative. A survey conducted by an online news organization shortly after our announcement found that 63 percent of voters said they would consider voting for a United Utah Party candidate in a future election.[5] We were heartened by that news.

On May 25, we submitted 2,700 signatures to the Utah Elections Office, making sure we had the sufficient number to exceed the threshold even if many were considered invalid. (And several hundred were.) That afternoon, Jim Bennett announced his candidacy, which elicited even more attention for this new party. At that time, we asked the elections office director if there would be a problem certifying our new party's signatures by the next afternoon—the deadline for candidates to file in the special election. He said his office could validate the signatures by that time and that he did not anticipate a problem with Jim Bennett being able to file as a UUP candidate. In retrospect, we wished we had gotten that statement in writing.

Something changed dramatically between our conversation that morning and later that afternoon, when I received a phone call telling me that we also needed to submit a constitution and bylaws for the new party. That was not in the requirements the elections office had posted on their own website for new political parties. But I scrambled and, within a few hours, emailed a constitution and bylaws. It was drawn largely from the existing documents for the Democrats and the Republicans. The reality is these would not necessarily be our governing documents, because we would adopt a constitution and bylaws at our first state convention in June and we would then submit those to the elections office per state ordinance. I assumed that those other parties' documents had passed muster once, so something like them would as well. I don't think they thought we could move that fast and instead would be flustered by the request. To me, this was a new hurdle intended to function as an excuse not to certify us quickly.

When we contacted the elections office the next morning, we were told it would be some time before the signatures could be certified, and therefore Jim Bennett could not file as a UUP candidate. Indeed, when he went to file that afternoon, he was rejected. His only option according to the elections director was to file as an unaffiliated candidate. Our candidate refused to do that at that time.[6]

The combination of the slow-walking of the signatures and the demand for a constitution and bylaws convinced me that some intervention had taken place between the time we had initially submitted the signatures and the time I was contacted about the additional documents. My speculation was that the governor or the lieutenant governor had directed the elections office not to allow Jim Bennett on the ballot. Since the elections office was a partisan unit controlled by partisan elected officials, they could use the process in a partisan manner. And, at first, there was not much we could do about it. In fact, ultimately, they would take the full thirty days they had by law to certify.[7]

Nor would the issue of certification be our last encounter with the Utah elections office. The next year, several people who had registered as United Utah Party members, including myself and one of our congressional candidates, found that their party registration forms had been altered. Some had been changed to unaffiliated while others had been made Republicans.[8] We complained to the state elections director, who claimed the problem was a mistake at the county level. It seemed odd to us that these "mistakes" in different counties would all happen at about the same time.

SUING TO GAIN BALLOT ACCESS

The preceding day, I was contacted by an attorney for one of the largest law firms in Utah who offered pro bono legal counsel for our new party. When the elections office declined to certify us in the time frame they had indicated and then refused Bennett's candidacy, I contacted the attorney again and we discussed the next legal step of a lawsuit against the state. My first response was to seek to avoid a lawsuit and then simply forego this election. Already, we were working toward the 2018 campaign. I worried that our first impression would be of a litigious political party.

However, Jim Bennett wanted to pursue the suit. And the attorney felt we could win if we sued. They would be bearing the costs, so we did not have much to lose. If we gained the image of a David against a Goliath, we might earn the sympathy of the public. So, we decided to go ahead and sue the state in federal court for delaying our certification and refusing to allow Jim Bennett to file as our candidate for the special election.[9]

The law firm hired an election law expert from out of state who prepared and argued the case for us. He contended that the state had plenty of time to certify the two thousand signatures in twenty-four hours. The candidates for the GOP primary had submitted signatures the following week and had been certified within twenty-four hours, even though each had to submit seven thousand signatures—more than three times the amount they had to certify for us. He claimed that the state had violated the civil rights of Jim Bennett by forcing him to file as an unaffiliated candidate.

The federal judge agreed with all the arguments of our attorney and ordered the state to place Bennett on the ballot.[10] We were elated by the outcome and that the state decided not to appeal. However, all of this had taken more than two months. By the time we had an official candidate, it was already August. We had lost two months to campaign for him.

Over the next two and a half months, Jim Bennett campaigned aggressively and the party sought to help him with fundraising and distribution of literature and signs. It was a big task for a very small party. We had only several hundred members at the time. The two major parties had hundreds of thousands!

The publicity regarding the Bennett campaign helped him qualify for the Utah Debate Commission debate to be held in October. He was the first non-major party candidate to qualify.[11] He was placed in the middle of the stage—between the Republican and the Democrat—which reinforced the verbal message. And he performed well.

However, the vote total was not what we expected. He received 9 percent of the vote. The combination of the lateness of his entry as well as the lack of organization contributed to the low vote total. But we also gained insights into the tendency of voters to return home rather than strike out to support a nonmajor party candidate. The chair of the state Republican Party confided to me a couple of weeks before the election that he thought Jim Bennett would win 18 percent of the vote. The exact figure suggested he had polling data that we did not have. Like Evan McMullin, our candidate was affected by this trend.

Moreover, the party was still new and people did not know who we were. We had formed only five months earlier. We had no history and many voters still were not sure about us, as confirmed by polls we conducted the next year.

We were pleased that Jim Bennett had polled well beyond what was typical for a third-party candidate in Utah elections. His vote total was more than the combined total of all the other third parties—Libertarian, Constitution, and Independent American.

The opposition from the state elections office, which was controlled by the governor and lieutenant governor, was, in a sense, flattering. If they had felt we were not in some way a threat, they would have gone forward with our party registration instead of taking the full legal thirty days to certify us. The Democrats also worried about what role we would play in their electoral fortunes. Some Democrats I knew questioned whether it was good to split the Democratic Party by creating essentially two Democratic parties. I found that some people I had worked with in the Democratic Party were not willing to even talk to me anymore.

ORGANIZING A NEW PARTY

We held our first convention in June of that year and selected officers. I was elected chair. The other officers all were former Democrats—two of them had run for office as Democrats previously. That imbalance worried me as we sought to reach out to moderate Republicans and unaffiliated voters. But Jim Bennett's high profile role as a candidate compensated for that imbalance. He had been heavily involved in Republican politics for most of his adult life. And his last name—shared with his three-term US senator father—solidified his Republican roots.

We also approved the constitution and bylaws. And we adopted a platform. Ours was intended to be a departure from the trend in party platforms. It was short. It fit on one page—single-spaced. It addressed what we considered the most important issues rather than a laundry list of issues pressed by various groups. We took evenhanded approaches to issues such as immigration, tax reform, abortion, gun control, and so on. We did identify ourselves as strong advocates of increased funding for public education. A key element of the platform was reform of the electoral system.

Now the hard work began of building a political party. We began by trying to create county organizations. We scheduled county party organizing conventions in the fall of 2017. That meant encouraging our supporters to come and to invite their friends and neighbors as well. We advertised in local media to inform voters in counties where we were focusing. We did not expect to organize in all twenty-eight counties within the state. Most were sparsely populated and Republican-dominated. But we did want to form organizations in the most populous counties, which we did. Within a year, we were organized in seven of the ten most populated counties in the state.

We also created various state party committees to handle functions we needed for the 2018 campaign. One was the research committee. Their task was to create policy briefs that would help candidates become informed on a wide array of issues. These two-to-three-page briefs covered issues such as tax reform, public education, environmental policy, gun regulation, and so on. My experience was that while candidates may have some familiarity with a single issue related to their occupation or personal interest—such as education for teachers or principals or tax policy for an accountant or financial advisor, or, for example, an environmentalist's interest in climate change—they had little knowledge of other issues they needed to be able to take positions on or talk to voters about.

Although the likelihood of being probed on issues by voters was low, one of the fears prospective candidates repeatedly voiced was that they did not know enough to talk to voters. Yet, the reality is that voters at the door or at meet-the-candidate events rarely had enough in-depth knowledge of issues to stump a candidate. Nearly all door-to-door encounters were civil, cordial, and superficial. Nevertheless, candidates needed to be informed, if for no other reason than to boost their self-confidence as candidates.

Another task of the research committee was the creation of district profiles to inform prospective candidates about who they would be running against and how they had voted in the past, what the district's boundaries and de-mographics were, and what the district's electoral history was. I would hand out these approximately five-to-seven-page packets to prospective candidates when I asked them to run. I found that it sent important messages. One was that the candidate became more aware of what he or she was getting into up-front. Also, it signaled that the party was serious about their running. We weren't simply asking them to sacrifice their time, energy, and money for months without support from the party organization.

The events committee planned the party's events. These included fundrais-ing dinners, picnics, and other socials. These activities helped party supporters get to know each other and communicated the vital message that they were not alone in their support of the party. The social aspect of politics was never my strong suit. I was glad there were people involved who were willing to take on event planning.

Another function of this committee was the party's presence in parades and county and city fairs. The events committee put together booths and built parade floats. In addition to the state fair, each county held their own fair and invited businesses and groups to rent booths. And some cities held their own fair. "Rodeo days," "Steel days," and "Strawberry days" were some of the names of the events cities held during the summer months to highlight their specialty. We rented booths in many of them in order to catch the attention of the thousands of people who passed by. Similarly, parades occurred all over the state throughout the summer.

The media committee undertook a large task as well—managing the message and its distribution in a fragmented media environment. They generated both traditional and social media messages. On the social media side, these consisted of tweets, posts, images, and ads on the party's social media platforms, while traditional media platforms included news releases, solicitations for interviews with the party chair, and newspaper op-eds. It helped that I already had relations with media in the state from past political activities.

We became innovative about how we could get traditional media attention. The candidates for the state legislature banded together to announce a legislative agenda, much as the Republicans had done in 1994 with the Contract for America. We piggybacked on current events to get in the story with a quote or a statement of our position. Two congressional candidates in 2018 announced their candidacies on the steps of the Capitol building, which helped them get television and newspaper coverage.

This committee also devised ads for cable television and Facebook to inform voters of who we were and what we stood for. Fortunately, a prominent former television anchor on the most-watched early evening news broadcast joined the party and became the face for many of our ads. My regret was that we couldn't recruit a prominent younger and female voice as well. As we had learned from our survey, younger people were our best demographic.

A critical committee was the one charged with fundraising. They helped organize fundraising events and drives and special outreach to individuals who could give larger donations. We lacked the resources to hire professional fundraisers outright. We did go through a succession of individuals who contracted with us to raise money for a commission. One succeeded, but she lasted only a few months. Finding someone who could successfully raise funds was one of the hardest tasks for me.

It was not too early to begin candidate recruitment. Two of the committees were charged with the task. One was focused on the federal and statewide races—the one US Senate race and the four congressional district races. The other had responsibility for identifying state legislative and county commission races throughout the state.

Ultimately, eighteen candidates ran for offices from Congress to the county commission.[12] We decided to skip the US Senate race because Mitt Romney entered the race. He was so widely popular in Utah that we did not want to sacrifice our image or our resources in a race against him.

As had been true when I was the county party chair, part of my job in candidate recruitment was to both encourage and discourage. There were several individuals who contacted me to announce they wanted to run for various offices. After some investigation of their backgrounds, I had to dissuade them from potential candidacies. For example, two were perpetual candidates for various offices—both partisan and nonpartisan. They had acquired a reputation as "nonserious" candidates. Another lived far from the congressional district he wanted to run in.

Some of the candidates were self-recruited. A former student, Eric Eliason, informed me he wanted to run for Congress in the first congressional district. He had become a successful businessman and was able to contribute hundreds of thousands to his own campaign.[13] He qualified for the Utah Debate Commission debate as well, which meant the party had qualified candidates twice in two years.[14] Eric Eliason was an ideal moderate candidate. He even won the endorsement of the largest newspaper in the state, a highly unusual act for a third-party candidate.[15] But he was running in the most Republican district in the state. He ended up winning 12 percent of the vote, which was the second-highest total for a nonmajor party congressional candidate in the nation that year.

Another self-recruit was a candidate for the state's third congressional district who had a long personal (and stormy) history with the incumbent, although she subsequently dropped out for medical reasons. We were able to replace her with another candidate who did not campaign and won only 2 percent of the vote. The original candidate, however, had the potential to damage our reputation as the "nice guys" in the state. She wanted to wage a personal campaign against the incumbent, who had been the mayor of the city where she lived. I advised her to keep the campaign about policy issues and the role of the party rather than launch personal attacks against the incumbent.

However, our third congressional candidate was one I worked diligently to recruit. She and her husband had built a development company that was enormously successful. She had deep roots to Utah—six generations—and could relate to Latter-day Saint women, which was another strong demographic for us. It took a couple of months of arm-twisting to encourage her to run. She finally decided to do so and started to develop her campaign by surrounding herself with paid advisers and workers.

Unfortunately, she found it difficult to take political advice from others. She paid for advice from those without political experience, which was expensive and not useful. To my surprise, she was uninterested in retail campaigning and had been assured by her inexperienced consultant that she could win by a late media campaign. It was a difficult experience trying to advise a candidate who was more interested in paying for bad advice than in taking free good advice and who had no desire to engage in the traditional activities of candidates.

In late July, she suddenly dropped out of the race. A couple of months later, she reregistered as a Republican and then a little over a year later launched a campaign for the Republican nomination for governor. It was a failure as well. She did not gather enough signatures to get on the GOP primary ballot, nor did she attempt to elicit support at the GOP convention. She needed to take one of the two routes to get on the primary ballot. However, the convention option was not really open to her since she ran on an anti-Trump platform in a state party that was intensely loyal to Donald Trump.

One of my anxieties came to pass with her. That was the prospect of a high-profile candidate abandoning the party and rejoining one of the two major parties. The message that sends is damaging to the party. Yet, this is a real fear for third parties. The siren call from the two major parties is loud. Not only does it affect voters at the last minute, as mentioned above, but it also can influence activists and even candidates. Of course, the latter are the more dangerous to the party because of their higher profile.

Our focus in 2018 was to assist our candidates. We gave money directly to candidates. Every candidate received a certain amount, but some got more if their races were more competitive and they were more active campaigners. We sought to keep the party's name in front of voters. I wrote a series of op-eds, and the party issued multiple press releases seeking to be relevant in the news media discussion about the party and the election generally.

In March, the week after candidate filing, we held our first party caucuses. Utah's caucus/convention system calendar begins with neighborhood precinct party caucuses. The Republicans host caucuses throughout the state, typically in schools. The Democrats hold similar caucuses in Salt Lake County, Moab, and Park City, which are Democratic Party strongholds. But their caucus locations dwindle significantly outside that county.

For both major parties, the caucuses' main purpose is to elect delegates to the county and state-level conventions. These caucuses often become heated meetings where supporters of competing candidates vie for delegates to add to their candidates' total at the conventions. Interest groups attempt to pack the caucuses to produce votes for their favored candidates.

Since the party organizations controlled the caucuses, they could determine who could participate. While Democrats opened their caucuses to any voter, Republicans opened theirs to Republicans only. Prospective participants who were not already Republicans were required to reregister at the door.

We decided not to perpetuate that system. We opened the caucuses to all voters, regardless of their party status. We also opened our county and state conventions to all party members and not just delegates. That meant anyone who was registered with the party could attend and vote at a party convention. The result was our caucuses did not have a formal role in the nominating process. They were forums for introducing the party to voters, identifying our supporters, recruiting volunteers, and making organization plans to assist candidates.

We held caucuses in nineteen locations around the state. (Third parties in Utah usually did not hold caucuses or may have had one in Salt Lake City.) More than nine hundred people showed up at those locations. That was a far cry from the Republican attendance across the state, which was about forty thousand, and the Democrats, which were about one-third of that. But since our party had less than half that number in actual registered members at the time, we thought that was an impressive turnout.[16]

As a new political party, we could be innovative. For example, we used webinar technology to broadcast to all of those locations. As the chair of the party, I was able to speak live to all the participants while others in other locations took turns, including the congressional candidates. We also used that technology to broadcast our state conventions to satellite locations around the state. The point was to bring political participation closer to the people rather than expecting them to travel to be involved. These were technological advances the major parties had not used.

Our familiarity with this technology became useful two years later when the COVID-19 pandemic hit and the party could not hold in-person caucus meetings or county or state conventions. Unlike the major parties, we continued to hold our caucuses, although we did so virtually.[17] We were not surprised they were not well attended, because the news media generally announced all caucuses had been postponed based on what the Republicans and Democrats had done.

BUILDING A PARTY IN A PANDEMIC AND A
TRUMP-DOMINATED ELECTION

Our candidates' electoral performance varied greatly depending on whether they were in a two-way or three-way race. Our vote total ranged from 2 percent in a rural state Senate race, where our candidate did not actively campaign, to 39 percent for a state House district race in the southern part of Salt Lake County where the candidate did campaign during the last two months before the election. Those in the three-way races tended to receive less than 10 percent of the vote, although one earned 15 percent. Three of our candidates—one for the state senate—passed the 30 percent threshold. One received 39 percent. On the aggregate, our eighteen candidates earned about 10 percent of the vote. It was a little more than what Jim Bennett had received the year before in his congressional race.

There was speculation that the party was Jim Bennett's effort to exact revenge on Republicans who had defeated his father for reelection in 2010. The rumor circulated because Jim Bennett had become the face of the party in 2017 with his congressional bid. But our performance showed that the party was much broader than one person. We demonstrated that we had captured a niche of support within the electorate. The question was whether we could move beyond that niche.

Not only did we want to do well, but we wanted to show we could do better than the Democrats. We were pleased that most of our candidates in one-on-one races with Republicans exceeded the record of Democrats who had run in those districts previously by a range of 5 to 7 percent. That meant, unlike the Democrats, we were picking up the votes of unaffiliated or moderate Republicans who could not vote for a Democrat and now had an alternative.

To make more of a dent, we needed to run more candidates in 2020 and earn a higher percentage of the vote. We went through the same process in 2020 that we had in 2018—fundraising, research, events, media messages, candidate recruitment, and so on. One advantage we had was more name recognition after having run candidates in 2018. However, we also were fighting the expectation that we should have won seats in 2018. Although we would have been happy to do so, we did not expect that our first attempt at multiple contests would gain us victory.

Our mantra from the start had been that we viewed our party as one that respected the opinions of the grassroots. It was not a party of elites. At the first convention, in a spontaneous act, I invited people in attendance who wished to stand to do so and explain why they were there and what they wanted out of this new party. Of the forty people there, half a dozen did that.

In January 2019, we held a breakfast meeting for past candidates, precinct chairs, legislative district chairs, and county party leaders to discuss what we should do going forward. We discussed for several hours the performance of the party in the 2018 campaign and what goals we should set for 2020. This meeting became a staple of 2020 and beyond. It was an opportunity for local party activists to register their opinions and help guide the party for the future.

We started early to recruit candidates for 2020. Once again, we created two committees. One difference was the emphasis on statewide races. While only one had existed in 2018, which we had skipped, there were four in 2020. We had no illusions about winning any of them. A statewide race was well beyond our means. It was possible we could recruit an affluent individual who would spend her or his own money. But we weren't counting on that. Ultimately, we were able to fill only one of the four races—the state auditor. A state treasurer candidate had signed up in the fall of 2019 and then, by February, backed out. Candidates for governor and attorney general were elusive, although we tried.

Our first candidate signed up in June. Then we gained others in the fall of 2019. The filing occurred in March. So, we were on track to have a significant slate in 2020.

One of my goals was to recruit a female candidate for governor. No political party had ever run a woman for governor in Utah. I wanted us to be the first. To that end, I approached heads of women's groups, former legislators, and a current small-town mayor. None of them, although all polite, expressed interest. At the same time, I did not want to run someone just because she was female. I wanted someone people would want to vote for. My failure to achieve that goal was a major disappointment of 2019–20.

In addition to a female candidate for governor, I sought gender parity across our entire candidate pool. About one-third of our candidates in 2018 were women. I hoped to increase that to 50 percent. I knew it would be an uphill task. Women are more reluctant to run. And they are definitely loath to run twice. That made it difficult to re-recruit those who had run before, although one of the female candidates in 2018 ran for the school board in her city two years later and won that nonpartisan race. Nevertheless, gender parity was our goal.

A new group—Mormon Women for Ethical Government—had formed in 2017 in response to the election of Donald Trump. These were Latter-day Saint women who were more moderate and wanted to take a stand against the type of politics that Trump practiced. The organization was not explicitly partisan. However, the participants tended to be moderate Republicans who had become disenchanted with their own party. They were a prime group for us to cultivate relationships with.

Since several of our supporters were their members, we reached out to them and sought their help in recruiting female candidates. In addition, I asked the candidate recruitment committees to make a special effort to identify prospective female candidates for state legislative and county council races. As it turned out, about half of those we approached to run were women. But, again, only about one-third of our candidates were women. It was another disappointment.

By the end of the filing, which was the middle of March, we had twenty-five candidates running. One withdrew within a few days of filing, due to work conflicts. Another filed without notifying us that he was doing so. He had filed for a county commissioner post in a rural county in central Utah. Worrying that he might be a fringe candidate who would embarrass us, I started to do a little research on him. It turned out he had been elected county sheriff seven times as a Democrat and had run unsuccessfully for the county commission four years earlier. I called him to introduce myself and learned that he had decided to switch parties because being a Democrat in rural Utah was no longer an option for a candidate. I was elated that he would not cause harm to the party. In fact, given his electoral history and wide name recognition, this was the candidate who had the best chance of winning his race.

After all the efforts to attempt to recruit candidates, the bottom line is whether they actually file. Utah has a one-week filing period. It is the moment of truth for party leaders who hope that a candidate does not back out at the last minute. In fact, that happened to our party in 2020. A physician who had previously run as a Republican for a state Senate seat decided to run for Congress. He had hired a campaign manager and was putting together a campaign organization. He had enough name recognition and money in the district to wage a decent, although not likely winnable, campaign.[18]

But, on the first day of filing, he told me he was not going to run. Instead, he ran for lieutenant governor with our former congressional candidate who dropped out in 2018 and had decided to run for the Republican gubernatorial nomination.[19] However, running as anti-Trump candidates in the Utah Republican Party in 2020 did not get them far. As mentioned earlier, they did not qualify for the primary and did not even compete at the party's convention, where they would have been anathema to the vast majority of delegates anyway.

On the other hand, some candidates who had repeatedly said "no" to the idea of running suddenly jumped in the race. One contacted me several times on the last filing day saying he was going to run and then he was not going to run, and back and forth. Finally, he called an hour before the county elections office closed and told me he was going there to file. I was pleased but also amused at the Hamlet-like scene I had witnessed that day.

As the filing closed, the starting gate formally opened for the 2020 campaign. We thought we had a good crop of candidates and a chance to make significant inroads into the strength of the two major parties in the state. Of course, what we could not anticipate was a global pandemic that would envelop the world in repeated lockdowns. The whole country shuttered its businesses, shops, restaurants, movie theatres, and government offices for a couple of months and then opened slowly after that. People would become scared of interacting with others, including greeting people at their door or attending county fairs, parades, and other public events.

The pandemic's toll on lives and health was devastating for many people in the United States, including in Utah. Our difficulties as a party were miniscule compared to that effect. Nevertheless, it did set back dramatically our efforts at outreach to the tens of thousands of voters we sought to connect with.

Like everyone else, we switched to virtual meetings. We urged candidates to do the same. But there was a larger problem than just physical contact. It was the overwhelming preoccupation with the pandemic. That was an understandable reaction. Nevertheless, it was difficult to get voters' attention during an electoral campaign.

There were no parades that summer. There were no county or city fairs. Our candidates could not go door-to-door to meet voters, because they did not want to have that personal interaction nor did they expect that many people would open their doors to a stranger in the midst of a pandemic. They did distribute literature. And they relied heavily on social media.

The party helped with social media. We spent tens of thousands of dollars on social media ads. Some were party-oriented—explaining what the party was and how we differed from the other candidates. Many, however, were candidate-specific ads intended to inform voters of our candidate in a particular district. We also used YouTube, Roku, Hulu, and other platforms for party or candidate-specific ads, particularly in districts or counties where candidates were actively campaigning.

After the pandemic hit, I knew 2020 was going to be a difficult year for our party and its candidates. Our success would be based on getting our candidates known to voters. That was going to be difficult when most of the mechanisms of interpersonal communication were unavailable. Candidates also were frustrated, as they were unable to engage in traditional activities. All of us were in unprecedented territory. And I worried that voters who were uninformed about options would default to what they knew—the two major parties, and particularly the Republicans.

Another problem in 2020 was the influence of the presidential election. The 2018 midterm election had been state-focused. We were not affected by the vote for the presidency, as occurred in presidential elections. In 2020, there was a massive Trump turnout; in fact, the 2020 election set a record for voter turnout.[20] And that increased turnout in Utah primarily was directed at Donald Trump. While in Utah Joe Biden received 250,000 votes more than Hillary Clinton had in 2016, Donald Trump picked up 350,000 more votes than he had in 2016. The extra vote was not simply due to McMullin voters supporting either Trump or Biden. McMullin won 243,000 votes in 2016 in Utah, which was slightly less than the gain for Biden alone.[21] And, those Trump voters likely kept voting Republican down the ballot and hurting both Democrats and United Utah Party (UUP) candidates.

Overall, our candidates did about the same in 2020 as they had in 2018, earning, on average, about 10 percent of the vote. It was a relief to me that we had not done worse. Our best candidate performance was from the former sheriff, who won 38 percent of the vote in a strong Republican pro-Trump county.

Our party had a goal of becoming the second party in the state, not another third. We made inroads toward that goal in 2020. In two counties, the number of UUP candidates on the local ballot (not statewide or congressional) equaled the number of Democrats on the ballot. In two other counties, including the second-largest county in the state, the number of UUP candidates exceeded the number of Democrats. In the second-largest county, which was Utah County, the Democrats fielded two candidates, while the UUP had eight. This disparity indicated that the Democrats had seriously atrophied since I had stepped down as chair nine years earlier. But it was also an indication of the shrinking of the Democratic Party's presence across the state outside of Salt Lake.

As it turned out, the Democrats did not field a candidate in the state auditor's race, although the Libertarians did. Our candidate received 13 percent of the vote, beating the Libertarian. That translated into 173,000 votes, which we thought was a strong performance for a third-party candidate, particularly for one who did not campaign.

In Utah, to remain on the ballot, one of the party's candidates must get at least 2 percent of the statewide vote. Our 2020 performance from the state auditor candidate guaranteed our ballot access. Two other parties—the Green and the American Independent—lost their ballot access because they failed to achieve that minimum.

But that was not our goal. Our goal was to acquire more votes toward the objective of winning elections. That was not easy to achieve in 2020. Yet, far more Utah voters supported a UUP candidate in 2020 than had ever before. We had run more candidates in more races in more counties and had collected more votes—approximately 270,000 across all candidates, compared with 160,000 in 2018 and 13,000 in 2017. I stepped down as chair in January 2021, but the UUP was poised to compete in the future.

LESSONS LEARNED

Obviously, starting a new party is not easy—even on a statewide rather than a national level. For example, the new Forward Party, initiated by former Democratic presidential candidate Andrew Yang and former New Jersey governor Christine Todd Whitman, faces a high hurdle in competing effectively against the two major parties No minor party at the national level has displaced a major party since the election of 1860, when the Whigs imploded and the newly created Republican Party emerged from the old party's ruins.

All the stresses of heading a county major party organization were present with a new party—the multiple tasks of candidate recruitment, fundraising, party organization, messaging—and are demanding for any party chair. Fortunately, there was no negative perception to overcome. Instead, there was no perception at all. Voters had no familiarity with the United Utah Party. The reality of a moderate party, even though they supported the concept, was new to them. In fact, that became one of our major hurdles—defining who we were as ourselves and not simply in reference to the two major parties. We could not be simply "not them." We had to define ourselves.

Without significant funds, though, it became difficult to do so. Entering the political landscape with a large amount of cash to spend on messaging would have increased our odds of "breaking through" with our message. Yet, getting one or more donors to donate those large amounts of money became impossible without some guarantees that the risk would pay off. There were no such guarantees.

Our gradual approach—that is, that we would incrementally build name recognition and brand awareness—was the only one we could afford. But it reinforced the message of failure as we did not win elections immediately. Increasingly, we began to concentrate our efforts. Not that we did not run candidates in multiple areas. Names on ballots and even whole campaigns by candidates helped improve brand awareness. But we poured more money and resources into particular areas with the hope that we could do better or win in those areas.

It was difficult to convince voters to abandon their preconceptions, that is, that there were two major parties you choose from. There were no other options to be considered, because those offered in the past were extremes, such as the Greens on the left and the American Independent Party or Constitution Party on the right. We knew we had an electability problem that would take some time to overcome.

Again, I had much to discuss in class about political parties, particularly third parties. However, I did not recruit in class. Students would bring up the United Utah Party in class and I would address what the party was and why it was founded. More often they would approach me during my office hours and ask if they could become involved. I directed them to the volunteer committee and then made no further mention of it with them to assure that I did not know whether they had followed through or not.

You Are Not Unique

One of the most important lessons for me in my own involvement was that there are many people who want the same goal. They are just waiting for someone to take the lead to form an organization, launch a campaign, jumpstart a movement to start the work of bringing that goal to pass. In this case, many people wanted an alternative to the two-party system that was more moderate. They thought it was a good idea, but they were not going to take the initiative.

So it is with many innovations. The interest is there. It takes only the spark to make it happen. Innovating can seem lonely and scary at times. We might wonder: Will I stick my neck out to create something and no one will care? Is it really the case that "if you build it, they will come?" There are plenty of examples of that not happening. A new business is started that soon fails. A much-touted product (such as the Edsel or New Coke) is soundly rejected by consumers. Or a high-budget film flops at the box office.

Yet, a new party, even one with a significant potential base of support, is not easy to start. Democrats and Republicans have inherent advantages of tradition, recognition, money, and organization. But, the expectation of pundits, and the hopes of Republican and Democratic Party leaders, was that initial victory should be achieved or the contest is not worth waging. Politics is not like a business market where a new company's ability to reach a 10 percent share of the market is considered a triumph. The UUP was breaking down support for the two major parties by gradually winning more votes over time. Nevertheless, while a company gains profits from a 10 percent share, a political party gains nothing tangible. Although it may be gradually changing hearts and minds, there is no immediate "revenue" in the form of seats in a state legislature or Congress.

Of course, I knew all of this. The question was whether the conditions in Utah were the same as they were nationally or in most other states. In Utah, there was no real two-party system in most of the state. The minority party had a disastrous reputation to contend with. The Democrats were not organized in most of the state. They had left a vacuum. Could it be filled? Could the United Utah Party grow to fill that vacuum?

Party Organizations Need Political Scientists

Another lesson I learned is that political scientists can help improve political discourse and activity. Frequently, I shared with activists what I knew from the literature to add a dose of realism to expectations. Many people felt that a third party would catch fire immediately, and my task was to explain that it could take several election cycles before that would happen. Or they believed we could get a majority of those identified with a political party to donate money to the party when, in reality, a small percentage do so.

I also sought to moderate the populist passions that are latent in the system (and sometimes quite manifest). For example, UUP members wanted to support term limits. Most would have preferred strict limits such as six years for the state House and eight for the state Senate, much like California's, as well as a subsequent lifetime ban on serving in that office. However, I argued successfully against such short terms or the inability to run again. I urged a balance between rotation in office and the need for a long enough term to gain expertise.

My job was to educate people both in and out of the classroom. That did not mean lecturing them at every opportunity. It did mean helping them understand the political system so they could make a difference within it. As well, it meant encouraging and recruiting them to political involvement. I introduced internship programs both within the Democratic Party and the United Utah Party and supervised students who gained their first experience in practical politics. In addition, there were many students who became involved in other ways with the party or with individual candidate campaigns.

Academics need to be willing to get in the trenches with others to change the political system. In other words, get the hands dirty in practical politics. That means more than devising models or writing more papers. It means contributing to political parties in meaningful ways as an extension of what we do in the classroom.

7. Community Service and Running for Office

I started on a tenure track as a political science professor in 1985 at a small state liberal arts college in upstate New York. My area was American politics, and I began teaching survey classes as well as upper undergraduate course offerings in campaigns and elections, political parties, and media and politics. My decision to teach those subjects was due to a long-term interest. Since my adolescence, I had been interested in government. My father was a career officer in the Navy, and I spent most of my childhood living on or near naval bases or in Washington, DC, near the Pentagon. We lived in northern Virginia twice before I turned twelve. Politics is in the blood within the Beltway.

In addition to teaching the subject matter, I urged the students to become involved in politics themselves. To stimulate them, occasionally I invited local politicians to speak to my classes to provide a real-world perspective. Throughout my career, I continued to do that. I have had US senators, US representatives, state legislators, political party chairs, mayors, city councilors, and school board members visit my classes, relate their experiences, and interact with students.

It was not long before I realized that I was a hypocrite. I was encouraging students to become active citizens and make a difference in government, but I was not doing so myself. It was at that point that I resolved I would become involved in my community or state (although the extent of participation varied at different stages of my life). And this engagement would be volunteer rather than paid, since I wanted to give back and not seek a monetary reward.

My involvement over thirty-five years included a variety of roles, as I have documented in this book already. Two I have not discussed so far are my service as a volunteer on city and school district commissions and committees and as a candidate for office. This is what this chapter is about.

CITY SERVICE

A neighbor approached me one day and asked if I would like to serve on a city commission. He was the city's recreation director and wanted to know if I wanted to participate in the city's Recreation Advisory Commission. He had the task of recommending members of the commission to the mayor, who made the appointment. I expressed interest and, when a vacancy occurred next, I was appointed.

I realized that had I lived in a different neighborhood, I would not have met him. Indeed, I might have lived in a neighborhood where no one served in an influential post in city government. And the commission was not something I would have volunteered for without his invitation. I know that invitations to become involved are crucial to the process of engagement and that there are many people who do not become involved because no invitation is offered. In my case, invitations to serve were offered by others at several points.

Frankly, political scientists may not necessarily be invited, unless they take some initiative to do so. Academics typically do not move in the same circles that city volunteers and candidates are drawn from. They tend not to join the local service clubs, mingle in business organizations, or live in the most affluent neighborhoods due to middle-class status.

But there are ways for political scientists who want to serve on a city, school district, water district, or some other district's committee to become involved without necessarily receiving an invitation. Local governments are always looking for someone to serve on these committees. They advertise in city newsletters or on social media or on their websites.

Inviting local politicians to speak in classes is another way to become familiar with those who make such appointments. Yet another is to join (and even head) nonprofit organizations serving the community in some way. Those organizations—from the Scouts to Habitat for Humanity to the local food bank—not only provide important service to community members in need but also introduce volunteers to other volunteers who may be influential in integrating people into community work.

Political scientists may join national organizations and consider that involvement to be similar. If the national organization has a local branch, such as the NAACP or the League of Women Voters, then local interaction is facilitated. However, if it is simply a national organization without a local in-person component, particularly where the individual member's contact is limited to giving donations and receiving emails, then it cannot accomplish the same social opportunities as a more local organization.

Initially, there may be some suspicion of the academic. He or she is too smart, will show up the other members of the commission or council, will lecture the others, and will be too socially awkward to contribute. All of these fears may be borne out in some cases, but not typically. However, academics have the advantage of intelligence, foresight, and experience with the need for collegiality—all important traits for service. An academic who does not attempt to exhibit an attitude of superiority, does not insist on using "big words" to impress others, and is willing to cooperate, compromise, and work hard will gain the respect of other members.

My neighbor's invitation led to nearly a decade of service on two city commissions and involvement in lobbying and initiative campaigns. I served for six years on that commission and became familiar with the parks and other recreation facilities of the city. As well, I became aware of the recreational needs that were not being met by the city. The city's fitness center needed to be updated. New city parks had to be built as new residential developments sprang up. Soccer and baseball fields were in short supply given the heavy demands of Little League teams.

Shortly after I joined the commission, I was elected vice chair. The newly elected chair had been on the commission for a year or two and told me he was not anxious merely to serve in the position. He wanted to do something. I agreed wholeheartedly with his sentiment. I had no career ambitions involved in this appointment. It was an effort to serve. And I did not want to attend meetings and repeatedly hear the recreation director reiterate the needs of the city that were not being met because of inadequate funding.

A few years earlier, the state legislature had passed legislation allowing counties (with the voters' approval) to enact a zoo, arts, and parks (commonly termed ZAP) tax as part of the county's sale tax. The tax amount was minimal—a one-tenth of one percent additional sales tax that would be devoted to those three specific purposes. The tax change was urged by Salt Lake County, which immediately held a vote to implement it. When the vote passed, the county began to apply the money to funding for county parks, arts organizations, and the local zoo.

As a commission, we discussed the new tax and wondered if voters in our own county would approve something similar. We concluded that if they would, the county could help the city with recreation and parks projects using this new tax money. Unfortunately, we were well into an election year and had to move quickly if we wanted to lobby the county commission to place the ZAP tax equivalent in our county. The county commissioners would have to approve this measure by the end of August, and we came up with this idea in July.

Since the tax would be used to support both parks/recreation and cultural arts, we decided not to attempt this effort alone. We reached out to the cultural arts community in our city to gauge their interest in joining a coalition to place this referendum on the ballot and then work for its passage with the voters, particularly in a short time frame. When they expressed interest, we began to draft a proposal and planned a date to place this on the county commissioners' agenda.

On that date, we appeared at their meeting and made a presentation. We pointed to the success of the Salt Lake County tax in improving cultural arts and recreation in their county. We urged the commissioners to allow the public to decide whether or not they wanted this tax, even if the commissioners themselves might be opposed to tax increases. All three of the county commissioners were known as fiscal conservatives, although one was considered more moderate while another was quite conservative. The third was in his last year since he had decided not to run for reelection after being convicted of a DUI. We had no idea how he would vote since he had nothing to gain or lose either way. To our surprise, he voted favorably, and the measure passed 2–1.

Now we faced a critical question. How do we educate the eighty thousand voters who would cast a ballot in this election with limited time and even more constrained resources? The fact is we didn't; only 38 percent voted in support. It is likely most voters had no information about it.

But we did see a silver lining in the vote. A majority of voters in our city had voted "yes." That gave us hope that if we could adopt a city tax rather than a county one, there was a good chance the voters would approve it. Yet, as the statute was written, that was not allowed.

Our next step was to see if we could convince the state legislature to allow cities and not just counties to adopt their own version of the ZAP tax. One of our local legislators agreed to sponsor the legislation. Other cities were taking the same steps, which increased our chances of victory in the legislature. Again, the success of the ZAP tax and the lobbying by cities who wanted to adopt it at the city level convinced the legislature to expand the law beyond counties.

At about that time, the city council created a cultural arts advisory commission intended to provide cultural arts with the same kind of public input that had existed with the recreation commission. The commission was populated with representatives of various cultural arts organizations—theatres, dance groups, community music organizations, and so on. I was asked to serve on that commission and expressed a willingness to do so. I was one of the few who did not represent an organization. Once again, I was elected vice chair. Along with the recreation advisory commission, our first task was to get a ZAP-type tax in our city.

Now that we had the authority to adopt such a tax, we needed to convince the city council to allow a vote. We scheduled a date to make a presentation to the city council to lobby them to allow a vote. We enlisted a group of supporters to attend the meeting in support of a few leaders of our coalition who participated in the actual presentation. Again, we explained the success of the ZAP tax as a model for our city. We discussed the recreation needs of the city—the need for more ball fields, a fitness center update, and so on. We also noted that two of the largest arts organizations in the county—two playhouses—were located in our city. Our city would become a mecca for cultural arts patrons.

To our surprise, a local legislator who was extremely conservative came to the city council meeting to speak out against allowing a vote of the people on this new tax. He appealed to their anti-tax attitudes. I spoke with him afterward to ask him why he was opposing the opportunity for the people to vote and decide for themselves. He said he did not believe government money should be spent on cultural arts and recreation. Just for my amusement, I asked him what he thought about government support for transportation. He said he opposed that as well. Then, I asked him about public education spending. He replied that he wasn't sure about that. His response expressed the views of the hard-line, anti-government people in our county. Unfortunately, he had a lot of support. He was elected to the legislature several times.

Despite his efforts, the mayor and the city council voted overwhelmingly to place the measure on the ballot and allow the voters to decide. At times, our city council had been dominated by the anti-government groups. Fortunately, this was not one of those times. Now the hard work would begin—educating voters and assuring that the support from three years before had not withered.

Our group, which consisted of representatives of both arts and recreation, began to have weekly meetings to strategize and implement this campaign. I was selected as the leader of the group. That choice probably stemmed from the fact that I was not from either camp. I belonged to both city commissions, but I was not a part of the arts community, since I did not represent any particular organization, nor was I part of the recreation community, because I did not come from any of the particular sports. My job was to unite these two communities who had not worked together before.

First, we needed a catchy title for our efforts—something that would be memorable for the voters. It could not be ZAP because that was already associated with somewhere else and we didn't have a zoo in our city. One person suggested something that included cultural arts and recreation and came up with the acronym CARE. We liked that title for the new tax—the CARE tax. It would send important signals about what our community cared about.

Then, we began to solicit free publicity. The cultural arts organizations handed out fliers at their events and sent mailings to their members explaining what the CARE tax was and how it would benefit the arts. Similarly, we asked the sports organizations—football, soccer, baseball, softball, and so on—to do the same for their many participants. We knew their organizations included many parents who would be interested in how this might affect their programs.

The city itself could not take a stand. The staff needed to be neutral. But the city could provide information to the voters, which it did in its monthly newsletter to residents. The elected leaders of the city could take a position, which they did. It was gratifying to have the mayor and city council on our side.

We used other tools to inform voters. We raised enough money to print signs and literature, which we distributed across the city with the help of these two communities. We also used free media, as I became the spokesperson for the group—doing media interviews, writing op-eds, and issuing press releases.

Three years after the county vote and four years after I had joined the recreation commission, the city voted in favor of instituting the CARE tax. The victory was sweet. Not only could the city fund recreation projects, but cultural arts organizations could be promoted. Our city would be the first in the county to approve this tax.

But the struggle did not end there. The legislature required that the tax be renewed every eight years. Seven years later, those who had been involved in the initial campaign began to discuss how to organize for the next vote. One major problem, however, was the way the money had been spent by the city council over those eight years. Nearly all of the money had been given to cultural arts organizations. Those organizations had lobbied for the money and convinced the council of their needs. However, the sports groups felt betrayed. They complained of deteriorating facilities at the ball fields and a general neglect of their needs. They threatened to vote against renewal because it would only mean a tax increase for them with no promise of any help from the money for recreation.

Once again, I became the leader of the campaign and had the unenviable task of getting the sports organizations back on board with a renewal of the CARE tax when they were inclined to oppose it. I met separately with the recreation-oriented groups to assess their feelings and determine what it would take to get them back in support. At the same time, the cultural arts community did not want to compromise, because they knew that any change in allocation would siphon money away from them.

I had to convince the cultural arts community that there was a risk the renewal would not pass if the sports groups were opposed. Not only would they not do the kind of campaign legwork they had done eight years earlier, but they could organize opposition. Their absence from our campaign would be a sign to the voters that the CARE tax was really only a cultural arts tax. And that kind of tax would not be popular, since support for recreation within the city was stronger than support for the cultural arts. One reason had to do with geography. The cultural arts productions drew patrons from other cities in the county. That meant many of their patrons could not vote in our city and were not concerned about what happened in the city. The recreation community, however, existed solely within the city, since the city organized the sports for city residents. Recreation was a big deal for many residents. And they would be city voters.

After discussions with both communities, our group proposed two changes to the way the money was handled by the city. One was the creation of a volunteer advisory committee that would give the council recommendations on how the tax revenue would be spent. That committee would consist of representatives from both communities on an equal basis. The second was a resolution by the council that there would be a roughly even split between funding for recreation and cultural arts in the future.

Those two changes satisfied the representatives of the recreation community and they signed on to the renewal campaign. Most of the cultural arts organizations accepted the need to compromise and guarantee a much larger share of the CARE tax funds to recreation needs. The largest of the organizations did not and attempted to lobby the city council to oppose the roughly equivalent allocation of funds. Fortunately, the council rejected their opposition and agreed to the two conditions.

With the support now of the two communities, the campaign undertook the same effort as before. This time an even larger majority supported the CARE tax, and the tax was secure until the next vote in the future.

CANDIDACIES

Even though many political scientists study people who run for office and those who vote for them, few take the step of running for office themselves. As political scientists, we leave that to the politicians or the citizens who run for various reasons other than winning. But should we?

Running for office is an experience that brings a new practical perspective to the political scientist that is difficult to duplicate in any other way, as explained by several political scientists in chapter 2. Experiments, and certainly not theories and models, do not impart the same kind of knowledge that putting one's name out in the public limelight does. There is something about being willing to put your mind and body where your mouth is that offers a rush of excitement, anxiety, and knowledge that is difficult to gain in conferences or through academic journal articles or books.

Geneseo School Board

Listening to many actual and erstwhile elected officials explain how they become involved in the first place has convinced me that one of the most difficult decisions is the initial one to run for elective office. Running for office was something I considered doing from the time I was a teenager. As I previously mentioned, I worked in a campaign for the first time in 1972. Even at that young age, I observed candidate campaigns at close range and began to anticipate the possibility of running myself some day in the future. Before I opted for an academic career, I thought applied politics might be my chosen profession. However, even after I became a political scientist, the thought remained that I should run for part-time office at some time. That time came sooner than I thought.

Only a year into my teaching job at SUNY Geneseo, I decided to run for the local school board. A major impetus in that decision was the fact that my daughter was enrolled in the local elementary school and my son would be in kindergarten the next year. The school district was small—one building housed K-12, although secondary school students were separated in different wings from the elementary school. Participating in parent-teacher conferences, attending school board meetings, and listening to school staff discuss their problems piqued my interest in attempting to make a difference. The elementary school building was designed during the 1960s when a common education theory touted the value of breaking down walls. All the K–6 classes were held in a large hall. Initially, students sitting at a desk anywhere in the hall could have seen students at a hundred other desks. Teachers would have had to compete for students' attention with many distractions from the sights and sounds of other teachers and students in other areas of the hall. The design would have been more disastrous had teachers not constructed their makeshift walls with bookshelves—all designed to block off their classrooms to avoid those distractions from other classes and create something closer to a separate classroom.

This was the kind of educational experimentation that bothered me. Education reform could be a step toward progress in student learning. However, too often seemingly good ideas on paper were pushed by national educational leaders or educational psychologists without regard to the consequences of implementation. I felt teachers and parents were the best determinants of the quality of educational reform, since they could see direct effects in the classroom and their own homes. I thought maybe I could take my approach into a school board that was deciding whether to adopt educational reforms.

School board members were elected at-large. Two of the positions were up for re-election that year. One of the members was a middle-aged woman who had been on the board for only one term. However, the general perception of her among the town residents was that she was not interested in her school board work and had been increasingly lackadaisical toward her job. She no longer had children in the school, which may have affected her attitude.

I thought this perception might be an opportunity to replace her with someone who was more energetic and who actually had children in the school. Plus, the section of the district I lived in was not represented on the board because the school board was elected at-large and no one had run from my area. That struck me as unfair for those of us who lived in that region of the district.

Another thought that occurred to me was that I would not lose anything if I ran for office. If I lost, I would not be no worse off than I was before. In fact, I expressed concern to one of the other candidates about that after I did lose. Would the school board and school administration be prejudiced against me because I had run but lost? She was adamant that would not be the case. Rather, they would take me more seriously because I had gained the support of others. Receiving the votes of hundreds of others would signal that I had support when I said something in a school board meeting.

Granted, campaigning would take time. And I would invest some money. For a school district of our size, it was hundreds of dollars not thousands or tens of thousands. But for someone who taught American politics courses that included discussion of campaigns and elections, I concluded the experience would only enrich my teaching. I could learn what it was like to be a candidate.

I came in third in a four-person race. Although I did not get into the top two, I did receive more votes than the incumbent, which I considered a small victory in that sense. However, in a larger sense, I won a personal major victory. I had been willing to put myself out there, to be not behind the scenes but the actual candidate. As a candidate, I needed to formulate a rationale for my run and then articulate it to others. I had to create campaign literature and take the time to distribute it. Also, I needed to go door-to-door and solicit votes. It was a rural community and that meant walking up driveways of houses on large lots or driving up to a farmhouse surrounded by acres of fields. I met many of my neighbors and listened to their concerns about the local school.

There also was a difference in my teaching. My classes became more informed, as I could talk about candidates, campaigns, and elections with more appreciation for those who participate, not just observe or discuss, the electoral process. I avoided "war stories" about my experience. But I realized I could discuss what candidates go through with more confidence because I had personally endured candidacy for elective office, however humble the actual office of a local school board member in a small, largely rural community.

Alpine School District School Board

My second run for elective office occurred ten years later. In the intervening years, I had left SUNY Geneseo and taken a job at the US Coast Guard Academy. As a faculty member there, I was a federal employee. The Hatch Act prevented me from running for office. I avoided electoral politics during the five years we lived there in order to comply with the law.

Then, I was hired at Brigham Young University. Once again, I became involved in our local schools since we now had four children enrolled in the local elementary school and junior high school. My wife and I attended parent-teacher conferences, we volunteered in our children's classrooms, and I attended school board meetings. The Alpine School District was the polar opposite of Geneseo. It was a geographically large school district that covered a dozen cities in the northern half of the county. At that time, there were approximately forty thousand children in the district.

We were aware before we moved to Utah that class sizes were uncommonly large. But we were not prepared for what we saw. The problem became personal to us when we dropped off our third-grade daughter in her classroom. There were forty-five children in a classroom designed for thirty. The teacher explained to the parents that the classroom was not typically that crowded. Only on the first day would everyone be present. Otherwise, the students would rotate in and out of the classroom on a three-week vacation schedule.

The school was a year-round school, which meant classes went on for eleven months with only the month of July off. The students were not in the classroom that long, but the teachers were. The class was divided into five tracks and each track was on a sixty-day-on, fifteen-day-off schedule. The plan received national attention and was emulated by other schools.[1]

Administrators claimed teachers preferred the year-round schedule because teaching for eleven months meant a salary increase. In reality, teachers hated the year-round schedule because they did not have enough time off. Yes, given the choice between lower salaries and higher ones, they chose the latter. But Utah had one of the lowest teacher average salaries in the nation. It was no surprise they wanted to earn extra income. Nor was it surprising many of them were completely burned out by May.

Year-round school was yet another example of educational experimentation that had gone awry. Within a few years, the school district abandoned year-round schooling, including at our school (the one that had originated the five-track plan). In its place, the district adopted the extended-day school plan rather than extended year. In the extended-day plan, teachers spent more time in school because one group of students came to school from 7:30 am to 2:15 pm while a second arrived at 9 am and remained until 3:45 pm. This plan allowed for some classes (those held earlier in the morning and later in the afternoon) to be smaller. But those in the middle remained large. The district was doing whatever it could to reduce class size while not spending more money to do it.

I quickly became familiar with the school board members and the superintendent as I repeatedly expressed my concerns about large class sizes. Another issue arose around that time that animated me to become involved with the school board on that topic as well. A new high school was being built near our home. However, the plan for boundaries placed our home in the existing high school for our area, which was twice as far away as the new school would be. Some people in our area simply petitioned the school board to change the boundaries. Or they determined they would send their children to the new school since the state required schools to enroll pupils from any part of the district, unless the school was closed because it had reached the enrollment maximum. (The school board declared that the new high school would reach that maximum upon opening and therefore declined to allow any student outside the new high school boundary to attend, even though it was not really at that maximum.) The school board countered with the argument that shrinking the boundaries of the existing high school would produce too few students for that school. That would create an inequity among the district's high schools. Moreover, and perhaps more importantly for many parents, the school's sports designation would drop to the next lower level if it was a smaller school. Football players, for example, no longer would play the biggest and most high-profile teams in the state.

Instead of merely complaining to the school board, I devised a plan that would place our neighborhood in the boundary area of the new school but potentially maintain enrollment for the existing high school. I attended a school board meeting, signed up to make a comment, and then laid out my plan—complete with a map of proposed boundaries. I suggested that the school board convert the existing high school into a magnet school. The magnet school concept was not new, but it had not been adopted in my area. My idea was that this school would become a magnet school for the arts. It was already known for its arts programs. As a magnet school, it would boost arts education to attract students from across the district who wanted to specialize in the arts.

The school superintendent was intrigued by the idea and even asked if I was saying that the school district should innovate. I am not sure if he was genuinely surprised at the concept of the school district innovating or if he was sending a subtle signal to the members of the board who were sitting there listening to the discussion. I answered emphatically that they should consider this proposal and seek to determine how many students might attend a magnet arts school in the district to study the feasibility of the change. Unfortunately, the school board ultimately was not interested in innovating or even examining the possibility. They rejected my idea. I wondered if the school board needed more vision.

The five school board members were elected to represent specific areas within the school district. Our school board member was an amiable retired high school teacher in his eighties. He had been a popular teacher in one of the high schools until he retired and later ran for the school board. The overcrowding in the schools did not bother him. When I asked him about it, he said he was always pleased when he had a lot of students sign up for his classes. He had no intention of attempting to rectify the situation. I felt he should be replaced.

However, I knew this would not be easy. These school board members were elected on a district basis. But the district still was much more populated than Geneseo. The district I would run in encompassed approximately one-half of a city of nearly 90,000 people. As was the case in Geneseo, I was still unknown. This would be an uphill battle.

I created a flier and began to go door-to-door to advertise my candidacy. My pitch was that I could bring innovation to the school board and particularly would support ways to reduce class sizes. I was not shy about saying that I thought we needed to devote more resources to public education, which would include a tax increase. I bought yard signs and, with some help from others, placed them in various locations around the district.

Not only was I running against the incumbent but also against a real estate developer with money to devote to the campaign and the head of an advocacy group for special needs children. The primary culled the field to two people for the general election. I did not make the cut, beating only the developer. I was disappointed but not surprised. Increasingly, I had found that campaigning for office was difficult while I was seeking to get promoted and helping my wife raise a family with young children. The time was not right for me, and I was quietly relieved I did not win.

School Board Advisory Committee

Following my unsuccessful run for the school board, I determined to remain involved. My goal of reducing class sizes still excited me. I just needed to find another way to accomplish it short of actually being a school board member.

I learned more about how school funding worked. I discovered that bonds were used to raise money for capital expenditures such as building new schools or renovating existing ones. Leeways, however, were votes of the people to raise taxes to staff schools. Too often the school district had proposed bonds but not leeways. A bond is more popular in the sense that voters can see an actual capital improvement—a new gym, or a new auditorium, or even a new neighborhood school. Plus, when bonds were paid in full, taxes dropped again.

Leeways, however, were less tangible. But unlike a bond where the tax increase disappeared when the bond was paid off, a leeway did not disappear as a tax. It was a permanent increase. However, the legislature in Utah had capped the amount a school district could raise in a leeway. But our school district was not yet at that cap.

I realized one way to hire more teachers and reduce class size was to adopt a leeway at the same time as a bond. Taxing up to the legislature's cap would not reduce class size dramatically. It would mean on average only a student or two fewer in a classroom. But I thought it would be a start.

I knew the school board was contemplating a bond. Rapid growth was the norm in our school district. While the southern part of the district was aging and school population declining, the northern section was burgeoning. New homes and subdivisions were popping up in formerly small cities. The area had become a tech haven with a plethora of new start-ups. The dot-com boom later was followed by a dot-com bubble, which burst in 2000. However, that had not yet occurred. And, amazingly, it would not slow growth for long. The northern section needed new schools at all levels as neighborhoods grew from the desert and families with young children moved into the new houses suddenly built there.

The timing seemed opportune to propose a leeway as well. I cajoled school board members as well as the superintendent. I attended school board meetings and urged a leeway. I argued that the time was ripe and that the demand for new schools the bond would bring would favor the leeway as well.

My continual lobbying paid off. The superintendent voiced support for the leeway, and the board followed him in voting for both the bond and the leeway to be placed on the ballot for the voters' approval. Now another struggle began—convincing voters to support both the bond and the leeway. They had the choice of accepting both, rejecting the leeway but accepting the bond, or discarding both. The last two options were not out of the question. A nearby school district board had recently proposed a bond that was soundly defeated by the voters. The same could happen in ours if the district did not do its work to convince the voters.

Perhaps as acknowledgment for my efforts, I was asked to serve on the school district's bond advisory committee. Our committee met weekly for several months to plot a strategy to win public approval. We recommended the bond include not only new schools in the north but also improvements in schools in the south that were needed and would gain public support of the bond across the district. We reviewed what the district itself could and could not do regarding the bond and leeway. They could not take a position on the issue. However, they could "inform" voters by sending information in district newsletters about the effects of passing the bond and leeway. As well, they could work with the Friends of Alpine School District, a nonprofit organization that could advocate for the bond and leeway. Friends raised money for a public relations campaign, collected endorsements, and launched advertising separate from the district.

Surprisingly, the Utah Taxpayers Association, a conservative (perhaps even reactionary) anti-tax organization in the state that carried clout with the business community, announced they did not oppose the bond or leeway in the Alpine School District. Even they acknowledged the need for additional funding for the district. The district was known as one of the poorest in the state, routinely scoring at the bottom in terms of per pupil spending. One might have hoped that they would have endorsed the proposal, but expecting them to approve a tax increase was too much to hope for!

On election night, we learned that both the bond and the leeway had passed, although the latter by a narrower margin. It was an exciting moment to see voters support an initiative I had proposed. Over the extent of my career of political involvement, many election nights would bring disappointment. But this one did not.

State Legislature

My interaction with school board members before and after my own run helped me understand that the real power over education policy lay with the state legislature. The legislature determined the amount of money devoted to education in the state through the weighted per pupil unit. Most of the money school districts used to pay teachers, administrators, and staff and to run programs came from the state. School districts did raise their own funds through property taxes. However, the state legislature controlled how much a school district could tax the property of their citizens.

The legislature not only determined the amount of money each district— and therefore each local school—received, but it also decided how it was going to be spent. The legislature passed bills that created, modified, or destroyed educational programs. They had the final say on what would be taught, how it would be taught, and how much financial support it would receive.

The micromanagement of education was particularly characteristic of the Utah legislature, because many legislators harbored a fundamental mistrust of educators. Some were charter school supporters who championed alternatives to the traditional public education system. Others pushed vouchers to provide financial encouragement for private schools. And still others advocated home schooling because they disliked what was taught in the public schools. The teachers' union was particularly despised by Republican legislators, since they were continually asking for more money for an educational system many legislators were attempting to supplant with charter schools, private schools, or homeschooling.

A member of the Alpine School Board who I had worked with on an effort to pass the leeway and bond in the district contacted me and urged me to run for the state legislature. Others involved with the school district did so as well. They knew I was a strong supporter of public education and would be an advocate for increased education spending. Moreover, two of the candidates who were already running were opponents of putting more money into public education. One was a cofounder of a charter school and wanted to use his position to further the cause of charter schools. The other related to me that he considered the teachers union to be nothing better than thieves who wanted to steal his wallet to pay for education funding. I could understand why those in the education community were desperate for someone to advocate in their behalf.

Of course, they wanted me to run as a Republican. The Republican Party dominated politics in my state and my county. At that time, no Democrat had won the governorship for twenty years and a US Senate seat for thirty years. The legislature had been controlled by the Republicans for more than twenty years. None of the more than a dozen legislators representing my county in the legislature identified as a Democrat, and neither did any of the county elected officials. By that time, the Democratic Party in the county had shrunk to a shell of its former self forty years before.

I was registered as unaffiliated, which was the legal term in our state for independent. When I had moved to Utah, there was no party registration—everyone was unaffiliated. However, shortly thereafter, the state legislature had instituted party affiliation boxes on voter registration forms. Then, the Republican Party closed their primary elections and forced voters to register as Republicans if they wished to participate. Republican precinct chairs visited homes and informed voters that, from now on, they needed to register as a Republican in order to vote in a GOP primary election. My wife and I declined to do so.

But the bigger issue was that I did not feel comfortable in the Republican Party in Utah. What little I knew of the party made me nervous about affiliating. I told the suitors who called me to run that I wasn't a Republican and that given how moderate I was, I didn't think I could win the Republican nomination.

They insisted that my moderate views would not be a problem that year. The Utah Education Association was planning a major push for educators to attend Republican caucuses and conventions and elect pro-education, moderate candidates. In other words, I would benefit from their efforts because I would be their preferred candidate.

Despite my reservations, I went ahead and filed to run. From the very beginning, my reservations only deepened. Immediately after the filing, the county Republican Party held an informational meeting for candidates. I was unable to attend and sent a representative, which turned out to be a wise choice. The party officials told all the candidates there they had to sign a pledge on the spot to support the platform. I wasn't there to do so and never did. It was offensive to me to demand that test of loyalty. Of course, they could not have enforced it. I was already filed as a candidate. But they could have worked against me. (Eventually, they did that anyway.)

The next objective was to win at the state legislative district meeting at the county convention where approximately one hundred delegates would decide who would become the nominee or at least go on to the primary. Only the top two vote getters would go on to the primary. And that would only occur if, in the final round of voting, the second-place candidate had received at least 40 percent of the vote. The primary was a distant thought that I began to realize I would not reach.

I began to make the rounds of delegates. Some of those elected were educators or those who the education community had encouraged to run as a delegate. They were sympathetic and promised support. But I quickly realized the education community had failed to elect a majority of delegates in my district. I was skeptical of their efforts after they publicly boasted of who they would elect. I feared that their braggadocio would animate the other side. And that is exactly what happened. Most of the delegates were the hard-line right-wing Republicans who were suspicious of public education, the government's role in much of anything, and any other social change. It was clear I was facing a largely hostile crowd.

Of course, I could have withdrawn from the race at that point and saved myself any embarrassment. But I felt that would have betrayed the education community who was counting on electing an ally rather than an opponent. Withdrawal in the midst of a campaign wasn't really something that matched my personality anyway. I stuck it out.

Or I could have told the delegates what they wanted to hear. I could have repeated back their anti-government, anti–public education views. In short, I could have joined their cause. But that was never an option. I told them I supported more public education funding and that we needed to raise taxes to bring that about. I explained that government could not solve all problems, but it could do much good. Perhaps the most disturbing heresy for them was the fact that I proclaimed that the Second Amendment was not absolute.

Admittedly, I was taking a kind of perverse pleasure in talking to these delegates who felt they needed to hear the different candidates out but squirmed nervously when someone challenged their orthodoxy.

The convention was as depressing as I suspected it would be. The officials would not tell the candidates how many votes each had won. They simply announced the two candidates who would go on to the next round (and eventually compete in a primary). They were the two who opposed public education support. Candidates were not allowed to watch the vote counting, but they could send a representative. Mine said he was watching the counting of ballots and then saw someone bring over ballots from another table that he didn't know existed. I left the convention feeling that the process potentially had been rigged because it was not transparent: I could only send one representative even though vote counting was going on in more than one location and no vote totals were announced. But I also knew that I had been in the wrong place anyway, particularly after the education community did not deliver.

At the same time, the experience confirmed a few points for me. One was that I did not belong in the Republican Party. I was far too moderate for these people. Another was that the caucus/convention system robbed the voters of the opportunity to participate. Such a system helps political parties limit participation to the most fervent and extreme activists. However, it was not beneficial to average voters who did not want to sit through a caucus or convention to have a say in their governance. Combined with a closed primary, the caucus/convention system was disastrous for voters since it would give them little say in who was nominated. And when that nomination process was tantamount to a general election, which is the case in many parts of the state of Utah, the average voter is completely excluded.

LESSONS LEARNED

Knowledge

My public engagement significantly expanded my understanding of my community. Before joining the recreation advisory commission, I knew nothing about the recreation activities and needs of my city. As a resident, I enjoyed city parks and the fitness center and my children joined city-sponsored sports teams, but I was unaware of how people used these resources and how they fit into the city's budget and planning. Nor was I aware of the deficiencies in those recreational needs. All of that knowledge I would not have acquired had I not become involved. And the same was true with the arts and education and a host of other issues I became acquainted with because of my involvement in city commissions, school board issues, and issues handled by the state legislature.

It also made me aware of the practicalities of government that academics often miss when posing theories or creating models. I began to question theoretical academic papers and articles on practical grounds. I wished the authors had used a broader set of methods to understand better what public officials really dealt with on a regular basis.

That practical knowledge also came from associating with people in the community who were not academics. Typically, I was the only academic on a city advisory commission or the school board committee. The delegates I interacted with or the average voters I met were nonacademics in nearly all cases. Gleaning their perspectives expanded my understanding of how ordinary voters thought about politics and interacted with government. Certainly, those I associated with could not qualify as a national random sample. But they constituted a cross section of local voters. They enlightened me in ways quite different from papers, articles, and books written by many academics.

Time

Public engagement is a costly investment. Running for office and serving in any capacity—appointed or elected—requires an expenditure of time. That means there is less time for other pursuits. As Ecclesiastes 3 says, there is a time and place for everything. Running for office was a major expenditure of time that I could not afford while I was still struggling to get tenure and gain promotion as well as helping raise young children. When our children were young, my involvement matched that stage in my life. Once I had been promoted to full professor and the children were grown (or nearly so), I was able to devote far more time to political activities.

Engagement with the community could be viewed as robbing time from the task of earning tenure and promotion. Even for those who have tenure or are full professors, such involvement can be viewed as a distraction from time spent on researching and writing articles and/or books or preparing for classes. Undoubtedly, it is time not devoted specifically to those tasks.

Yet, as mentioned in chapter 2, those who engage in politics or the life of the community generally find a connection with their teaching and perhaps research. They find the involvement broadens their perspective about how politics works. They are experiencing politics firsthand rather than just reading about it from academic sources. It can enrich the content of lectures as students gain real-world insights from their professor that enhance the textual materials.

During my quest for full professor, I published extensively. By the time I was promoted to full professor, I had written seven journal articles or book chapters and three books (one coauthored) and had compiled an edited volume. I continued to publish vigorously following that promotion. But I reached a point a few years after achieving full professor when I determined that I could cut back on the number of books I was writing (not stop writing) and use what I had learned to help my community.

The question of time is one each person must answer on their own. The timing is right for one person when it may not be for another. But the commitment to giving back to our communities should remain and be expressed during most of our lives in some form.

One and Done

Losing an election is a painful experience. Of the eight elections I have run in (five for political party office and three for government office), I have lost half. That is not bad for a batting average, but it is not the mark of a successful political career.

Yet it is critical not to stop attempting to make a difference when you lose. Prominent politicians provide encouragement. Ronald Reagan won the presidency on his third try. Similarly, Joe Biden ran three times before winning. Both were past typical retirement age, particularly Biden, but they persisted when others would have given up.

During his mayoral campaign, I met a successful businessman who ultimately lost his race. He had come from a poor background and built a thriving business. He had become wealthy and well-respected in the community. Now, he wanted to give back to the community. But he lost the election. When I encouraged him to use the experience to plan to run again in the future, he dismissed my idea. He told me he had decided that if he did not win that race, he would get out of politics. I was disappointed but not unfamiliar with the sentiment.

Pulling out of the process because of one loss, one setback, does call into question the motivation of the individual in terms of community service. Yet, it may be the individual feels that he or she has been rejected on a personal basis and that trying again would only compound that rejection. Of course, that is not the case. Voters typically have no intent of rejecting a candidate personally, except, perhaps, at the presidential level. Rather, they disagree with what the candidate is offering in terms of policy direction. Or the other candidate simply is more popular, which is not to say the losing candidate necessarily is unpopular. Or, as is true in partisan elections, party matters.

Similarly, failure to achieve a certain goal is not necessarily an excuse for no longer attempting to make a difference or even reaching that specific objective.

After three defeats, I decided that being a candidate may not be for me. But I could still make a difference.

One of my department colleagues pointed that out to me recently. He had just lost a race for city council and was wondering what to do next. He told me that I had succeeded in affecting the community and the state without actually serving in a public office. He was correct. I had found ways to serve without winning elective office.

What Is Winning?

However, what is winning? Undoubtedly, the average person looking at electoral politics would say that it is getting at least one more vote than the opposition candidate. And that would be true.

To me, I won by gaining the experience of running for office. I won by looking beyond my own myopia. I saw other people's problems and realized that they needed help to solve those problems. They looked to their representative to do that for them. Even though I did not become that representative, by campaigning to fulfill that role I thought about how I would serve them. I won by not being satisfied to stay on the sidelines while battles were waged. Instead, I fought to effect change. I joined the fray.

In doing so, I sent a message to others. Some of my students knew I was running or had run. They saw a professor who was not content to talk about and study governance, behavior, public policy, and so on, but was willing to participate in a greater role than voting or donating to someone else's campaign. I hope that motivated them to do so as well.

Yes, taking power to effect change through a public office is important. And I attempted to do just that. Yet, there are other "wins" in the process that should be recognized as well.

Conclusion: Overcoming the Barriers to Engagement

When Paul Wellstone ran for the US Senate for the first time, a former Minnesota governor advised him: "I know you are a professor and will be tempted to talk about all kinds of issues. Don't! Go into cafes, and listen to people, and then make it simple."[1]

This scenario may be similar to what political scientists feel will happen if they became engaged in practical politics. The complex will have to be made simple. The knowledge of the professor will be discounted in favor of the "wisdom of the masses."

The advice Wellstone received was wise. But it doesn't mean he did not have something meaningful to contribute himself, including drawing from his experience as a political science professor. Wellstone, like other professors, can bring the ability to communicate with those less well versed in a particular subject. After all, that is exactly what a political science professor does while teaching. In addition, political scientists can apply their own research and the research of others in practical environments. Even when they are handling unfamiliar topics and problems, such as public budgeting or zoning laws, professors can employ their analytical skills to arrive at well-researched and reasoned solutions.

Academics may fear practical politics because of the intellectual distance between them and voters. There is no question that an academic running for office or dealing with constituents in a public office needs to bridge that gap. That requires listening to and understanding voters' concerns. But voters also respect academics. Certainly, they don't want to be talked down to. They do appreciate when someone values their perspectives, however they also understand that they often lack knowledge of the issue and want the problem to be dealt with by someone who has that knowledge.

Humility is vital for the academic to succeed in the world of practical politics. At the same time, the professor should not discount his or her ability to make a difference in that world, and even that their contribution can be valuable. The balance may be difficult, but it is achievable.

Understandably, there are issues political scientists who desire to be engaged civically must confront, and yet there are benefits that accrue from involvement. Some changes will also need to occur in how colleges and universities address civic involvement by faculty, including by political scientists. Those topics are discussed next.

FACULTY ISSUES FOR CIVIC ENGAGEMENT

Student Involvement and Interaction

Political science majors often seek opportunities to apply their interest in politics and the community in real-world settings. These come in the form of internships and volunteering. Faculty who are civically engaged themselves, particularly in political organizations or campaigns, can utilize a ready supply of students who are interested in being involved, particularly with a faculty member they are familiar with. But faculty need to be careful.

How to handle student involvement can be a tricky matter for political scientists who are civically engaged. This is particularly true for those who run electoral campaigns, but it also is true for those who are passionately involved in their own causes. Students may be sincerely interested in the same cause as the professor or genuinely support the professor's election. However, there may be other motives, which could be implicit and perhaps not even well formed in the students' minds. The desire to please to get the professor's praise and reward would not be an uncommon incentive for aiding the professor. Or, more ominously, the student may worry that the lack of support for the professor's causes may result in subtle forms of punishment.

Some of the political scientists featured in chapter 2 explain how they address this issue. One approach is a direct one: telling students there is no connection between involvement in the professor's campaigns and success in the class. Thomas Ellington recounts that he has been explicit with students that they do not need to work for his campaigns or agree with them to do well in the class: "I always am aware of the power dynamic between me and my students."[2]

Another tactic is to dissuade student involvement in the professor's particular activity. Thomas Volgy, who ran for office seven times (three times for the city council, twice for mayor, and twice for the US House), says he never recruited students to work on his campaigns and specifically discouraged students in his classes from being involved with him. Similarly, Glen Duerr set a policy of not including students in his campaign who were in his classes. That policy was easier for him because he lives thirty minutes away from the campus and few students are in his city. He also adds that he avoids any discussion of his campaign in class during the election period.[3]

Similarly, when I was a party chair working with local candidates, I also taught a course titled American Political Parties and required students to become involved in a campaign during the semester and write periodic reports on their activity. But I did not want to know which students were working on campaigns of candidates I was working with. Nor did I want to know what was going on in opposing campaigns or have those candidates wonder if I did. To avoid the conflict of interest, I asked a colleague to read and grade those reports. He willingly obliged, which kept me away from any knowledge of what was occurring within any candidate's campaign through student reports. I was grateful to him for serving in that role during that period.

Yet, the issue is broader than simply campaign involvement. Professors can exercise influence over students in terms of initial political direction. How to temper that influence to avoid it being self-serving or reinforcing of the professor's partisan or ideological preferences is a question political science faculty continually must pose. Ian Brodie, who is self-admittedly highly partisan, drew a line in terms of stimulating student involvement, explaining that he encouraged students who wanted to get involved in politics but never tried to move them in a particular direction unless they already expressed interest in doing so.[4]

Professors need not shy away from expressing personal political views in class, particularly when queried by students. The question is how to make students feel respected even if they know you don't agree with them on certain issues because they view your extra-academic political activity. Shane Nordyke says she hopes that "when students see my advocacy for policy positions in my role, they see it as someone engaging on issues I care about and are inspired to do the same for things they are interested in."[5] But those "things they are interested in" may be in opposition to what the professor is advocating.

Again, even though I was intimately involved in partisan activities at various points in my career, I talked with students about getting involved in my party only after they had expressed interest in doing so. Most students wanted to get involved with other parties or candidates I was not affiliated with. So, I encouraged them and attempted to facilitate that involvement through my contacts with politicians in other parties.

Also, I invited various politicians and party leaders to speak to my classes. To demonstrate my neutrality, these speakers were balanced throughout a semester, which means I often invited people I disagreed with politically—sometimes strongly. But I did not feel it was appropriate for me to use the forum of a classroom to skew the message in the direction of my personal views. The result was that students often gravitated to a speaker who I disagreed with, asking them questions afterward, inquiring how they could be involved, and sometimes asking me to supply them with contact information so they could follow up. I always and willingly obliged them. If they could find a path to engagement through this person, and that participation jelled with their own particular beliefs, I was delighted to facilitate that.

Many times, I have met former students in various political settings such as conventions, debates, political fairs, and the like where they were working with politicians whose views I opposed. Often, they thanked me for helping them get involved. Sometimes they knew I believed differently and other times they may not have, but they were grateful I had helped them. My goal was not to indoctrinate; it was to facilitate their engagement in a way that they were comfortable with, even if that contrasted with my own views.

Academic Neutrality

An issue related to neutrality in encouraging student involvement and engaging in the classroom is the image of academic neutrality—in the discipline and in the public eye. Can academics be viewed as academics while also serving as policy makers or even simply becoming involved in the policy-making process? Can our research or analysis be accepted as legitimate if we are viewed by our colleagues or by the public generally as politically active in a partisan manner or at the least as favoring a particular political agenda?

As a right-leaning academic, Keith Whittington admits he worries about that. He understands that, simultaneously, he is making scholarly arguments while also advocating in other settings. However, he asserts he is not unduly blending the two. "If I thought my scholarship or my teaching was being 'infected' by my advocacy interests, I would definitely think that something had gone wrong. The difficulty, from my perspective, is how to know when that has happened."[6]

Shane Nordyke, who serves on a local school board, worries about that as well. She suggests that a political scientist contemplating engagement in public office consider how she or he will separate the political identity from the professional one. "Even in a non-partisan office, our positions on particular policies flag us as having particular political preferences."[7]

Charles Kupchan also experienced that dilemma, particularly when he took on the role of academic while advising policy makers. He related that after serving in the Clinton administration, he wrote a *Washington Post* op-ed critical of the administration's policy on expanding NATO. He talked with a high-ranking administration official who, he related, "said something 'like you know what's going on here—we thought you were on the team.'" He responded that it was his role as an expert to speak up. As a consequence, he concluded that when he was not in a government position, he would not go to meetings or attempt to get privileged information from policy makers because he wanted to preserve his independence.[8]

There may not be an easy solution to this dilemma. Partisans outside academe may misunderstand the scholarly role of an academic who engages in practical politics, just as academics may disdain the political role of a colleague or member of the discipline. However, a political scientist who engages politically will have to face the reality that criticism will come from various quarters. Frankly, it comes with the territory of political engagement.

However, the cost may be smaller than we think. As we have seen from these cases, some of the most respected members of the discipline are politically engaged. They run for office, serve in office, and work in appointive positions but also retain their identity as academics and are active in the discipline. These cases are presented as models of the ability to be both politically and professionally active.

Timing

The main task of a junior faculty member who wishes to remain employed, particularly at the current institution, is to gain tenure. And, at most higher education institutions, that process places community service/civic engagement below teaching and scholarship, as well it should. Timing in one's career becomes an important criterion in deciding whether to engage civically, particularly in an institution where civic engagement by faculty is not highly valued. Michael Munger advises political science professors contemplating civic engagement to wait until after tenure before undertaking activities beyond the university.[9] Indeed, that was the pattern for most of the faculty I highlight.

Others offer the same advice. Ted Morton added that a professor should make certain family is taken care of as well. Before getting involved, "take care of these priorities and financial security first," he recommends.[10]

That is not to say that a political scientist could not play some role prior to the tenure decision. It does mean that extensive roles—such as running for office, serving in office, or starting a new nonprofit—may be best saved for a career point when there is more certainty about permanent status.

Sacrifice

Civic engagement is not without cost to other aspects of one's career. Scholarship may be diminished, perhaps even some university service. Some people have the capability to juggle multiple balls simultaneously and handle each of them well. But most of us sacrifice something in order to serve.

Again, the political scientists featured previously are examples of how a satisfactory career can be pursued while also being civically engaged. For some that means being widely recognized for their scholarship. For others, it means receiving teaching awards. Still others have served as academic administrators at various times. The sacrifice may be in the form of even more extensive preparation for class lectures. It may be an article not pursued or a book not written. It is more likely those projects are simply delayed rather than discarded.

Another element of sacrifice is removal from our comfort zone. As discussed earlier in this chapter, academics initially may feel they are in strange surroundings—ones where decisions need to be made, positions need to be taken, research is applied. For example, Glen Duerr confesses that he is "fairly introverted. Yet, I take it as a major responsibility to serve the people well and to utilize my academic skills and public policy analysis training for the betterment of the city."[11]

Another point of sacrifice is public criticism. Campaigns and public service have become blood sport activities for many people, particularly in the age of social media. Glen Duerr recounts that it "is not fun being negatively described by some people in front of public audiences" or to be the subject of "occasional negative phone calls, emails, and social media posts."[12]

INDIVIDUAL BENEFITS OF ENGAGEMENT

While there are costs to practical involvement and issues to be resolved by each individual, they can be outweighed by the benefits. They apply to the faculty member but also to students, the institution, and the community. Obviously, the outcome of this cost-benefit analysis will depend on the situation of the individual. But I want to state what they are, particularly for the professor who may consider only costs.

Networks

Networking with other academics is strongly encouraged within the profession. We accomplish this not only through participation in panels at academic conferences and workshops but also through graduate school connections, joint authorship or editing, section activity, and the like. Such networking aids faculty members in various ways, including mentoring, research collaboration, publication opportunities, and pedagogical sharing.

Obviously, students also benefit indirectly when professors are current in terms of theories, methods, and ongoing research. At times they can participate—either as graduates or undergraduates—in the research that springs from those networks in the form of joint projects. Some students benefit more directly from the traditional academic networks, particularly those who are PhD-bound and seeking connections for graduate school admission and collaboration with graduate faculty.

However, most students don't directly benefit from such networking. These are the students—the vast majority of those we come in contact with—who will pursue nonacademic careers. The networking they directly benefit from is the type that connects them with internships and career opportunities. That kind of networking is difficult for most academics. Yet, it is the type most needed by students.

Faculty who are civically engaged themselves are more likely to engage in that form of networking. They come to know government officials—local, state, or even federal interest-group representatives, candidates, political party leaders, political consultants, nonprofit organization leaders, and so on. They can refer students to these individuals. They can assist with competitive internships. They are more aware of job opportunities within politics.

There is a flip side to networking. If an academic is too closely associated with a particular group or political party and simultaneously hostile to opposing groups or parties, then the networking can be narrow. Even if association is typically to one group, it is important to maintain good relations with others of opposing parties to avoid damaging networks and limiting student opportunities.

Even though in my own political involvement I was heavily involved with party politics at various points, I still attempted to maintain cordiality with those who I disagreed with and even worked against. That took the form of sponsoring bipartisan panel discussions and inviting a broad array of politicos to guest speak in my classes. In addition, respectful discourse toward all helps preserve relationships even when there are strongly opposing views.

Having said that, I admit that there were some individuals who were on an opposing side who would not communicate with me and, therefore, I could not be of assistance to students regarding that politician. For example, I wrote a column for a Utah newspaper for several years. In several of my columns, I criticized the governor on various issues and matters. Even though there were other times I praised him for an action or stance he took, he focused primarily on the criticism and would not respond to me. (Although I later learned he was hostile to our department generally and not just me.) I was not always successful, but I sought civility across party lines for ethical reasons but also because I wanted to set an example for students and not constrict the available networks I could plug them into.

Impact on Scholarship

Political scientists who are politically engaged, as well as active scholars, can gain insights from their involvement that, in turn, can be applied to research. Peter Feaver says his government experience led to research strains he did not previously consider. For example, while in the White House, he worked on foreign policy strategy. Since then, he has devoted some of his research agenda to issues related to grand strategy.[13] Similarly, Jeffrey Berry at Tufts University says that his real-world experiences with nonprofits have "shaped the way I think about non-profits" and that what he writes and teaches about nonprofits and his own engagement are "so intertwined over time that it is difficult to sort out causation."[14] John Portz describes his involvement as "an opportunity to take some of what I teach about and study and apply it in a way that contributes to our community."[15] Ian Brodie says his involvement has altered his scholarship by making him concentrate on the political context rather than on the simple narrow policy. As well, it has helped him see the importance of the human dimension in political decision-making rather than simply structural forces.[16]

Similarly, Kristi Andersen's foray into local electoral politics reshaped her thinking about the salience of partisanship in local elections as compared to socioeconomic status. She was recruited by Democratic Party officials and received support from the party in order to turn the town "blue" but found that party mattered much less at the local level of electoral politics than it did at other levels. She gained support from professionals and new residents, regardless of party, while losing the vote of long-time residents and working class voters, even though many were Democrats. "We convinced a number of non-native Republicans that we were well-qualified, agreed with them on important local issues, and were in fact more similar to them in background and outlook than were the traditional Republican elites."[17]

She also learned quickly how much voting matters to politicians. Facing limited time and resources, she and others on her slate focused on active voters and paid little attention to less frequent voters and none at all to those who were not registered. She termed unregistered voters as "effectively non-people" who were "effectively denied an opportunity to make their views known to the candidates" because "they became categorized as non-participants and, therefore, people whom it was rational to ignore."[18] Her practical experience helped her comprehend the perspective of candidates as they approach voters.

For years I taught a course titled American Political Parties. However, I did not publish in that area. At least, not until I became involved in the formation of a minor party. Now, I understood firsthand the challenges third parties faced. I also began to consider the circumstances that might lead to a successful third-party venture, at least in terms of policy influence if not electoral victory. I studied more intensely the literature on third parties and decided there was a vacuum I could fill. That led to the idea of editing a volume of original work on contemporary minor parties in the United States, as I discussed earlier.

Impact on Teaching

Students are inclined to see the professor as well aware of the content of academic journals and monographs but not necessarily of the "real world" of politics. Professors may offer real-world examples of concepts, but they are most likely to be examples based on the experiences of others; less so their own experiences, because they simply lack them.

However, as several of the political scientists above noted, students are most interested in personal stories. When a professor can relate the concept to their own political experience, the student views them as a more complex individual rather than the academic stereotype. They can see that the professor understands what they are discussing both from an academic and a practical point of view. Also, they can explain when a textbook discussion does not relate to practical politics.

Others offered additional benefits. Michael Munger at Duke believes his civic engagement has helped him become a better teacher because his candidacies have made him "much better at framing arguments." Adam McGlynn, who is a professor at East Stroudsburg University as well as a local school board member, believes his dual role is good for his students. When first elected, he commented: "I believe this will really help my students," because he could provide real-world knowledge of the issues he discussed in his education policy courses.[19] As well, Marc Howard has offered students meaningful insights into the world of the criminal justice system and given some of them not only empathy but also the satisfaction of knowing they helped exonerate someone who had been unjustly incarcerated.[20]

Ted Morton "made a lot of new friends that I otherwise would never have met," he says, because of his public service. But the experience, he relates, also "gave me a more realistic understanding of the motives and behavior of elected officials."[21] He also says he has come to be less critical of politicians in the classroom since he became one: "I've concluded that it is easier to criticize this process [of compromising to create and maintain coalitions] from the sidelines than to do it in real time. . . . While I am still critical of decisions made by elected officials, I am a lot less self-righteous."[22]

This logic might argue for political science professors being drawn largely from practitioners. But that is not what I am suggesting. Rather, it is the combination of an understanding of the literature with practical experience that is most rewarding for students. Otherwise, students may be inundated with "war stories." Even though they may be interesting, they may not further the students' comprehension of concepts.

Personal experience as a supplement to the literature students are reading and discussing can be a rich resource, particularly whether there is a connection between what is being taught in the classroom or discussed in the book and what occurs in real-world politics. The professor with some personal experience can provide that complement and demonstrate those applications for students.

Teaching/Research Connections

So much of the learning academics engage in comes in the classroom or the library. But Kristi Andersen sees community engagement as an opportunity for academics to learn new subjects through service. It is an opportunity for "learning about new subjects: municipal law, daycare regulations, farmland protection grants, architecture and adaptive re-use of old buildings, environmental protection of water bodies—you name it!"[23]

In some cases, the connections between a political scientist's research and teaching and civic engagement are obvious. Peter Feaver's expertise in US foreign policy translated easily into his service on the White House National Security Council staff. Jeffrey Berry at Tufts teaches nonprofits and community activism but also is a leader of a nonprofit himself.

Much of the involvement described in previous chapters has involved local government. Yet, most areas of teaching and research in political science do not correspond to local government. Thomas Volgy's area was international relations, not state and local politics, even though he did serve in Tucson's local government. But he did coauthor a book on poverty among working classes in the United States that was suggested by his community service. And he enriched his teaching on foreign policy and international politics through examples of how elites make decisions.[24]

Impacting the Community

Clearly, civic involvement by political scientists can impact the community in which they live, locally or globally. Marc Howard's project has meant inmates are preparing themselves for a life outside prison. And the lives of many have been affected by the three individuals who his students have helped to exonerate and free.

Thomas Volgy ran for mayor of Tucson, Arizona, on the key issue of campaign finance reform. While mayor, he instituted the city's novel campaign finance system. Candidates could receive public matching funds but only if they met stringent requirements on spending limits. The reform dramatically reduced the amount of money spent on local elections.[25]

Regardless of the avenue the political scientist takes to become civically engaged, the act of involvement can reduce the distance between academics and our neighbors. Academics easily can become isolated from the broader community. We can limit our associations to those who work at the university, who hold doctoral degrees, and who share our views on a host of issues. Simultaneously, we can become somewhat condescending toward others who do not share our educational background or interests. That distance can lead to misunderstanding and some degree of hostility toward academics.

It is easy to forget that the higher educational institutions where we work operate largely through the sustenance provided by that larger community. Tax dollars are one form of support. Another is donations to the institution. And yet another is the very act of community members sending their children to the college or university.

Civic engagement by political scientists can help bridge the gaps between the ivory towers and the communities in which academics live. According to Kristi Andersen, community involvement is a great opportunity to develop friendships with others in the community.[26] Thomas Ellington relates that his civic service has profoundly impacted his connection with his community: "I have gotten to know people I probably would have never met otherwise. . . . I love this place and my neighbors in a way that I don't think I could have imagined if I had not made a commitment to public service. I hope that my community is better because of the work I have done, but I absolutely know that I am better because of my involvement with my community."[27]

INSTITUTIONAL CHANGE

The choice of whether or not to engage in the larger community beyond campus is shaped to a large degree by the institution's approach to civic engagement. Some colleges and universities have taken steps to facilitate extra-academic involvement. However, others have been slower to adopt such changes. Here are specific actions institutions can take to make civic engagement easier for their faculty, including political scientists.

Stopping the Tenure Clock

Many of those political scientists who were interviewed for this book advised junior faculty to concentrate on meeting established tenure requirements and waiting until their post-tenure career to become involved in practical engagement areas such as government service, nonprofit leadership, or electoral campaigns. However, in some cases, that involvement can be useful to the academic and the institution pre-tenure. An offer to serve in a government role may not come later and the opportunity is lost. Exposure to practical politics at that point may help inform the junior faculty's research and teaching in ways that would benefit their careers. It also might aid them in developing networks that would be useful for students.

Institutions should adopt pre-tenure policies that include stopping the tenure clock while the faculty member is on unpaid leave in an area of service that would enhance their teaching and research. Adopting a policy rather than leaving it to individual negotiation would signal to junior faculty that they are not discouraged from accepting offers to leave academe for a year or two. In addition, a policy reduces the possibility of selectivity based on prejudice. Without a policy, administration leaders may pick and choose who they will allow to leave based on their own political biases.

It is true that the consequence may be the faculty member leaves academe entirely. Several of our cases in chapter 1 did exactly that. However, if the leave is unpaid, there is not a significant financial cost to the university. And stopping the tenure clock encourages the individual to come back, while not doing so may discourage a return.

Recognizing Civic Engagement

Another tool for encouraging public service beyond the campus is to recognize it. Departments, colleges, and universities recognize achievements in scholarship and teaching, but such acknowledgment of excellence in civic engagement is much less common. Kristi Andersen suggests that colleges and universities do a better job of crediting faculty who are involved in community service: "Colleges and universities can recognize faculty members in their internal and external communications ('Professor X has been recognized by the United Way . . .')."[28]

This could be done in a couple of ways at least. One is, as she suggested, a university- or college-wide announcement highlighting some public service by a faculty member. This could be accomplished through a campus newsletter or a presidential or dean speech or an email from a high administrator that is distributed across the campus.

Another is to create awards for civic engagement, much as is done for teaching and scholarship. These awards should recognize exemplary public service by a faculty member such as the creation or leadership of a nonprofit organization, longtime membership on the board of a local charitable organization, service in governmental office, and so on. Political science departments should do this. But they should be given at college or university levels as well.

Counting Public Service as University Service

One of the issues faced by institutions is whether civic engagement can be substituted for other activities. Should civic engagement "count" as a substitute for the prime responsibilities of an academic, that is, teaching, research, and service to the institution? This is not an abstract debate. It is one that institutions must address as they consider files where a political scientist is an activist—perhaps as a candidate, an elected official, or a leader or prominent member of an interest group.

There is not an easy solution. Substitution could be granted within the realm of "service." Rather than narrowing that term to service within the institution or within the discipline, it could be expanded to include forms of service to the community as well. Most faculty still will choose university or college service. Even those who seek to use community service will not be completely absolved from responsibility for institutional service.

Ian Brodie explains that the University of Calgary is clear in emphasizing scholarship and teaching. But he did assume his outside referees for his tenure and promotion cases took into consideration his political involvement.[29] Peter Feaver says he is glad that his department faculty at Duke have not had public involvement counted against them. It does not, however, serve as a substitute for teaching and research, and it does not make tenure-worthy a case that is lacking in scholarship and teaching.

Colleges and universities could offer more encouragement for public service by counting it as equivalent to service within the university. That would require specific mention of public service within the tenure document section regarding service. And provisions could be added that measure that service, such as letters from nonacademic colleagues of the political scientist in a governmental position or a nonprofit organization leadership role.

Too few university tenure policies mention service beyond the community. Service is defined more narrowly. For example, Colby College's policy explains that "service to the candidate's department/program, to the College, and to the discipline should be taken into account." Similarly, Williams College lists particular activities, but all of them are service to the institution with no mention of service beyond it.[30] Middlebury College includes the traditional list of service activities within the college but then adds "other activities that benefit Middlebury College," while Loyola Marymount University recognizes "community services that are consistent with LMU's mission." Some, such as Vanderbilt, may mention "service through University outreach" in vague terms but not specifically mention public service.[31]

Others specify forms of service but do not mention government service. For example, the Idaho State University College of Arts and Letters' tenure policies regarding community service include speaking to community groups, serving on organization boards, and analyzing data for government or private groups, but it does not list service in government. It does add that such activities are not limited to those listed.[32] However, a specific mention of government or public service would be useful to communicate that such activity matters to the university.

Some have included specific mention of public service as a possible criterion for tenure and advancement. For example, the University of California, Santa Barbara tenure policies include acknowledgment of such service: "Recognition . . . should also be accorded for able service to the community, state, or nation." The College of Liberal Arts and Sciences at the University of Kansas specifically mentions public service in its tenure policies: "The form of accepted and valued service varies greatly among the disciplines represented in the College, and may include scholarly service to the discipline or profession, service within the University, and public service at the local, state, national, or international level."[33]

Civic Engagement should be explicitly included as a form of service, although it need not be a requisite form of service. For example, Stetson University faculty standards for service include specific mentions of both campus engagement and civic engagement: "While not required, community service contributions included as evidence for tenure and promotion should bear a relationship to the candidate's field of expertise and the mission of the University." Similarly, the University of Texas at Austin also includes in its tenure policies a specific section on "Service to the University and to the Nation, State, and Community." One of the types of service discussed there is "community-engaged service," although it does not specify what that might be.[34]

One suggestion is that institutions offer course reductions as incentives for those who take on substantive service roles outside academe. That may be a step too far for many institutions. Yet, it may redound to the institution's benefit if a faculty member becomes an important public official in a small town or city where positive town-gown relations are vital and the administration could use an advocate within the local government.

Running for office is a place where course reductions could be particularly useful. Policies that require unpaid leaves naturally dampen enthusiasm for launching a campaign for public office. However, a course reduction arrangement would be helpful. Or at the minimum a course transfer agreement that allows the faculty member to take a course reduction while running a campaign that requires more than part-time campaigning.

It is critical, however, that these policies become explicit and publicized rather than simply negotiable. If the faculty member knows the institution will offer accommodation for a run for office, he or she will be more inclined to consider a run and initiate the process of notification of administrators. Without that knowledge, they may be discouraged.

Administrators may fear that these changes would lead to movement away from university service in various forms and toward public service. The reality is that few faculty members would use public service as a substitute for university service. Even fewer would do so for very long. It is unlikely there would be a plethora of political scientists using public service in lieu of internal university or college service, but those who do would benefit the faculty, students, the institution, and the community.

Accommodation

If the general consensus of the discipline or the higher educational institution is that civic engagement is simply an extra that the faculty member could pursue on their own time but otherwise is a distraction, then accommodation will be rare. But, as has been shown, there exist clear benefits of civic involvement for the institution itself. Therefore, accommodation should be made for those who seek to serve civically. Policies should reflect an appreciation for faculty engagement.

Again, universities and colleges often make accommodations in certain cases. But that approach does not encourage faculty, who do not know what the institution's reaction will be to their request for accommodation. Rather, the ability to serve, indeed the encouragement to serve, should be explicit in university policies. As Thomas Ellington notes, "the university is meant to be an institution that contributes to the common good of society, and practical involvement is one way that faculty members can model active citizenship."[35]

Some institutions view public engagement positively and act accordingly. For example, Charles Kupchan was fortunate in that Georgetown was accommodating to his public service. When he took a position with the Obama administration in 2014, he was automatically granted a two-year leave. Similarly, the University of Calgary accommodated Ian Brodie's and Ted Morton's government service opportunities.[36]

The college or university should encourage civic engagement, but it must do so in a nonpartisan way. Lack of transparency raises the prospect of the accusation of bias, such as when one faculty member of one political party receives accommodation when another doesn't. When policies are clear and accommodation is routine, and not a gift of the university, the institution avoids the appearance of bias.

Opposition Advocacy

Higher education institutions ideally operate in a politically neutral setting where faculty can express varying political views and become involved in divergent causes without fear of sanction or censure. Of course, the reality is quite different. Some private institutions are sponsored by churches with distinctive worldviews and little tolerance for those who oppose the sponsoring institution's political positions.

Nor are public colleges and universities immune to political pressure. State legislatures may seek to withdraw funding or in some other way punish an institution whose faculty member has offended legislators. Some legislators may make funding contingent on faculty silence on issues vital to the legislature. University administrators may be hesitant to defend academic freedom in an atmosphere ripe for retribution.

As a result of the less-than-ideal political settings in which higher education often operates, faculty may be reluctant to speak out on issues or become involved in political organizations, particularly if such advocacy conflicts with prevailing local views or the institution's emphases. That is a powerful disincentive to civic involvement.

Thomas Volgy suggested that, "at a minimum, universities should assure that the economic well-being of their faculty is not at risk when they engage politically." That means they should not use termination or, less drastically but still disconcerting, the denial of promotion—or even threaten such an outcome—to punish those who engage.

But there is more that needs to be done. University administrators should offer explicit promises to faculty that, whatever their political involvement, their jobs or promotion or tenure opportunities will not be at risk. This may include educating state legislators about the costs to the institution and higher education generally in the state when professors feel constrained about participating fully in the political process, even when that participation may conflict with the state's preferences. For example, three University of Florida political science professors were slated to be paid expert witnesses in a case over voting rights that pitted them against the state's position. As a consequence, the University of Florida decided the faculty could not be paid as expert witnesses when testifying against the state.[37] This kind of intimidation is exactly what needs to change.

Collegial Acceptance

Finally, one of the most difficult changes will not be institutional, but attitudinal—relying, in other words, on whether the culture of the department will accept the decisions of some faculty to become civically engaged. That culture of acceptance or discouragement can make a difference in how individual faculty view their own potential involvement. It is rarely directly addressed in formal reviews. Rather, it is usually signaled informally in conversations with junior faculty.

Some departments have developed a culture of appreciating civic engagement. The University of South Dakota is one, as both Shane Nordyke and Julia Hellwege demonstrate. Another is Duke. According to Michael Munger, he was encouraged by colleagues in his electoral campaigns. David Price, who served for many years in Congress, continued to hold his faculty appointment while in Congress.

The presence of a culture does not mean that every faculty member will be civically engaged. Faculty should not feel compelled to be civically engaged—either by formal policy or by an academic culture. However, such culture does ensure that there is acceptance of those who are so engaged. Noelle Brigden, who started a nonprofit in El Salvador, found appreciation for her civic engagement within her department. Her department includes people with an array of methodological approaches, but she feels her colleagues value her contribution and provide a resource for her.[38]

The intent of this book is to help change that culture to aid future political science professors in convincing colleagues that civic involvement is beneficial and should not be detrimental to their careers. It will take more than one book, obviously. But hopefully the case will be made again and again until cultures change and political scientists can feel comfortable making the difference—both on and off campus—that we have the ability to make.

Notes

INTRODUCTION: ACADEMIC DISENGAGEMENT

1. Edward S. Corwin, "The Democratic Dogma and the Future of Political Science," *American Political Science Review* 23 (1929): 569–592.

2. Albert Somit and Joseph Tanenhaus, *The Development of American Political Science: From Burgess to Behavioralism* (New York: Irvington Publishers, 1982), 11–21.

3. Somit and Tanenhaus, *The Development of American Political Science*, 46–47.

4. See John Milton Cooper Jr., *Woodrow Wilson: A Biography* (New York: Knopf, 2009).

5. Frederick H. Jackson, *Simeon Eben Baldwin: Lawyer, Social Scientist, Statesman* (New York: King's Crown Press, 1955).

6. Noel Pugach, "Embarrassed Monarchist: Frank J. Goodnow and Constitutional Development in China, 1913–1915," *Pacific Historical Review* 42 (November 1973): 499–517; John T. Seaman Jr., *A Citizen of the World: The Life of James Bryce* (London: Tauris Academic Studies, 2006); Somit and Tanenhaus, *The Development of American Political Science*, 43.

7. Robert Cuff, "Harry Garfield, the Fuel Administration, and the Search for a Cooperative Order During World War I," *American Quarterly* 30 (Spring 1978): 39–53; Barry D. Karl, "Charles E. Merriam: An Introduction to the Man & His Papers," University of Chicago Archives, at http://storage.lib.uchicago.edu/pres/2011/pres2011 -0055.pdf (accessed December 21, 2021); Somit and Tanenhaus, *The Development of American Political Science*, 139–140.

8. "Emmette Redford: Elected APSA President 50 Years Ago," Department of Government, University of Texas, August 24, 2009, at https://sites.utexas.edu/government /emmette-redford-elected-apsa-president-50-years-ago/ (accessed December 30, 2021); Edmund Spevack, *Allied Control and German Freedom: American Political and Ideological Influences on the Framing of the West German Basic Law* (Munster: Lit Verlag, 2001).

9. Somit and Tanenhaus, *The Development of American Political Science*, 84.

10. See Richard F. Fenno, *Home Style: House Members in Their Districts* (Boston: Little, Brown, 1978).

11. For a discussion of this approach to political science, see Raymond Seidelman, "Political Scientists, Disenchanged Realists, and Disappearing Democrats," in *Discipline and History: Political Science in the United States*, ed. James Farr and Raymond Seidelman (Ann Arbor: University of Michigan Press, 1993), 311–325.

12. Somit and Tanenhaus, *The Development of American Political Science*, 64–74, 111.

13. See William Foote Whyte, "Instruction and Research: A Challenge to Political Scientists," *American Political Science Review* 37 (August 1943): 692–697.

14. See Edward S. Corwin, "The Democratic Dogma and the Future of Political Science," *American Political Science Review* 23 (August 1929): 569–592.

15. James Farr and Raymond Seidelman, eds., *Discipline and History: Political Science in the United States* (Ann Arbor: University of Michigan Press, 1993), 249.

16. Somit and Tanenhaus, *The Development of American Political Science*, 176–180.

17. For a sample of the debate, see Heinz Eulau, ed., *Behavioralism in Political Science* (New York: Atherton, 1969); Austin Ranney, ed., *Essays in the Behavioral Study of Politics* (Urbana: University of Illinois Press, 1962); Charles A. McCoy and John Playford, *Apolitical Politics: A Critique of Behavioralism* (New York: Crowell, 1967); Bernard Crick, *The American Science of Politics: Its Origins and Consequences* (Berkeley: University of California Press, 1959).

18. Ralph Ketcham, *Public-Spirited Citizenship: Leadership and Good Government in the United States* (New Brunswick, NJ: Transaction Publishers, 2015), 101.

19. "The 2020 Awards," *Political Science Today*, March 17, 2021, at https://www.cambridge.org/core/journals/political-science-today/article/2020-apsa-awards/99CD7AFC5F08C0762834FAAFF62250F9 (accessed December 21, 2021).

20. Keith Whittington, "The Intellectual Freedom That Made Public Colleges Great Is Under Threat," *Washington Post*, December 15, 2021, at https://www.washingtonpost.com/outlook/2021/12/15/academic-freedom-crt-public-universities/ (accessed December 21, 2021).

CHAPTER 1. ENGAGEMENT AS A PRACTITIONER

1. Leslie Davis and Richard Fry, "College Faculty Have Become More Racially and Ethnically Diverse, But Remain Far Less So Than Students," *Pew Research Center*, July 31, 2019, at https:/ /www.pewresearch.org/fact-tank/2019/07/31/us-college-faculty-student-diversity/ (accessed August 4, 2022); Bridget Turner Kelly, "Though More Women Are on College Campuses, Climbing the Professor Ladder Remains a Challenge," *Brookings*, March 29, 2019, at https://www.brookings.edu/blog/brown-center-chalkboard/2019/03/29/though-more-women-are-on-college-campuses-climbing-the-professor-ladder-remains-a-challenge/#:~:text=Women%20made%20up%2031%20percent%20of%20full-time%20faculty,earning%20college%20degrees%20has%20tripled%20during%20this%20period (accessed August 4, 2022).

2. Dawn Langan Teele and Kathleen Thelen, "Gender in the Journals: Publication Patterns in Political Science," *PS: Political Science & Politics* 50 (April 2017): 433–447; Daniel Maliniak, et al., "The Gender Gap in International Relations," *International Organization* 67 (October 2013): 889–922; Vicki Hesli Claypool and Carol Merson, "Does Diversity Matter? Evidence from a Survey of Political Science Faculty," *Politics, Groups, and Identities* 4 (2016): 483–498; Beth McMurrie, "Data Support Charges of Gender Bias in Political Science," *Chronicle of Higher Education*, August 20, 2013, A17.

3. For an exhaustive biographical treatment of Moynihan, see Godfrey Hodgson,

The Gentleman from New York: Daniel Patrick Moynihan (New York: Houghton Mifflin, 2000). See also David E. Rosenbaum, "Moynihan to Take a Post at Syracuse School of Public Affairs," *New York Times*, December 12, 2000, B2; "Senator Daniel Patrick Moynihan: There's a Story to Be Written Here," Wilson Center, January 1, 2001, at https://www.wilsoncenter.org/article/senator-daniel-patrick-moynihan-theres-story -to-be-written-here (accessed December 15, 2021).

4. Daniel Patrick Moynihan and James Q. Wilson, "Patronage in New York State, 1955–1959," *American Political Science Review* 58 (June 1964): 286–301; Nathan Glazer and Daniel Patrick Moynihan, *Beyond the Melting Pot: The Negroes, Puerto Ricans, Jews, Italians, and Irish of New York City* (Cambridge, MA: MIT Press and Harvard University Press), 1963.

5. For a discussion of his academic appointments at Wesleyan and Harvard in between the Johnson and Nixon administration service, see Hodgson, *The Gentleman from New York*, 121–144.

6. "Hubert H. Humphrey Award," American Political Science Association, at https://www.apsanet.org/PROGRAMS/APSA-Awards/Hubert-H-Humphrey-Award (accessed December 15, 2021).

7. "Daniel Patrick Moynihan: Late a Senator from New York Memorial Addresses and Other Tributes in the Congress of the United States," 108th Congress, First Session, Washington, DC: US Government Printing Office, 2003.

8. Dudley Clendinen, "East, a Senator from Carolina, a Suicide at 55," *New York Times*, June 30, 1986, 1.

9. See, for example, John P. East, "The Conservative Mission," *Modern Age* 25 (Fall 1981): 338–344; John P. East, "The American Conservative Movement of the 1980s: Are Traditional and Libertarian Dimensions Compatible?" *Modern Age* 24 (Winter 1980): 34–38. See also, John P. East, "Pragmatism and Behavioralism," *Political Research Quarterly*, December 1, 1968, at https://doi.org/10.1177%2F106591296802100405 (accessed December 2, 2021).

10. Martha Waggoner, "North Carolina's Junior Senator Commits Suicide, Police Say," *Associated Press*, June 29, 1986, at https://apnews.com/article/3068cacfc00e4e139 d79968a5c167bc7 (accessed December 2, 2021).

11. Waggoner, "North Carolina's Junior Senator Commits Suicide, Police Say."

12. "Funderburk East's Choice for Senate," *Kannapolis Daily Independent*, October 11, 1985, 24.

13. Clendinen, "East, a Senator from Carolina, a Suicide at 55," 1; Waggoner, "North Carolina's Junior Senator Commits Suicide, Police Say."

14. For a treatment of the Wellstone 1990 campaign, see Dennis J. McGrath and Dane Smith, *Professor Wellstone Goes to Washington* (Minneapolis: University of Minnesota Press, 1995).

15. Bill Lofy, *Paul Wellstone: The Life of a Passionate Progressive* (Ann Arbor: University of Michigan Press, 2005), 23–28.

16. Paul Wellstone, *How the Rural Poor Got Power: Narrative of a Grass-Roots Organizer* (Minneapolis: University of Minnesota Press, 1978). For a critical review, see

W. B. Stouffer, review of "Paul Wellstone, *How the Rural Poor Got Power: Narrative of a Grass-Roots Organizer,*" *Social Science Quarterly* 50 (September 1979): 346–347.

17. Senator Paul Wellstone, *The Conscience of a Liberal* (Minneapolis: University of Minnesota Press, 2002), 5.

18. McGrath and Smith, *Professor Wellstone Goes to Washington*, 33–34.

19. Lofy, *Paul Wellstone*, 36–38; Wellstone, *The Conscience of a Liberal*, 5–7.

20. Lofy, *Paul Wellstone*, 40–42.

21. Lofy, 55–61.

22. Wellstone, *The Conscience of a Liberal*, 4.

23. Wellstone, 5.

24. Wellstone, 8.

25. John Geddes, "The Life and Times of Jack Layton," *Maclean's*, June 17, 2011, at https://www.macleans.ca/news/canada/the-making-of-jack-layton/ (accessed June 26, 2022).

26. Geddes, "The Life and Times of Jack Layton."

27. Jack Layton, *Speaking Louder: Ideas That Work for Canadians* (Toronto: McClelland and Stewart, 2006), 38.

28. Layton, *Speaking Louder*, 39–40.

29. Jack Layton, *Homelessness: The Making and Unmaking of a Crisis* (Toronto: Penguin Canada, 2008); Layton, *Speaking Louder.*

30. "Timeline: Jack Layton's Life," *Global News*, August 22, 2011, at https://globalnews.ca/news/146960/timeline-jack-laytons-life/ (accessed January 26, 2022).

31. "David E. Price: Full Biography," at https://price.house.gov/about (accessed January 20, 2022).

32. David E. Price, *The Congressional Experience: An Institution Transformed*, 4th ed. (New York: Routledge, 2020); David E. Price, "Intensified Partisanship in Congress: Institutional Effects," in *Governing in a Polarized Age: Essays on Elections, Parties, and Political Representation in Honor of David Mayhew*, ed. Alan S. Gerber and Eric Schickler (New York: Cambridge University Press, 2016), 371–376; David E. Price, "Reflections on Congressional Government at 120 and Congress at 216," *PS: Political Science & Politics* 39 (April 2006): 231–235; David E. Price, "Congressional-Executive Balance in an Era of Congressional Dysfunction," *PS: Political Science & Politics* 49 (April 2016): 485–489.

33. Dawn Baumgartner Vaughan and Dan Kane, "Democrat David Price Will Retire After More Than 30 Years Representing NC in Congress," *News & Observer*, October 18, 2021, at https://www.newsobserver.com/news/politics-government/article255057582.html (accessed January 20, 2022); Mark Green and Kenneth Wollack, "The House's Decade of Democracy Partnerships," *The Hill*, December 1, 2015, at https://thehill.com/blogs/pundits-blog/international/261586-the-houses-decade-of-democracy-partnerships (accessed January 20, 2022).

34. Steve Hartsoe, "Rep. David Price: We're in a Perilous Moment," *Duke Today*, January 19, 2022, at https://today.duke.edu/2022/01/rep-david-price-were-perilous-moment (accessed January 20, 2022).

35. Aaron Navarro, "Two Longtime House Democrats Announce Retirement," CBS News, October 18, 2021, at https://news.yahoo.com/two-longtime-house-democrats-announce-224910141.html?fr=sycsrp_catchall (accessed December 1, 2021).

36. E-mail correspondence with author, January 22, 2022.

37. E-mail correspondence with author, January 22, 2022.

38. E-mail correspondence with author, January 22, 2002.

39. Walter Isaacson, *Kissinger: A Biography* (New York: Simon & Schuster, 1992), 315.

40. Niall Ferguson, *Kissinger, 1923–1968: The Idealist* (New York: Penguin, 2015), 328.

41. Ferguson, *Kissinger, 1923–1968*, 328.

42. Ferguson, 329.

43. Ferguson, 386–389.

44. Ferguson, 791–797; Isaacson, *Kissinger*, 129–133.

45. Isaacson, *Kissinger*, 546–586.

46. Peter Collier, *Political Woman: The Big Little Life of Jeane Kirkpatrick* (New York: Encounter Books, 2012), 25–26, 48–54, 71–72.

47. "Dictatorships & Double Standards," *Commentary*, November 1979, at https://www.commentary.org/articles/ja"ne-kirkpatrick/dictatorships-double-standards/ (accessed December 17, 2021).

48. Collier, *Political Woman*, 25–26, 48–54, 71–72.

49. Tim Weiner, "Jeane Kirkpatrick, Reagan's Forceful Envoy, Dies," *New York Times*, December 9, 2006, A1.

50. Collier, *Political Woman*, 169–200.

51. See Ann Blackman, *Seasons of Her Life: A Biography of Madeleine Korbel Albright* (New York: Simon & Schuster, 1998).

52. Robert D. McFadden, "Madeleine Albright, First Woman to Serve as Secretary of State Dies at 84," *New York Times*, March 23, 2022, at https://www.nytimes.com/2022/03/23/us/madeleine-albright-dead.html (accessed April 25, 2022).

53. Charles P. Henry, *Ralph Bunche: Model Negro or American Other?* (New York: New York University Press, 1999), 31–39.

54. Brian Urquhart, *Ralph Bunche: An American Odyssey* (New York: W. W. Norton, 1993), 60–61, 93–94.

55. Urquhart, *Ralph Bunche*, 94–99.

56. Henry, *Ralph Bunche*, 120–131, 142–146.

57. Henry, 156–158.

58. Henry, 242.

59. "Stephane Dion," *The Canadian Encyclopedia*, at https://www.thecanadianencyclopedia.ca/en/article/stephane-dion/ (accessed December 29, 2021).

60. Stephane Dion, "The Quebec Challenge to Canadian Unity," *PS: Political Science and Politics* 26 (March 1993): 38–43.

61. See Stephane Dion, *Straight Talk: Speeches and Writings on Canadian Unity* (Montreal: McGill-Queen's University Press, 1999); "Investiture Speech as doctor

Honoris Causa of Professor Doctor D. Stephane Dion," University Carlos III of Madrid, November 13, 2002, at https://www.uc3m.es/ss/Satellite/UC3MInstitucional/en/TextoMixta/1371219411404/ (accessed December 29, 2021).

62. "Investiture Speech as Doctor Honoris Causa of Professor Doctor D. Stephane Dion"; Mike Cohen, "The Time Had Indeed Come for Stephane Dion to Leave Politics," *Suburban*, January 10, 2017, at https://www.thesuburban.com/blogs/cohen_confidential_with_mike_cohen/the-time-had-indeed-come-for-st-phane-dion-to/article_2b878254-d748-11e6-85ad-6bb536a1944b.html (accessed December 30, 2021).

63. Hon. Stephane Dion, Routine Proceedings, House of Commons, Canada, May 16, 1996, 2864, at https://www.ourcommons.ca/DocumentViewer/en/35-2/house/sitting-48/hansard#2864 (accessed December 27, 2021).

64. Canwest News Service, "Dion Positions Himself as Potential Kingmaker," Canada.com, November 26, 2006, at https://web.archive.org/web/20120213175651/http://www.canada.com/nationalpost/news/story.html?id=09fe377b-49bf-441b-9f23-6efd71abe000&k=50781 (accessed December 29, 2021).

65. Aaron Wherry, "The Redemption of Stephane Dion," *Maclean's*, November 4, 2015, at https://www.macleans.ca/politics/ottawa/the-redemption-of-stephane-dion/#gallery/the-trudeau-cabinet-annotated/slide-1 (accessed December 29, 2021).

66. "Most Admired Man and Woman," *Gallup*, at https://news.gallup.com/poll/1678/Most-Admired-Man-Woman.aspx (accessed March 23, 2022).

67. Condoleezza Rice, *Condoleezza Rice: A Memoir of My Extraordinary, Ordinary Family and Me* (New York: Delacorte Press, 2010), 203–206, 211; Glenn Kessler, *The Confidante: Condoleezza Rice and the Creation of the Bush Legacy* (New York: St. Martin's Press, 2007), 15.

68. Rice, *Condoleezza Rice*, 228–259.

69. Kessler, *The Confidante*, 15–19.

70. Kessler, 159–164; Mark Mazzetti, "Bush Aides Linked to Talks on Interrogations," *New York Times*, September 24, 2008, at https://www.nytimes.com/2008/09/25/washington/25detain.html (accessed March 30, 2022).

71. "Profile of Professor Tijjani Muhammad-Bande," United Nations, at https://www.un.org/pga/73/wp-content/uploads/sites/53/2019/04/Profile_Ambassador-Tijjani-Muhammad-Bande_Rev2.pdf (accessed March 5, 2022).

72. Khaled Yacoub Oweis, "Who Is Tijjani Muhammad-Bande, United Nations General Assembly President?" *National News*, January 11, 20202, at https://www.thenationalnews.com/world/who-is-tijjani-muhammad-bande-united-nations-general-assembly-president-1.962862 (accessed March 5, 2022); United Nations, "Put Human Rights at the Centre of Coronavirus Response Urges Muhammad-Bande," *UN News*, June 2, 2020, at https://news.un.org/en/story/2020/06/1065312 (accessed March 5, 2020); "Interview with H.E. Professor Tijjani Muhammad-Bande, President of the 74th Session of UN General Assembly," *All Africa*, September 15, 2020, at https://allafrica.com/stories/202009151056.html (accessed March 5, 2022).

73. See Tijjani Muhammad Bande and Shehu Shalihu Muhammad, "The Role of the Civil Service in Nigeria and the Challenges of Efficient Service Delivery," *African*

Administrative Studies 72 (2009): 39–50; Tijjani Muhammad Bande, "Managing Diversity in the Civil Service: A Brief Examination of the Nigerian Case," paper presented at the United Nations Expert Group Meeting on Managing Diversity in the Civil Service, New York, May 3–4, 2001, at https://citeseerx.ist.psu.edu/viewdoc/download?doi=10.1.1.577.4405&rep=rep1&type=pdf (accessed March 5, 2022).

74. Judy Klemesrud, "Young, Small, Bright, and Powerful—and a Key to the City's Future," *New York Times*, January 15, 1976, 41.

75. Susan Chira, "Emphasis on Action: Donna Shalala," *New York Times*, December 12, 1992, 11.

76. "President Donna Shalala's Biography," University of Miami, at http://www.miami.edu/index.php/about_us/leadership/office_of_the_president/president_donna_e_shalalas_biography (accessed December 16, 2021).

77. Mark Caputo, "Shalala, Ex-Clinton Foundation Head, Weighs Congressional Bid," *Politico*, January 23, 2018, at https://www.politico.com/story/2018/01/23/donna-shalala-miami-congressional-bid-359511 (accessed December 16, 2021).

CHAPTER 2. ENGAGEMENT AS AN ACADEMIC

1. E-mail correspondence with author, April 3, 2022.

2. Kristi Andersen, "What I Learned (and Re-Learned) When I Ran for Local Office," *PS: Political Science and Politics* 40 (July 2007): 507–510.

3. Andersen, "What I Learned (and Re-Learned) When I Ran for Local Office."

4. E-mail correspondence with author, April 3, 2022.

5. E-mail correspondence with author, November 9, 2021.

6. "About Doc Farber," University of South Dakota, at https://www.usd.edu/arts-and-sciences/farber-fund/about-doc-farber (accessed December 7, 2021).

7. E-mail correspondence with author, November 9, 2021.

8. "Karen Pooley Continues to Advocate for South Bethlehem," Sustainability—Lehigh University, March 3, 2020, at https://sustainability.lehigh.edu/karen-pooley-continues-advocate-south-bethlehem (accessed December 10, 2021).

9. E-mail correspondence with author, October 18, 2021.

10. Whitney Smith, "USU Professor Hopes to Follow Other Faculty Elected to Public Office," *Hard News Café*, Utah State University, October 1, 2011, at https://hardnewscafe.usu.edu/usu-prof-hopes-to-join-other-faculty-whove-been-elected-to-public-office/ (accessed December 13, 2021); e-mail correspondence with author, October 28, 2021.

11. E-mail correspondence with author, October 28, 2021.

12. E-mail correspondence with author, October 28, 2021.

13. E-mail correspondence with author, October 28, 2021.

14. Damon Cann, "The Structure of Municipal Political Ideology," *State and Local Government Review* 50 (June 2018): 37–45.

15. E-mail correspondence with author, November 19, 2021.

16. E-mail correspondence with author, November 19, 2021.

17. E-mail correspondence with author, January 13, 2022.

18. E-mail correspondence with author, December 16, 2021; Tari Renner, "Political Science Professor Tari Renner Breaks Down His Two Mayoral Campaigns and What They Reveal About the Changing Face of Local Election Politics," *IWU Magazine*, Winter 2013–14 edition, at https://www.iwu.edu/magazine/2013/winter/renner -election.html (accessed December 16, 2021).

19. E-mail correspondence with author, December 16, 2021.

20. Tari Renner, "Running Uphill," *IWU Magazine*, Spring 2005, at https:// digitalcommons.iwu.edu/iwumag/vol14/iss1/4/ (accessed December 16, 2021); Tari Renner, "Political Science Professor Tari Renner Breaks Down His Two Mayoral Campaigns and What They Reveal About the Changing Face of Local Election Politics," *IWU Magazine*, Winter 2013–14 edition, at https://www.iwu.edu/magazine/2013 /winter/renner-election.html (accessed December 16, 2021).

21. Bob Aaron, "Prof Takes Political Science from Classroom to County Board," News and Events, University Communications, 1999, at http://digitalcommons.iwu .edu/news/821 (accessed December 16, 2021).

22. E-mail correspondence with author, December 16, 2021.

23. E-mail correspondence with author, November 17, 2021.

24. E-mail correspondence with author, November 17, 2021.

25. E-mail correspondence with author, November 17, 2021.

26. See Danny Hayes and Jennifer L. Lawless, *Women on the Run: Gender, Media, and Political Campaigns in a Polarized Era* (New York: Cambridge University Press, 2016); Jennifer L. Lawless and Richard L. Fox, *Running From Office: How Young Americans Are Turned Off to Politics* (New York: Oxford University Press, 2015); Jennifer L. Lawless, *Becoming a Candidate: Political Ambition and the Decision to Run for Office* (New York: Cambridge University Press, 2012); and Jennifer L. Lawless and Richard L. Fox, *It Still Takes a Candidate: Why Women Don't Run for Office*, rev. ed. (New York: Cambridge University Press, 2010).

27. E-mail correspondence with author, November 17, 2021.

28. E-mail correspondence with author, December 11, 2021.

29. Christine Hall, "Michael Munger," *Chronicle*, October 28, 2008, at https://www .dukechronicle.com/article/2008/10/michael-munger (accessed December 15, 2021).

30. E-mail correspondence with author, December 11, 2021.

31. Leah Boyd, "Duke's Michael Munger Decides to Run for NC House, Emphasizes School Choice and Alcohol Taxes," *Chronicle*, January 24, 2020, at https://www .dukechronicle.com/article/2020/01/duke-michael-munger-nc-house-representatives -school-choice-alcohol-taxes (accessed December 15, 2021).

32. Ian Brodie, *At the Centre of Government: The Prime Minister and the Limits on Political Power* (Montreal and Kingston, Canada: McGill-Queens University Press, 2018), vii.

33. Brodie, *At the Centre of Government*, xii–xvi.

34. E-mail correspondence with author, January 4, 2022.

35. E-mail correspondence with author, January 4, 2022.

36. E-mail correspondence with author, January 4, 2022.

37. John Dilulio, "The Coming of the Super-Predators," *Washington Examiner*, November 17, 1995, at https://www.washingtonexaminer.com/weekly-standard/the-coming-of-the-super-predators (accessed March 24, 2022); Alex S. Vitale, "The New 'Superpredator' Myth," *New York Times*, March 23, 2018, at https://www.nytimes.com/2018/03/23/opinion/superpredator-myth.html (accessed March 24, 2022); Carroll Bogert and Lynnell Hancock, "Superpredator: The Media Myth That Demonized a Generation of Black Youth," *Marshall Project*, November 20, 2020, at https://www.themarshallproject.org/2020/11/20/superpredator-the-media-myth-that-demonized-a-generation-of-black-youth/ (accessed March 24, 2022); Richard Morin, "Leading with His Right," *Washington Post*, February 26, 2001, at https://www.washingtonpost.com/archive/lifestyle/2001/02/26/leading-with-his-right/17663a11-1ddb-43f8-99d2-eeb4651af5d2/ (accessed March 24, 2022).

38. Morin, "Leading with His Right"; James Traub, "The Criminals of Tomorrow," *Public Interest Law Reporter* 2 (1997): 1.

39. E. J. Dionne and John Dilulio Jr., *What's God to Do with the American Experiment?* (Washington: Brookings Institution, 2000); John Dilulio Jr., "The Lord's Work," *Brookings Review* 15 (Fall 1997): 27–31.

40. Dana Milbank, "Dilulio Resigns from Top 'Faith-Based' Post," *Washington Post*, August 18, 2001, at https://www.washingtonpost.com/archive/politics/2001/08/18/diiulio-resigns-from-top-faith-based-post/7acf3a7d-e87a-4633-bb79-1b26473cc700/ (accessed March 24, 2022).

41. John Dilulio Jr., "Obama and the Faith-Based Initiative," *First Things*, February 6, 2009, at https://www.firstthings.com/web-exclusives/2009/02/obama-and-the-faith-based-init (accessed March 24, 2022); Laurie Goodstein, "Leaders Say Obama Has Tapped Pastor for Outreach Office," *New York Times*, January 28, 2009, at https://www.nytimes.com/2009/01/29/us/politics/29faith.html (Accessed March 24, 2020).

42. E-mail correspondence with author, November 19, 2021.

43. "Two Projects Chosen for President's Challenge for Racial Justice and Equity Response Funding," Marquette University News Center, May 10, 2021, at https://www.marquette.edu/news-center/2021/two-projects-chosen-for-president-s-challenge-for-racial-justice-and-equity-response-funding.php (accessed December 14, 2021).

44. Noelle Brigden, "Trauma-Informed Research Methods: Understanding and Healing Embodied Violence," in *Researching Gender-Based Violence: Embodied and Intersectional Approaches*, ed. April D. J. Petillo and Heather R. Hlavka (New York: NYU Press, 2022).

45. Hillel Italie, "College Educators Form Alliance to Defend Free Expression," *Associated Press*, March 8, 2021, at https://apnews.com/article/us-news-entertainment-e1ef82436852d77fd59b841d8a6b2c9a (accessed January 20, 2022).

46. Adam Liptak, "Conservative Lawyers Say Trump Has Undermined Rule of Law," *New York Times*, November 15, 2018, A19; "New Statement from Checks and Balances on President Trump's Abuse of Office," *Checks and Balances*, October 10,

2019, at https://checks-and-balances.org/new-statement-from-checks-and-balances
-on-president-trumps-abuse-of-office/ (accessed January 20, 2022).

47. Keith Whittington, *Speak Freely: Why Universities Must Defend Free Speech* (Princeton, NJ: Princeton University Press, 2019).

48. E-mail correspondence with author, January 10, 2022.

49. E-mail correspondence with author, January 10, 2022.

50. E-mail correspondence with author, January 10, 2022.

51. See https://prisonsandjustice.georgetown.edu/.

52. Annie Kane, "Prisons and Justice Initiative Launches Maryland Bachelor's Degree Program," *Hoya*, April 15, 2021, at https://thehoya.com/prisons-and-justice -initiative-launches-maryland-bachelor-degree-program/ (accessed January 19, 2022).

53. See www.douglassproject.org.

54. E-mail correspondence with author, January 10, 2022.

55. E-mail correspondence with author, January 10, 2022.

56. Marc Morjé Howard, *Unusually Cruel: Prisons, Punishment, and the Real American Exceptionalism* (New York: Oxford University Press, 2017).

57. E-mail correspondence with author, January 10, 2022.

58. E-mail correspondence with author, January 10, 2022.

59. Jason Buch, "Follow the Money: Part II," *Texas Observer*, November 22, 2021, at https://www.texasobserver.org/follow-the-money-part-ii/ (accessed January 27, 2022); Huw Jones, "Luxembourg Fund Industry Is a $5.4 Trillion 'Black Box,' Investigation Says," *Reuters*, February 8, 2021, at https://www.reuters.com/business/finance /luxembourg-fund-industry-is-54-trillion-black-box-investigation-says-2021-02-08/ (accessed January 27, 2022).

60. Ben Weider and Meghan Bobrowsky, "Questionable PPP Loans Amount to at Least $20 Million," *Governing*, September 10, 2020, at https://www.governing .com/finance/questionable-ppp-loans-amount-to-at-least-20-million.html (accessed January 27, 2022).

61. E-mail correspondence with author, January 26, 2022.

62. Andersen, "What I learned (and Re-Learned) When I Ran for Local Office," 507–510.

CHAPTER 4. UTAH DEBATE COMMISSION

1. See Alan Schroeder, *Presidential Debates: Fifty Years of High-Risk TV*, 2nd ed. (New York: Columbia University Press, 2008).

2. Jordan Williams, "Debate Commission Cancels Oct. 15 Trump-Biden Debate," *Hill*, October 9, 2020, at https://thehill.com/homenews/campaign/520448-debate -commission-cancels-oct-15-debate (accessed September 27, 2021).

3. "Media Advisory: First Presidential Debate of 2020 Draws 73.1 Million Viewers," *Nielsen*, September 30, 2021, at https://www.nielsen.com/us/en/press-releases/2020 /media-advisory-first-presidential-debate-of-2020/ (accessed September 27, 2021).

CHAPTER 5. SERVICE TO A MAJOR PARTY

1. Nathan Johnson, "County Dems Will Choose Party's Future," *Daily Herald*, May 8, 2007, A1.

2. Nathan Johnson, "Democrats Elect Local Leadership," *Daily Herald*, May 9, 2007, A1.

3. Bob Bernick Jr. and Lee Davidson, "Utah Demo Platform to Right of U.S. Plank," *Deseret News*, August 22, 2008, at https://www.deseret.com/2008/8/22/20270611/utah -demo-platform-to-right-of-u-s-plank (accessed October 28, 2021).

4. Office of Legislature Research and General Council, Utah Legislature, "Utah's Population Growth: State, County, and City Changes 2000–2010," Briefing Paper, January 2012, at https://le.utah.gov/lrgc/briefings/2012.Jan.CensusPopulationFinal.pdf (accessed October 14, 2021).

5. Tad Walch, "Utah County Demos Try a New Tack: YouTube," *Deseret News*, October 16, 2007, at https://www.deseret.com/2007/10/16/20047375/utah-county-demos -try-a-new-tack-youtube (accessed December 6, 2021); Jeremy Duda, "Utah County Dems Launch New Web Site," *Daily Herald*, October 16, 2007, A1.

6. Marc Haddock, "Utah County Democrats to Honor Former Governor Olene Walker," Deseret News, May 17, 2010, at https://www.deseret.com/2010/5/17 /20112622/utah-county-democrats-to-honor-former-gop-gov-olene-walker (accessed October 28, 2021).

7. Lee Davidson, "Utah Demo Wants End to Attacks on Romney," *Deseret News*, August 16, 2008, at https://www.deseret.com/2008/8/16/20269646/utah-demo-wants -end-to-attacks-on-romney (accessed October 28, 2021).

8. Robert Gehrke, "Dems Use Romney to Sell Candidates in Utah County," *Salt Lake Tribune*, November 2, 2018, at https://archive.sltrib.com/article.php?itype =NGPSID&id=10879059 (accessed October 28, 2021).

9. Dennis Romboy, "Why Mitt Romney Loses Points with Utah Republicans, Scores Big with Democrats," *Deseret News*, January 24, 2021, at https://www.deseret .com/utah/2021/1/24/22242586/mitt-romney-poll-disapproval-mike-lee-republican -donald-trump-election-fraud-joe-biden-democrat (accessed May 24, 2022).

10. Joe Pyrah, "Dems Raising More Money in County Races," *Daily Herald*, April 30, 2008, A3.

11. "Utah County Democrats Host Open House," *Salt Lake Tribune*, July 29, 2009, at https://archive.sltrib.com/article.php?itype=NGPSID&id=12935151 (accessed October 28, 2021).

12. Paul Rolly, "Voucher Fallout: Some Republicans Running as Dems in Utah County," *Salt Lake Tribune*, January 30, 2008, at https://archive.sltrib.com/article.php ?itype=NGPSID&id=8020072 (accessed October 28, 2021); Marc Haddock, "Some Utah County Republicans Switch Sides," *Deseret News*, March 23, 2010, at https:// www.deseret.com/2010/3/23/20104019/some-utah-county-republicans-switching -sides (accessed October 28, 2021).

13. Amy K. Stewart, "Ex-WSU Chief Will Run for Legislature," *Deseret News*, February 1, 2008, at https://www.deseret.com/2008/2/1/20068072/ex-wsu-chief-will-run-for-legislature (accessed October 28, 2021).

14. Donald W. Meyers, "Utah County Dems Honor Orton's Legacy," *Salt Lake Tribune*, May 2, 2009, at https://archive.sltrib.com/article.php?itype=NGPSID&id=12281124 (accessed October 28, 2021).

CHAPTER 6. FOUNDING A NEW MINOR PARTY

1. Lisa Riley Roche, "Mitt Romney: Trump Is 'a Phony, a Fraud,'" *Deseret News*, March 3, 2016, at https://www.deseret.com/2016/3/3/20583951/mitt-romney-trump-is-a-phony-a-fraud (accessed October 19, 2021).

2. Dennis Romboy, "New Poll Shows Evan McMullin Leading Trump, Clinton in Utah," *Deseret News*, October 19, 2016, at https://www.deseret.com/2016/10/19/20598604/new-poll-shows-evan-mcmullin-leading-trump-clinton-in-utah (accessed May 24, 2022).

3. Lee Davidson, "Governor Herbert to Utah Legislature: Forget Special Session," *Salt Lake Tribune*, May 18, 2017, at https://archive.sltrib.com/article.php?id=5303169&itype=CMSID (accessed May 24, 2022).

4. Dennis Romboy, "Frustrated Utah Republicans, Democrats Form Centrist Party, *Deseret News*, May 22, 2017, at https://www.deseret.com/2017/5/22/20612841/frustrated-utah-republicans-democrats-form-new-centrist-political-party.

5. Lisa Riley Roche, "Nearly Two-Thirds of Utahns Open to Voting for New United Utah Party Candidates," *Deseret News*, June 28, 2017, at https://www.deseret.com/2017/6/28/20614936/poll-nearly-two-thirds-of-utahns-open-to-voting-for-new-united-utah-party-candidates (accessed October 25, 2021).

6. Lisa Riley Roche, "New United Utah Party Leader Jim Bennett Announces Bid for Chaffetz's Seat," KSL.com, May 26, 2017, at https://www.ksl.com/article/44391418/new-united-utah-party-leader-jim-bennett-announces-bid-for-chaffetzs-seat (accessed October 25, 2021); Steve Griffin, "Jim Bennett Tries to Enter Race for 3rd Congressional District, But State Won't Let Him," *Salt Lake Tribune*, May 28, 2017, at https://www.ksl.com/article/44391418/new-united-utah-party-leader-jim-bennett-announces-bid-for-chaffetzs-seat.

7. Lisa Riley Roche, "United Utah Party a Step Closer to Official State Recognition," *Deseret News*, June 26, 2017, at https://www.deseret.com/2017/6/26/20614810/new-united-utah-party-a-step-closer-to-official-state-recognition (accessed October 25, 2021).

8. Lisa Riley Roche, "Stake Looking into Reports United Utah Party Members' Party Affiliations Being Switched," *Deseret News*, May 13, 2018, at https://www.deseret.com/2018/5/13/20644976/state-looking-into-reports-united-utah-party-members-party-affiliations-being-switched (accessed October 25, 2021).

9. Ryan Morgan, "United Utah Party Sues for Access on Special Election Ballot," *Deseret News*, June 21, 2017, at https://www.deseret.com/2017/6/21/20614537/united-utah-party-sues-for-access-on-special-election-ballot (accessed October 25, 2021).

10. Dennis Romboy, "Judge Orders State to Put United Utah Party Candidate on Special Election Ballot," *Deseret News*, August 3, 2017, at https://www.deseret.com/2017/8/3/20634468/judge-orders-state-to-put-united-utah-party-candidate-on-special-election-ballot (accessed October 25, 2021).

11. Lisa Riley Roche, "Curtis Avoids talking About Trump in Debate, but Allen, Bennett Kept Bringing Him Up," *Deseret News*, October 18, 2017, at https://www.deseret.com/2017/10/18/20635293/curtis-avoids-talking-about-trump-in-debate-but-allen-bennett-kept-bringing-him-up (accessed October 25, 2021).

12. "Candidates File for Congressional, Utah Legislative Races," *Deseret News*, March 14, 2018, at https://www.deseret.com/2018/3/14/20641630/candidates-file-for-congressional-utah-legislative-races (accessed October 25, 2021).

13. Lee Davidson, "Rep. Rob Bishop's Biggest Challenge May Come from a United Utah Party Candidate—Who Has Nearly \$200K in Campaign War Chest," *Salt Lake Tribune*, July 20, 2018, at https://www.sltrib.com/news/politics/2018/07/20/rep-rob-bishops-biggest/ (accessed October 25, 2021).

14. Benjamin Wood, "United Utah Party Candidate Qualifies for Official Utah Election Debate; Poll Indicates Wider Gap in Love-McAdams Race," *Salt Lake Tribune*, September 5, 2018, at https://www.sltrib.com/news/politics/2018/09/05/united-utah-party/ (accessed October 25, 2021).

15. "Tribune Editorial: Eric Eliason Is First District's Choice for Real Change," *Salt Lake Tribune*, October 21, 2021, at https://www.sltrib.com/news/2018/10/21/tribune-editorial-eric/ (accessed October 25, 2021).

16. Jacob Klopfenstein, "United Utah Party Caucuses Exceed Expectations with 900 Attendees," *KSL.com*, March 22, 2018, at https://www.ksl.com/article/46286106/united-utah-party-caucuses-exceed-expectations-with-900-attendees (accessed October 25, 2021).

17. Dennis Romboy, "Utah Democrats, GOP Cancel In-Person State Conventions, Postpone Caucus Night," *Deseret News*, March 12, 2020, at https://www.deseret.com/utah/2020/3/12/21176714/coronavirus-utah-republican-party-democratic-party-election-convention-caucus (accessed October 25, 2021).

18. Dennis Romboy, "Ex-Republican Launches Bid for Congress as United Utah Party Candidate," *Deseret News*, January 30, 2020, at https://www.deseret.com/utah/2020/1/30/21115373/ex-republican-launches-bid-for-congress-as-united-utah-party-candidate-2nd-district-stewart-gop (accessed October 25, 2021).

19. Sahalie Donaldson, "Gubernatorial Candidate Names Doctor as Running Mate," *Deseret News*, March 19, 2020, at https://www.deseret.com/utah/2020/3/19/21186960/gubernatorial-candidate-jan-garbett-names-doctor-as-running-mate (accessed October 25, 2021).

20. Bethany Rodgers, "Utah's Voter Turnout in This Election Certified as State's Highest on Record," *Salt Lake Tribune*, November 24, 2020, at https://www.sltrib.com/news/politics/2020/11/24/utahs-voter-turnout-this/ (accessed October 21, 2021).

21. "Historical Election Results," VoteUtah.Gov, at https://voteinfo.utah.gov/historical-election-results/ (accessed October 21, 2021).

CHAPTER 7. COMMUNITY SERVICE AND RUNNING FOR OFFICE

1. For more discussion of year-round instruction and the Orchard Plan, specifically, see Patricia Gandara, "Extended Year, Extended Contracts: Increasing Teacher Salary Options," *Urban Education* (October 1992): 229–247; Nancy Veatch, "An Evaluation of the Orchard Plan: A Year-Round Efficient Educational Program" (MA thesis, University of California, Davis, 1991).

CONCLUSION: OVERCOMING THE BARRIERS TO ENGAGEMENT

1. Paul Wellstone, *The Conscience of a Liberal* (Minneapolis: University of Minnesota Press, 2002), 15.

2. E-mail correspondence with author, February 14, 2022.

3. E-mail correspondence with author, October 18, 2021, and November 19, 2021.

4. E-mail correspondence with author, January 4, 2022.

5. E-mail correspondence with author, January 13, 2022.

6. E-mail correspondence with author, January 10, 2022.

7. E-mail correspondence with author, January 13, 2022.

8. Interview with author, January 28, 2022.

9. E-mail correspondence with author, December 11, 2021.

10. E-mail correspondence with author, January 10, 2022.

11. E-mail correspondence with author, November 19, 2021.

12. E-mail correspondence with author, November 19, 2021.

13. E-mail correspondence with author, January 28, 2022.

14. E-mail correspondence with author, December 11, 2021, and February 2, 2022.

15. Joanna K. Tzouvelis, "Watertown School Committee Chair Will Not Seek Re-election," *Wicked Local*, July 7, 2021, at https://www.wickedlocal.com/story/watertown-tab/2021/07/07/three-school-committee-seats-up-re-election-chair-not-run/7871955002/ (accessed December 13, 2021).

16. E-mail correspondence with author, January 4, 2022.

17. Kristi Andersen, "What I learned (and Re-Learned) When I Ran for Local Office," *PS: Political Science and Politics*, 40 (July 2007): 508.

18. Andersen, "What I learned (and Re-Learned) When I Ran for Local Office," 508.

19. "Political Science Professor Elected as Nazareth Area School Director," *ESU Insider*, December 3, 2015, at https://quantum.esu.edu/insider/political-science-professor-elected-as-nazareth-area-school-director/ (accessed December 15, 2021).

20. E-mail correspondence with author, January 10, 2022.

21. E-mail correspondence with author, January 10, 2022.

22. E-mail correspondence with author, January 10, 2022.

23. E-mail correspondence with author, April 3, 2022.

24. E-mail correspondence with author, October 18, 2021.

25. Jim Nintzel, "Mister Coffee: Can Tom Volgy's Unorthodox Campaign Unseat Congressman Jim Kolbe," *Tucson Weekly*, October 22, 1998, at https://www.tucsonweekly.com/tw/10-22-98/feat.htm (accessed December 13, 2021); Dave Devine,

"Why Tucson's Campaign Matching-Fund Program is a Winner," *Tucson Weekly*, October 2, 1997, at https://www.tucsonweekly.com/tw//10-02-97/curr2.htm/ (accessed December 13, 2021).

26. E-mail correspondence with author, April 3, 2022.

27. E-mail correspondence with author, February 14, 2022.

28. E-mail correspondence with author, April 3, 2022.

29. E-mail correspondence with author, January 4, 2022.

30. "Colby Faculty Handbook," Colby College, Revised June 2021, at https://www.colby.edu/provost/wp-content/uploads/sites/121/2021/06/Faculty-Handbook-2021-June-2021.pdf (accessed 17 March 2022); "Williams College Faculty Handbook," at https://faculty.williams.edu/files/2016/08/Williams-faculty-handbook-2016-17.pdf (accessed March 17, 2022).

31. "Middlebury Handbook," Middlebury College, at https://www.middlebury.edu/handbook/pages/ii-ug-college-policies/faculty/faculty-rules (accessed March 17, 2022); "Faculty Handbook & Handbook Addenda," Loyola Marymount University, 2019, at https://academics.lmu.edu/media/lmuacademics/provost/documents/LMU%20Faculty%20Handbook%202019-2020%20FINAL%20BW.pdf (accessed March 17, 2022); "Principles, Rules, and Procedures for Promotion and the Award of Tenure," Faculty Manual, Vanderbilt University, at https://faculty.williams.edu/files/2016/08/Williams-faculty-handbook-2016-17.pdf (accessed March 17, 2022).

32. "Promotion and Tenure Guidelines (Approved May 2020)," Arts and Letters, Idaho State University, at https://www.isu.edu/cal/promotion-and-tenure-policy/ (accessed March 17, 2022).

33. "Appointment and Advancement: A Publication of the Committee on Academic Personnel Prepared in Consultation with the Associate Vice Chancellor for Academic Personnel (Revised 9/21)," University of California, Santa Barbara, at https://ap.ucsb.edu/policies.and.procedures/red.binder/sections/%5B1_75%5D%20Appointment%20and%20Advancement.pdf (accessed March 17, 2022); "Promotion and Tenure Procedures for the College of Liberal Arts & Sciences," University of Kansas Policy Library, at https://policy.ku.edu/CLAS/promotion-tenure (accessed March 17, 2022).

34. "Standards for Tenure and Promotion to Associate Professor," Stetson University, at https://www.stetson.edu/administration/provost/media/Standards%20and%20Evidence%202018-06-28.pdf (accessed March 17, 2022); "General Guidelines for Promotion and Tenure of All Faculty Ranks—2020–2021 Academic Year," The University of Texas at Austin, at https://utexas.app.box.com/v/2020-21generalguidelines#:~:text=II.-,Service,.,-III (accessed March 17, 2022).

35. E-mail correspondence with author, February 14, 2022.

36. Interview with author, January 28, 2002; e-mail correspondence with author, January 4, 2022, and January 23, 2022.

37. Lindsay Ellis and Emma Pettit, "I'm Speechless: What Prompted the U. of Florida to Tell Professors Not to Testify?" *Chronicle of Higher Education,* November 2, 2021, at https://www.chronicle.com/article/im-speechless (accessed April 28, 2022).

38. E-mail correspondence with author, November 19, 2021.

Index